The Acoustic Guitar

VOLUME II

University of Oklahoma Press
Norman and London

The Acoustic Guitar

Adjustment, Care, Maintenance, and Repair

VOLUME II

Don E. Teeter

By Don E. Teeter

The Acoustic Guitar: Adjustment, Care, Maintenance, and Repair (Norman, 1975)
The Acoustic Guitar: Adjustment, Care, Maintenance, and Repair, Volume II (Norman, 1980)

Library of Congress Cataloging-in-Publication Data

Teeter, Don E
  The acoustic guitar.

  Includes bibliographies and index.
  1. Guitar—Maintenance and repair. I. Title.
ML1015.G9T44   787.6'12'0288   79–5962
ISBN: 0–8061–1607–2

Preface

Hello. I'm back again, just like the proverbial bad penny. Before proceeding any further, I wish to take this opportunity to thank each and every one of you who has read Volume I of *The Acoustic Guitar: Adjustment, Care, Maintenance, and Repair.* The critical approval has been fantastic. Of the many reviews and articles clipped and forwarded my way by the University of Oklahoma Press, I have received only one bad review to date, from some alleged scholar who was disgruntled because I didn't delve into the intricacies and mysteries of classical-guitar construction. The poor guy missed the point altogether. The book was on guitar repair, not guitar construction.

He condemned my various jigs and hand-made tools as mere carpenter's gimmicks. For a scholar, that was practically unforgivable stupidity. Any real instrument repairman should be aware that a carpenter's background, especially a finish carpenter's, is a definite asset in one's favor owing to the knowledge of woods, finishes, and so on.

As for my "untraditional" use of jigs, custom designed tools, and techniques, I say, "So what?" If one has to make a living in this extremely tedious and difficult line of work, there is nothing wrong with using a faster, more modern, untraditional method if it accomplishes a given job properly—usually with more precision owing to the consistency of jigging—in less time. Let's face it: we repairmen are definitely not in this business for our health, and if someone insists on doing the job utilizing the slower, more time-consuming expensive traditional methods, I consider that his loss. Any time I can find a quicker, if unconventional, technique that will produce the necessary results, I intend to use it.

Perhaps the strongest point of controversy has risen from my somewhat peculiar and unorthodox method in refretting an instrument. The response to this technique has ranged from outright praise (from repairmen who have had to face the very real and tenacious problem of instrument returns because of the working out of driven-in frets, a particularly perplexing problem in older instruments resulting from wood deterioration) to out-and-out derision from others whom I suspect have not yet given the technique a fair

try. I've received many telephone calls from repairmen all over the nation who have tried the technique, switched over to it, and wanted to thank me for the idea.

To be honest about it, I really anticipated a lot more flack from this technique than has developed. The refretting chapter in Volume I, however, has probably received more revamping in this supplement than any other. Don't get me wrong. I still use the basic technique of setting the frets in epoxy and clamping them rather than pounding them in with a hammer, but I have expanded the technique to include the use of a relatively new invention of mine, a tool that I call a string tension simulation jig. I suspect that this jig might be patentable, but anyone with enough intelligence to use the jig could duplicate it for his own use without violating a patent right, so I have chosen to share the idea with anyone who cares to use it.

Those of you who have encountered a really "squirrely" neck and fingerboard, perhaps one that even straightens up nice and true when the string tension is relaxed, will appreciate this tool to no end. I believe mine is original. I've never heard of anyone else using such an animal. This jig will actually duplicate the irregularities of a warped and twisted neck to a gnat's whisker (very close) *with the strings and frets removed* and will hold these irregularities while you dress or plane them out.

Some necks, such as those on the Martin line of instruments, have no provision for bow adjustment, and the proper amount of forward bow can actually be calculated into the jig setting before the dressing or planing takes place. Intriguing, isn't it? It removes the last vestige of guesswork from refretting.

Also, with the ever-increasing invasion of plywood instruments from Japan, Taiwan, Korea, the Philippines, and elsewhere, and the ever-increasing prices of these instruments, it is (perish the thought) becoming more worthwhile to have these instruments repaired rather than relegate them to the trash heap. A large percentage should be trashed—or hung on a wall with a plastic posy in the soundhole—but there are some that can be salvaged.

Accordingly, I am including a chapter in this book deal-

Fig. 1—A pair of oldies but goodies! A 1934 000–45 Martin (customer's) and a 1938 D–45 sunburst Martin (author's guitar).

ing with some of their peculiarities and the techniques that I use to salvage them. I know, I know, you probably hate to work on them as much as I do, but they are becoming a definite factor in the instrument-repair business and are a headache that we have to live and deal with—like it or not.

In Volume I, I tried to evolve my techniques utilizing as

Fig. 2—Back view of the pair of old 45 Martins.

many basic tools as possible, but unless you are a machinist with access to a machine shop, some of the work on the new tools and jigs will have to be farmed out, such as the heliarcing and milling of the slots on the beam of the string tension simulation jig. However, the initial expense incurred will be well worth it in the long run from the time and effort saved.

This volume is an extension of and supplement to my

Fig. 3—Another pair of goodies, both mine. An 1860 1–34 series "New Yorker" Martin and "Pretty Baby II", an instrument that I designed and made for myself. It is designed around a classical-shaped body but has an x-braced top for light gauge steel strings.

original book and is intended not to take its place but to be used in conjunction with it. I shall refer to the books as Volume I and Volume II for clarity when explaining a particular technique that I do not wish to repeat in this volume. There will be some repetition, however, when I think there are certain things that need to be doubly stressed or

Fig. 4—The back view of the "New Yorker" and "Pretty Baby".

where I think I may be able to clarify certain areas. After all, I have learned a tremendous amount since completing the original manuscript back in 1972, and I have been able in some instances to simplify my techniques. I am, as all of us in the guitar repair field should be, in a constant learning process. I consider a day that goes by without my learning or encountering something new, no matter how small, as a day wasted.

Since the publication of *The Acoustic Guitar*, there have been several other books written on the subject. I still hold

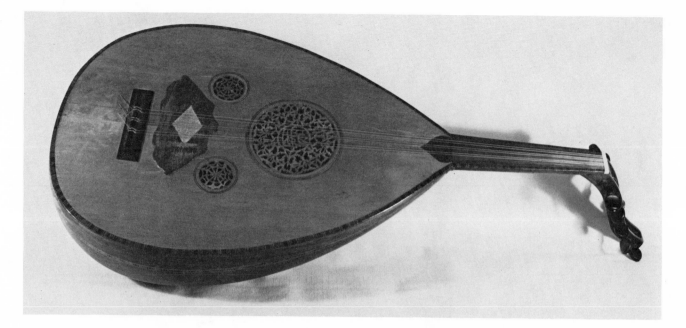

Fig. 5—A little variety makes an instrument repairman's life more interesting. This is an Arabic oud (fretless lute).

with the idea of purchasing everything written on the subject for reference or background material. You may wish to use techniques other than mine, and if they work out better for you than mine do, by all means use them. "There's more'n one way t'skin a cat," as the old saying goes.

Interest in instrument repair has blossomed in the past few years, to the extent that there are several schools offering training courses in instrument repair and construction. You will find some of them listed in the back of this volume. One of these, the Roberto-Venn School of Luthiery, in Phoenix, Arizona, uses my first book as reference in guitar repair and I have spoken at the school.

Before closing this preface, I suppose I should clarify another area. Several hundred people have asked me who was responsible for the photographs and drawings in Volume I. I confess that I'm the one responsible for both the photo-

graphs and the drawings in Volume I, as well as in this volume. I used an A1 Canon SLR 35-millimeter camera. Taking the photographs wasn't so bad because nature photography is a hobby of mine, but those drawings were murder! I had to drop everything and learn the rudiments of mechanical drawing to do them.

Please use this volume with an open mind and a great deal of patience. I hope that it will be accepted as well as the first book. All the various jigs, tools, and techniques are used regularly in my shop, and I trust they will serve you as well as they have me. Again, I thank you for your enthusiastic support.

Don E. Teeter

Oklahoma City

Contents

The Acoustic Guitar
VOLUME II

More on Tools Used in Guitar Repair

I still use basically the same hand and power tools that I outlined in Volume I, but I have made a few additions. Most of my new tooling falls under the heading of specialty tools explained in the next chapter.

Part of my new standard tools are used in maintaining the tools that I already have, and that's primarily what this chapter is about—maintenance.

I have added a second bench grinder. My original bench grinder now sports a wire brush on one end and a cloth buffing wheel on the other. One of the wheels on my new grinder is used exclusively for sharpening drill bits and is set up with a permanently mounted twist drill sharpening jig— a very handy gadget. Of course, you can "eyeball"-sharpen your bits—I did for years—but if you should get the angle on one flute slightly off from the other or slightly wider, an off-center point is the result, and you end up with a drill bit that will wander or follow the wood grain to one side or the other. On metal it will burn up much faster and wallow out a hole—if it lasts long enough to drill a hole. Any of the available jigs will ensure a centered point and equal angles to each flute. They're well worth the money for precision work.

The wheel on the other end of the new grinder is used for rough grinding my chisels, plane blades, knives, etc. Here's a valuable tip. Most of the readily available green or gray grinding wheels are bad about clogging up and burning the edges of your tools unless you keep quenching them constantly. Brookstone Hard-To-Find-Tools offers a white vitrified aluminum oxide grinding wheel that is just about the ultimate for sharpening tools. It doesn't clog up easily— unless you're grinding on nonferrous metal—and will remove nearly twice the material that standard wheels will in the same length of time with little or no burning. Still, it's a good idea to quench your tool regularly to keep down the heat. I highly recommend this white grinding wheel. The Brookstone (address in the back of Volume I) catalog number is J–3728. They also offer a silicon carbide wheel dressing stick, #J–3799, for sharpening and maintaining the trueness of the white or any other grinding wheel that's well worth the price.

Brookstone also offers a universal plane blade and chisel honer, #J–2062, that works in combination with a hone for sharpening plane blades or wood chisels. It's no problem to set and hone a 25- or 30-degree angle on your tools. I rough-sharpen occasionally on the white wheel, finish on a hone with the holder, and strop on a piece of well-worn 600-grit Wetordry (Figure 7) sandpaper for a razor edge. My sharpening schedule for my wood chisels is to grind them every three or four months, hone once a month, and strop daily on the constantly used chisels. I sharpen my planes when needed, usually on the hone with the holder.

Whetstones have a bad habit of clogging up, even when used properly with honing oil (see Figures 8 and 9) and invariably need cleaning when you're in a hurry and can't take the time to soak. A quick way to clean them is to spray the clogged surface with WD-40, hit it with a hand wire brush, and wipe with a clean cloth. Shoot it with WD-40 a second time and wipe again. Presto, a clean surface. Apply fresh honing oil and go to work.

A sharp tool is the only way to go. Dull tools cause too many accidents. I've ended up with more cuts from dull tools than from sharp ones. You know that the sharp ones are more dangerous so you are automatically more careful with them.

I use various knives and keep them razor-sharp. The two X-acto knives (Figure 10) with the rounded ends are my favorites. Originally they had sharp points like the blades next to them, but I resharpened and honed them to the finished configuration shown in the photo on purpose. You can cut through masking tape (carefully) and not scratch the finish below as would happen with a needle-sharp point. I hone these blades every six or eight weeks and polish them every day on a heavily rouged cloth buffing wheel. Common red jeweler's rouge is available from most industrial or plating supply houses. The rouged wheel polishes the blades to a smooth, hair-shaving edge.

When I need a sharp-pointed blade such as in fine trimming for grafting, digging splinters from my hand, etc., my favorite is a surgeon's scalpel (Brookstone). You can buy the handle and select the type of throwaway blades you prefer.

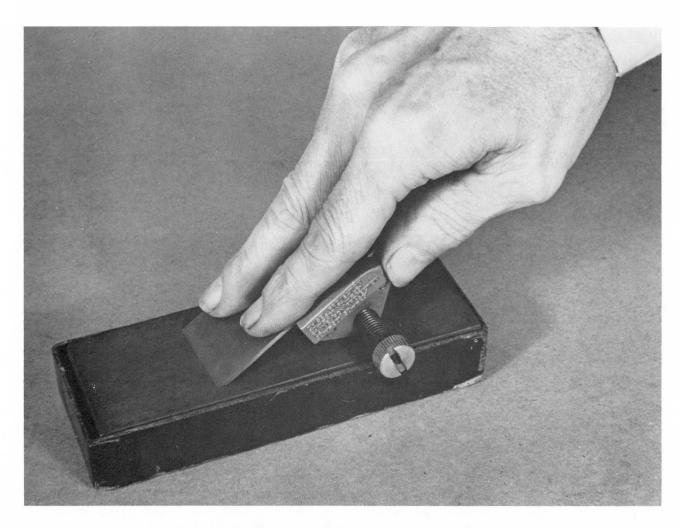

Fig. 6—Chisel and plane blade holder used with a hone to hold the cutting edge at the desired angle to the stone for sharpening. Available from Brookstone, Hard–To–Find–Tools. Their address is in the back of Volume I.

Fig. 7—Stropping a chisel's edge after honing on a piece of worn 600–grit Wetordry sandpaper to achieve a razor–edge. Lay the sandpaper over a hard flat surface such as a thick piece of Plexiglas or a saw table.

Fig. 8—Macrophotograph of a dirty, oil–and–chip–filled fine India whetstone. A stone this dirty does a poor job of sharpening knives, chisels, etc.

Fig. 9—A macrophotograph of the same India stone after cleaning with WD–40. See the text for the procedure.

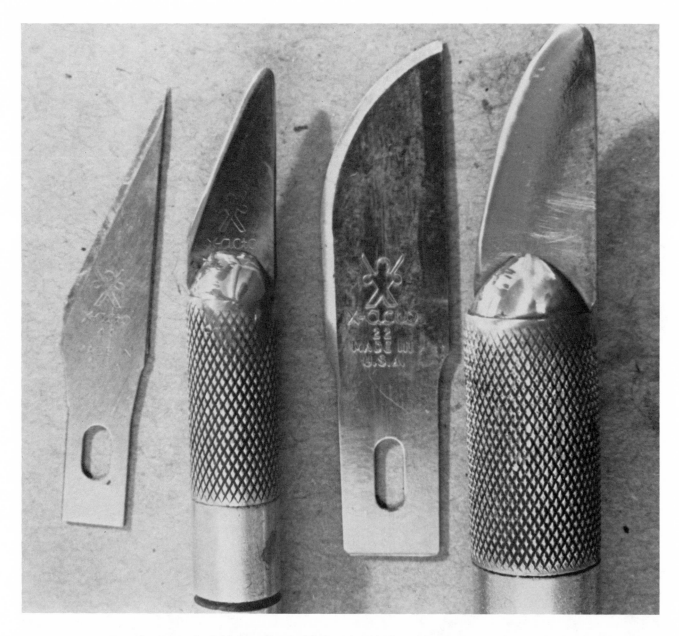

Fig. 10—X–acto knife blades with rounded, honed, and polished tips (see text) compared to the original blades. These are excellent for trimming masking tape with minimal marring of the finish underneath as when masking of a bridge, etc.

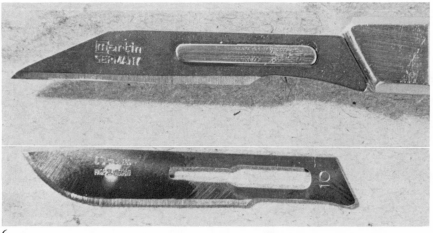

Fig. 11—A surgeon's scalpel with two of the many available disposable blades. These are excellent for working on impacted plywood areas, grafting, and digging out splinters from your fingers.

Of course, you'll want to sterilize the scalpel blade before you use it to dig out splinters from your hand.

I mentioned WD-40 earlier. The last thing we want on an instrument's wood that is to be finished is oil, and WD-40 is a great greaseless, oilless lubricant for the threads on metal "C" clamps and bench vises. It stops rusting, too. WD-40 is also good for freeing rusted or seized metal parts, tension rod nuts, bridge adjustment pieces, etc. It also works beautifully to keep your lathe and electric drill chucks operating smoothly. Use it also in lubricating your vernier caliper beams and micrometers. I keep a can handy at all times.

Another item that is often neglected until it starts giving trouble is the electric motor used to power your equipment. Most motors are vented to outside air and have small internal vanes or "fans" that draw in the air for cooling purposes. Along with this cooling air comes dust, particularly when used on a belt sander or bandsaw. These should be blown out periodically with an air hose before enough dust can accumulate to cause trouble. Use plenty of air pressure and work from both ends of the motor alternately until no more dust comes out. The primary trouble point is in the starting circuit. Dust builds up and keeps it from shifting from the starting to the running phase. Sometimes the poor motor draws so much amperage trying to shift that it will trip a circuit breaker. A small shot of WD-40 on the shaft where the shifting mechanism works, after blowing out the dust, helps to keep it working freely.

Unless your motors are equipped with sealed ball bearings, the main shaft bearings should be lubricated periodically. Every two to six months is often enough, depending on the work load of the particular equipment. You will usually find small rubber push-in or metal screw-in plugs in the bearing housings at each end of the motor. Unplug the cord for safety, remove the plugs, and give them a good snort of 30-weight motor oil. Be sure to replace the dust plugs when you are finished.

Another item often neglected is the air compressor. Clean the dust from the air intake filters often and keep a regular check on the crankcase oil reservoir. Don't overfill unless you want oil in your air supply, but don't let it get low or you might be buying a new compressor pump after a connecting rod comes through the crankcase.

Bandsaws need only occasional maintenance besides caring for the motor and changing dull blades. I've replaced the two sealed ball bearings that back up the blade twice in the past eighteen years. Check them for freeness whenever you change a blade. If they are locked or hard to turn, replace them.

The flat side guides that stabilize the blades from each side above and below the table should be removed and checked every six months or so. When they start grooving, they may be reversed once for a new smooth surface. After reversing, buy a new set of guides to have on hand when the other ends wear out.

Each time you replace the bandsaw's blade, clean off the rubber tires on the large wheels with a stiff bristle brush, especially if you have been using a skip-tooth blade for cutting nonferrous metal, and check the sealed bearings on each wheel for freeness. The wheel should coast for several turns with a good spin from your hand. Always clean out the accumulated dust while you have the guards off, and, after installing a new blade, spin the tires by hand for several revolutions to center the new blade. *Never start* the saw without the wheel guards in place. A broken blade (it happens even with new blades) whipping off an unguarded saw can be worse than diving headlong into a prickly-pear patch.

Before I forget it, I want to mention something that is *very important*. Anytime you buy new tools, a set of instructions and a parts list is included (or should be). Buy a large manila folder or its equivalent and keep all of your papers and parts lists in this folder. I started doing this one day after I spent over an hour looking for a parts list so I could order a new bearing. Keep everything together and in one place and you'll always know where to look for it. It can save you, and a parts house, a lot of time trying to find a part number.

The Dremel Moto Tool is a relatively trouble-free tool, but it does need maintenance once in a while. The more expensive models have ball spindle bearings and will last for years under everyday usage with an occasional armature brush replacement. I get about three years' use before sending them back to the factory for a complete overhaul, but the bushing types need the bushings replaced after a year's constant use. Grasp the chuck and try to wiggle it sideways. If you can feel a definite movement or if the tool makes a funny "chattering" sound while running, the bearings are suspect and probably need replacing. I own two Moto Tools because I won't be without one (my right arm) for the four to six weeks needed to send it back. You can either return it yourself or have your local dealer do it for you. A complete overhaul is usually about half the price of a new tool and usually lasts just as long.

As mentioned in Volume I, dental burrs and cutters of all descriptions are available from your local Dremel dealer, your local dentist, or a dental supply house. I usually hit up my dentist for some used ones every time I go in for a checkup.

For slotting bridges a $\frac{3}{32}''$ router bit is needed. They used to be available from woodworking suppliers under the name "veining bits." They had small shanks that would fit the Dremel chuck and used bronze sleeves to size them up to fit the standard $\frac{1}{4}''$ router shank. They seem to have been discontinued and are now ground on a $\frac{1}{4}''$ shank. The smallest router bit offered by Dremel is $\frac{1}{8}''$, so in the spe-

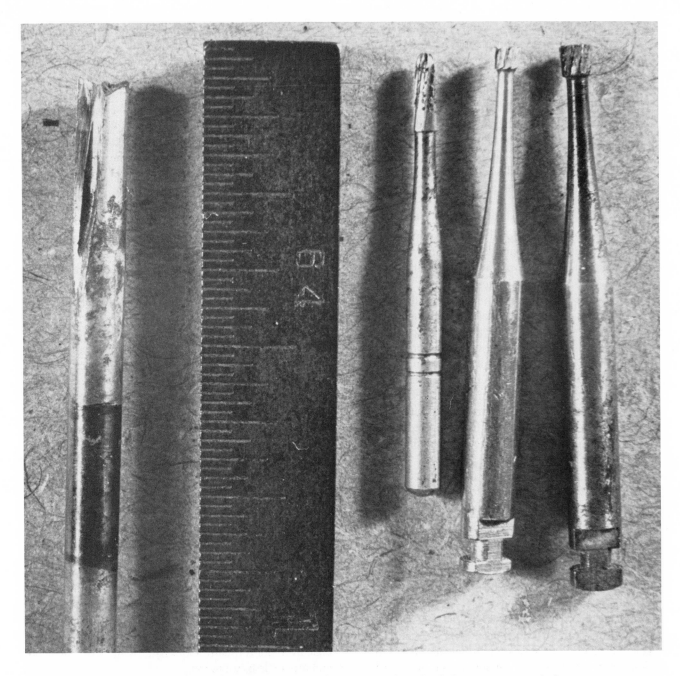

Fig. 12—A homemade, double–flute router bit, a ¹⁄₆₄" graduated rule for perspective, and three dental burrs that I use in pearl inlay work and refretting. Macrophotograph.

cial tool chapter I tell you how to make your own router bits using the Dremel, a small cutting wheel, and a handmade jig.

You will need some cork padding if you decide to make a copy of my string tension simulation jig in the next chapter. Save the scraps. Check the cork facings occasionally on your wooden cam and spool clamps and use the scrap cork to reface these as needed. It's better to take a few minutes to recork a clamp than to spend several hours to repair a marred finish.

Another essential item for any woodworking shop is a fire extinguisher, or, better yet, several of them—one for each room of any size and two or more for a large room. They must be of the proper type, too. No CO_2 or liquid types around electrical equipment. Use only the A-, B-, and C-rated multipurpose dry-powder types. Six pounders are a

Fig. 13—More useful Dremel accessory tools. The 1/32" graduated rule is for perspective. A cutting wheel and mandrel, two carbide burrs handy for working in metal, etc., a 1/4" commercially available router bit, and a miniature wire brush.

handy size and should be checked periodically to ensure that they are still up to a full charge. Once used, they should be immediately recharged, even if only partly discharged. Powder can lodge under the valve and let the propellent leak down. Nothing is as useless as an empty fire extinguisher.

And, please, mount an extinguisher *outside the door* to your spray room or booth. If a fire starts inside a spray room, you sure don't want to have to fry your hide trying to reach the extinguisher through the fire.

Good tools will last for years with simple routine maintenance. Take good care of them. Keep everything clean, sharp, and lubricated. Down time on needed tools is lost money, and that's the bottom line when you make your living with your tools.

2

Specialty Tools, How to Make Them

A Drawknife for Working in Close Places

Drawknives are handy for roughing out neck contours, but the blade width on the smallest commercially made drawknife I've ever been able to find is one inch. This makes it next to useless for roughing out the tight curves in the heel of a guitar's neck.

I got exasperated one day and made one from an old three-cornered file that works very well. I didn't bother to anneal it but left it the original hardness. It not only takes a razor edge, but it keeps it. You can shave a thin sliver or whack off a big chunk, and it takes only minutes to rough out a heel curve.

Parts and materials.

1 piece—7″ three-cornered file or one that measures ⅜″ across the widest part of the flat side.
2 pieces—⅜″ O.D. by 3½″ copper tubing.
2 pieces—wooden file handles with metal ferrules.

The first step is to grind the teeth from one side of the file and hone it smooth. This will be the bottom of the drawknife. Mark off a 2½″ section in the center of the file and grind it down until the back of the file is ⁷⁄₃₂″ high instead of ⅜″ as shown in "A" of Figure 14. It should taper from ⁷⁄₃₂″ at the back to a sharp edge at the front. Be sure to quench often while grinding to prevent overheating and drawing the temper from the file. If the ground area turns blue, throw it away and start over, for you have allowed it to get too hot. After grinding out this 2½″-long notch, grind the back edge of the bottom in the same area (shaded part in "A"), round.

Measure off 1⅜″ on each side of the notch and saw off the excess ends of the file with a carbide-impregnated hacksaw blade. Don't try a regular hacksaw blade; it won't touch a file. All you'll succeed in doing is ruining the teeth. An alternate method is to grind a groove around the file and place it in a bench vise with the part to be removed above the vise's jaws. Then wrap a rag around the exposed end to stop any dangerous flying chips (a file will shatter like glass) and give it a sharp rap with a ball-peen hammer. It should snap off at the groove.

Grind each end round for ⅜″ to where they will fit into the two pieces of copper tubing. Wrap a *wet* rag around the central portion of the file and braze the tubing to each end of the file. Bend the tubing parallel to the bottom of the file at approximately a 60-degree angle.

Drill out the handle's holes to fit the ⅜″ O.D. tubing, press onto the tubing, and pin as shown in "B" of Figure 14.

The final step is to hone the cutting edge from the top and bottom and spray with WD-40 to prevent rusting. Wipe dry and it's ready to use. *Be very careful* with this tool; the file-hard edge is treacherous, and the slightest slip will cause big trouble, but if used properly and cautiously until you become accustomed to it, it will be an invaluable tool for rough-carving necks.

Small-Angle Square

This small-angle square is ideal for use inside a guitar when working blind through a sound hole to determine the proper angles for laying out a new bridge plate. Slip it into place, spread the legs, then use it to set a regular sliding T-bevel square to lay out a template for the new bridge plate. It is small enough to fit in between the various angled struts where the average angle square would be useless because of its size.

Parts and materials.

1 piece—¹⁄₃₂″ by ½″ by 6½″ aluminum.
1 piece—⅛″ by ½″ by 2¾″ aluminum, fiberboard, or what-have-you.
1 piece—⅛″ by ¾″ round head stove bolt with nut and washer.
1 piece—small spring (optional).

The drawings and photograph in Figures 15 and 16 are

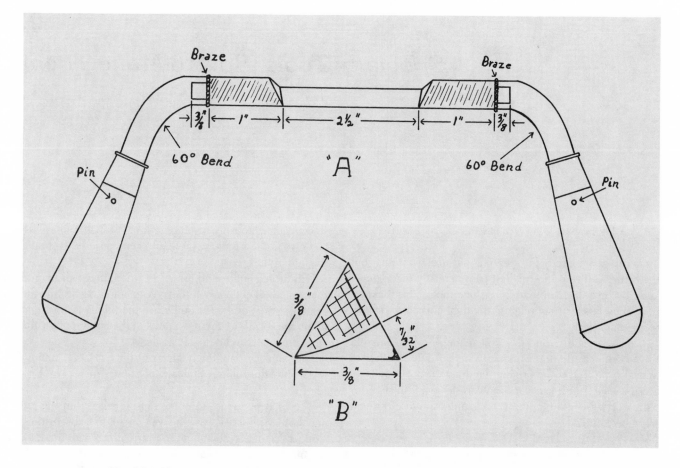

Fig. 14—Close quarters drawknife. "A" gives the general configuration while "B" shows a cross section of the central cutting area. The shaded areas of "B" represent material ground away.

pretty well self-explanatory. The aluminum strap is bent into a shallow U to fit over the center piece. Drill the ⅛" hole and assemble, then round the pivot end of the angle square. Smooth all the edges until they are free of burrs and the tool is ready for use. Figure 16 shows the angle square in use.

FRET BURNISHERS

These tools are very useful for putting the finishing touches on a fret job, particularly if the tops of the frets have been dressed to any degree or if they have been re-crowned with special fret files. The files leave a rough appearance, and a burnisher used first with 400-grit then with 600-grit Wetordry sandpaper will clean them to almost a chrome-plated appearance. Photographs in the refretting chapter will show how they are used, so I won't go into that here.

Make a burnisher for each size crown of fret wire you will be using, although in a pinch a burnisher made for a slightly larger crown will work satisfactorily on a smaller crown by slanting it first to one side, then the other.

Materials for the fret burnisher.

1 piece—³⁄₁₆" by 1¾" *very* hard wood (rosewood, ebony, lignum vitae, etc.)
1 piece—½" by 1" by 5" hardwood for the handle (I used maple for the handle).

Cut out the pieces to the dimensions in Figure 17 and sand or cut away the shaded areas. Glue the hardwood burnishing block into the handle slot, clean up, finish-sand, and wax heavily with a good paste wax (nonsilicone). Check the refretting chapter on how to hold the burnisher and sandpaper. I think that you will find that the shape I have designed fits comfortably in your hand.

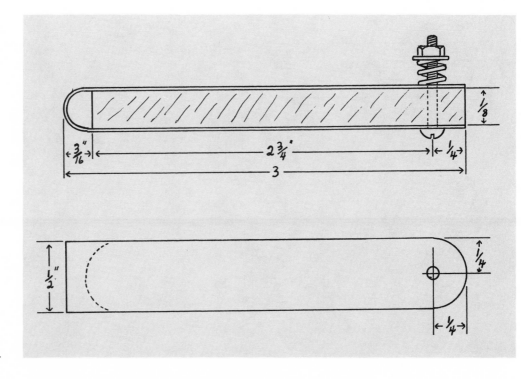

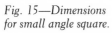

*Fig. 15—Dimensions
for small angle square.*

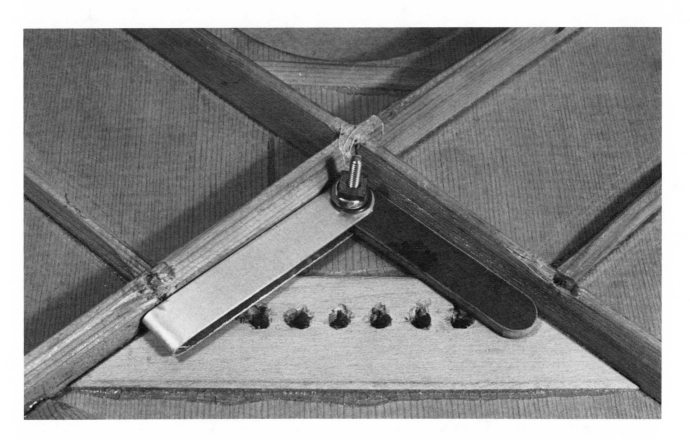

Fig. 16—A small homemade angle square used for checking strut angles to make templates for new bridge plates while working blind through the guitar's sound hole. (Shown on scrap top for photographic purposes).

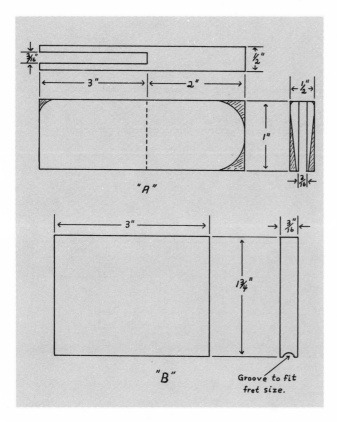

Fig. 17—Components for the fret burnisher. "A" is the handle, "B" is the blade. The shaded areas are cut or sanded away after the blade slot is cut into the handle.

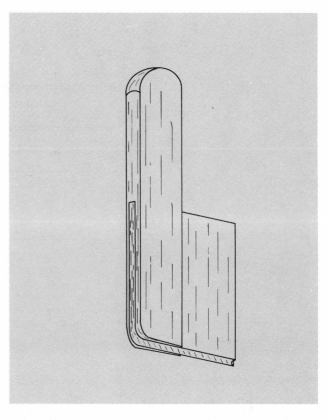

Fig. 18—Assembled fret burnisher. See the fretting chapter for instructions on using this tool.

MORE DREMEL JIGS

SHAPER TABLE FOR THE DREMEL MOTO TOOL

The Dremel Moto Tool can be used with a #229 router attachment to make a nice miniature spindle shaper. This shaper table can be used with various router bits, large burrs, miniature sanding drums, or the #402 Dremel mandrel (Figure 19) with slitting saws or cutting wheels for all kinds of jobs. It may be used with the stock guide furnished with the router attachment, the specially reworked guide shown in Volume I, pages 37 and 38, Figures 28 and 29, or the table guide shown in the drawings and photographs here.

I use the shaper table with the #407 sanding drum to finish out the back contours of Guild and certain models of Gibson bridges and making the ³⁄₃₂″ router bits needed for the two bridge slotting jigs that I have designed. Instructions for making the miniature router bits follow the plans for the bridge slotting jig in this chapter.

Parts and materials for the shaper table.

1—#229 Dremel routing attachment.
2 pieces—³⁄₁₆″ by 2″ flat-head wood screws with two ³⁄₁₆ washers and wing nuts.
6 pieces—#7 by 1½″ flat-head wood screws.
8 pieces—#7 by ¾″ flat-head wood screws—actual number required will depend on the type of base plate used for the router attachment, whether you use the standard plate or a custom plate and so on.
1 piece—¾″ by 8″ by 12″ plywood (cabinet quality) for the table top. You may use ½″ plywood in lieu of the ¾″ if desired.
1 piece—¾″ by 10″ by 17″ plywood for the table legs. It will be split into two pieces as shown later.
1 piece—¾″ by 1¾″ by 14″ plywood for the table guide.
1 piece—⅛″ by ¾″ by 14″ Plexiglas or aluminum to face the table guide.
Miscellaneous scraps of ¼″ and ½″ plywood as shown in the table guide drawings.

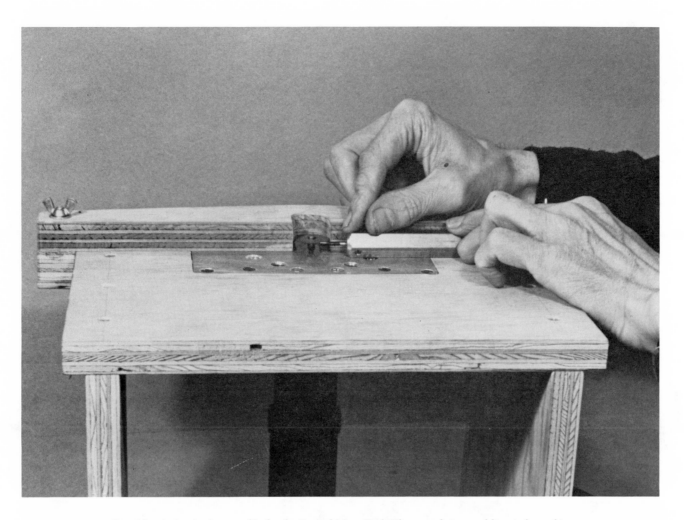

Fig. 19—*A simple shaper table for the Dremel Moto Tool. The setup being used here is for making* ³⁄₃₂″ *double–flute router bits for the bridge slotting jigs. The shaper table may be used with burrs, router bits, miniature sanding drums for shaping the backs of fancy bridges, etc.*

Lay out the table top and drill the six holes for the #7 wood screws as shown in Figure 20. I do not give dimensions for laying out the cutout area for the router base. This must be cut out to fit the particular base-plate configuration you plan to use. The three main things to pay attention to on the table makeup are to have the edge of the router base flush with the edge of the table, the flat surface of the base plate flush with the table top, and the spindle of the Dremel Moto Tool centered on the lengthwise (12″) measurement. The crosshatch shading in Figure 20 indicates the approximate area to be cut out for the Dremel router attachment, and the regular shaded area is routed deep enough for the router base plate to fit flush with the table top.

The ³⁄₄″ by 10″ by 17″ piece of plywood is laid out and sawed on the slanted saw mark shown in Figure 21. The 8″ sections of the legs are glued and screwed to the table as shown in Figure 21. The 9″ ends of the legs are at the bottom, and the slant is to the router (back) side of the table for stability. Figure 22 shows the table with the legs attached and the cutout made for the router attachment and base plate.

Construction of the table guide (Figure 23) is pretty much self-explanatory. Glue the ³⁄₄″ by ¹⁵⁄₁₆″ plywood blocks to each end, drill the ³⁄₁₆″ holes, cut out the center notch, and glue the Plexiglas (or aluminum) facing on the working edge. The ¼″ plywood pieces and ³⁄₁₆″ by 2″ stove bolts are for locking the guide to the table top.

If you want to go the fancy route, Dremel includes plans for a shaper table complete with drawers beneath the table for holding burrs, cutting tools, etc., with the router attachment set.

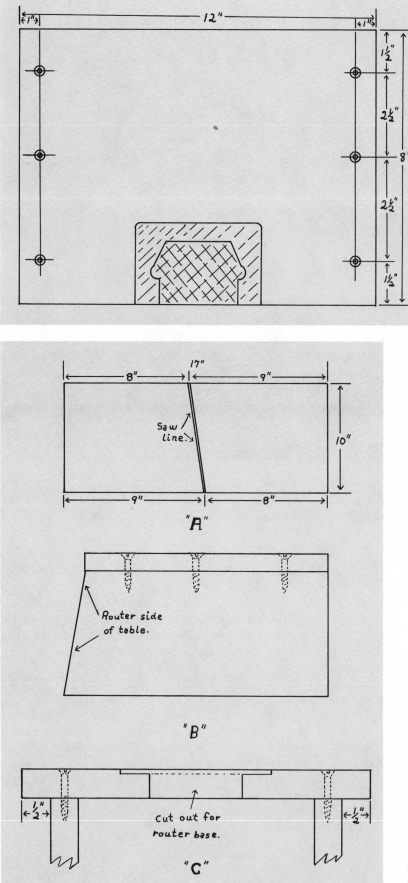

Fig. 20—The shaper table top. The six holes are drilled to ⁵/₃₂" and countersunk for #7 wood screws. The shaded areas are determined by your router base. The double–shaded (crosshatched) area is cut out completely and the single–shaded area is routed to the thickness of your router baseplate. The baseplate screw holes are patterned for your particular base.

Fig. 21—Shaper table continued. "A" is the table's legs cut from a single piece of ¾" plywood. "B" shows the side view of the legs and top assembled. The angled leg is the back or router side of the table and the angle is for stability. "C" is the back view of the table.

Fig. 22—Shaper table continued. The table and legs have been assembled after the cutout for the #229 Dremel routing attachment has been made. The baseplate for the routing attachment is my own design, but you may use the original baseplate if desired.

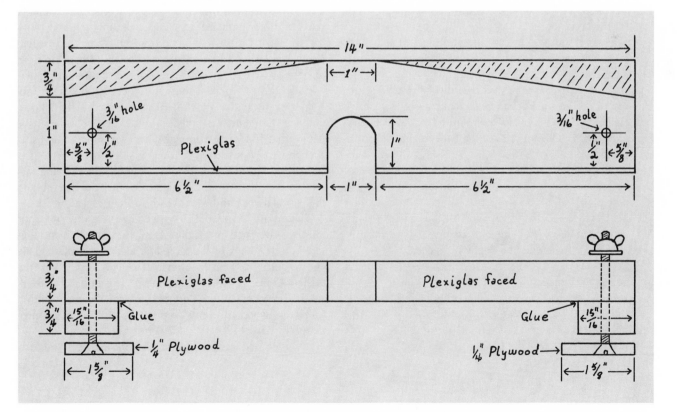

Fig. 23—Shaper table continued. Top and front view of the guide fence. It is constructed of ¾" plywood and the edge is faced with Plexiglas. The shaded area is to be cut away.

BRIDGE SLOTTING JIG FOR THE DREMEL

In Volume I, page 128, Figure 109, I show a method for cutting bridge saddle slots using the Dremel Moto Tool with a Dremel #199 saw blade. This works fine. The one disadvantage to the method is that it only cuts a slot .125 (⅛″) deep. A slot ⁹⁄₆₄″ to ⁵⁄₃₂″ deep would give more support to the saddle but would require a different setup.

A sliding table or a fancy crossfeed system under the spindle of a high-speed drill press with a router or milling cutter would be one way to go, but my small drill press simply is not fast enough. However, the 30,000 rpm Dremel Moto Tool is ideal for small router bits, and I chose to design a universally adjustable jig around it.

The first jig I designed involved the Dremel drill press, but I had problems cutting a true slot, so I discarded it for my present jig. I went whole hog and even designed a screw feed mechanism for the jig, and it works beautifully. I know that it looks complicated to build, and it was. I probably spent two or three weeks off and on arriving at a workable combination, but if you follow instructions closely, it's not all that hard. The difficult part was arriving at the original design and dimensions.

To simplify making the jig, I have broken it down into component assemblies and will give the needed parts lists at the beginning of each such assembly. I will start with the basic table assembly.

Materials for the basic table assembly.

1 piece—6″ by 12″ by ¾″ good cabinet-quality plywood for the table top.
4 pieces—1″ by 6¾″ by ¾″ plywood glued together to make two pieces 1″ by 6¾″ by 1½″ thick for the table legs.
2 pieces—1″ by 6″ by ½″ thick hardwood (I used scrap rosewood) for the backup guide locking pieces.
2 pieces—1″ by ½″ by ½″ plywood to be glued to the bottoms of the front ends of the backup guide locking pieces.
2 pieces—1″ by 1½″ by ¼″ plywood to be glued to the bottoms of the back ends of the backup guide locking pieces.
1 piece—1″ by 12″ by ¼″ plywood for the backup guide.
1 piece—⁷⁄₁₆″ by ¹¹⁄₁₆″ by 8″ hardwood (rosewood or ebony) for the guide rail–depth adjuster.
4 pieces—³⁄₁₆″ by 1¾″ flat-head stove bolts with washers, hexagonal nuts, and wing nuts.
2 pieces—³⁄₁₆″ by 1³⁄₁₆″ drill rod or other plain ³⁄₁₆″ metal rod.
2 pieces—¼″ plain flat washers.
4 pieces—#7 by 1½″ flat-head wood screws.

Cut the pieces, glue, drill, and assemble them as shown in Figures 24 to 27, and the basic table assembly is complete. If you look closely at Figure 27, you will notice the two ¼″ washers slipped over the studs and between the guide rail–depth adjustment bar and the table. Their use will be explained a little later.

The next step is making the pivot-and-slide assembly. This assembly will hold the Dremel and router attachment in position and allow it to slide lengthwise over the table as well as pivot up out of the way and also make one of the height adjustments.

Pivot and slide assembly parts list.

1 piece—#229 Dremel router attachment.
1 piece—⁵⁄₁₆″ by 9½″ drill rod (polished).
2 pieces—1″ by 1¼″ by 1½″ hardwood (rosewood, maple, mahogany, etc.).
1 piece—1¹⁄₁₆″ by 1″ by 2¾″ *very hard* wood (rosewood, ebony, hardrock maple, etc.).
1 piece—¼″ by 1″ by 2¾″ hardwood (same as above) to cap the pivot block piece.
4 pieces—#7 by 1½″ flat-head wood screws.
2 pieces—#5 by ⅝″ flat-head wood screws.

There are several critical dimensions to watch in making the pivot-block-and-shaft assembly so that the pieces will slide free and true without binding. The lengthwise ⁵⁄₁₆″ shaft hole *must* be drilled true and should be done with a drill-press vise and an accurate drill press or on a metal lathe. The two ¼″ holes for the router base shafts *must* be spaced exactly and drilled to a perfect 90-degree angle to the shaft hole. In fact, if I have to make another pivot block for my jig, it will be machined from brass stock. This shaft must slide free on the ⁵⁄₁₆ guide shaft with little or no slop, and the ¼″ cap must lock the two router-base shafts tight.

Only the ¼″ plated rods and the plastic Moto Tool holder of the router attachment set are used. The flat base and edge guide are discarded, and the excess plastic on the Moto Tool holder is trimmed off for visibility while using the jig. (See Figure 29).

Make and drill the pieces as laid out in the drawing, assemble the pivot assembly, and screw the pivot assembly to the basic table assembly as shown in Figures 30 and 31.

The jig may be used as is by feeding the router by hand, but I've designed a simple screw feed mechanism that screws to the back of the table and feeds the router slowly and smoothly as I turn a crank. This leaves one hand free to handle an air hose while slotting the bridge blank. A steady flow of air on the router bit, especially when slotting resiny rosewood, prevents burning up the router bit prematurely. A ³⁄₃₂″ bit gets hot in a hurry.

A screw feed gadget sounds complicated, but mine is

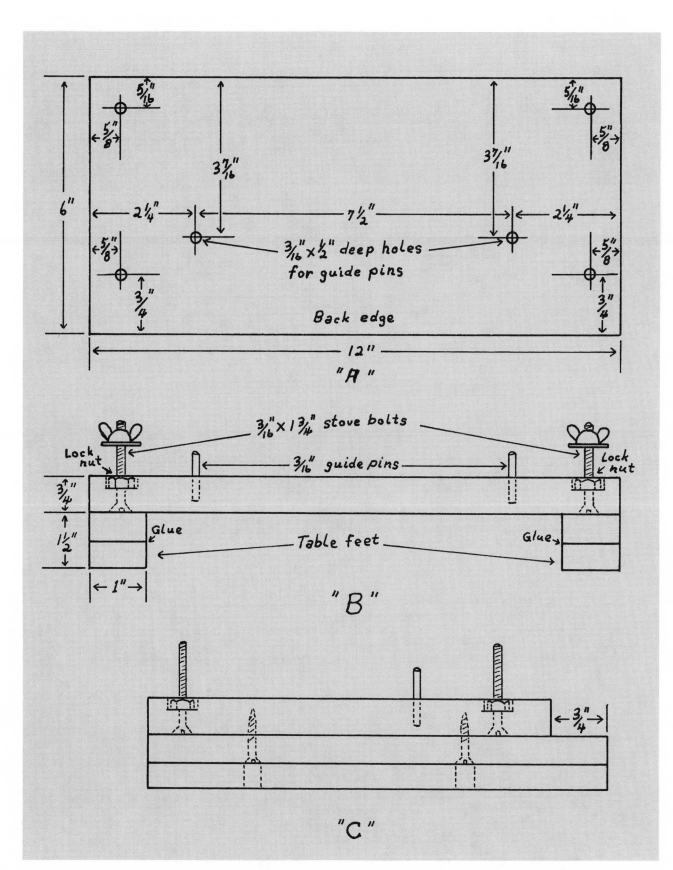

Fig. 24—Bridge slotting jig for the Dremel. "A" is the basic table layout. The four corner holes are drilled ³⁄₁₆″ and countersunk on both sides, tapered for the head underneath, and drilled for ³⁄₁₆″ lock nuts to fit flush on the top. "B" shows the front view with the legs, stove bolts, and guide pins in place. "C" is the end view of "B".

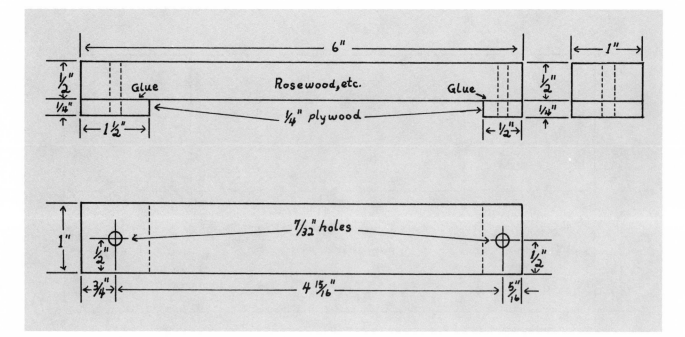

Fig. 25—Bridge slotting jig continued. Backup guide locking pieces. Two of these are needed.

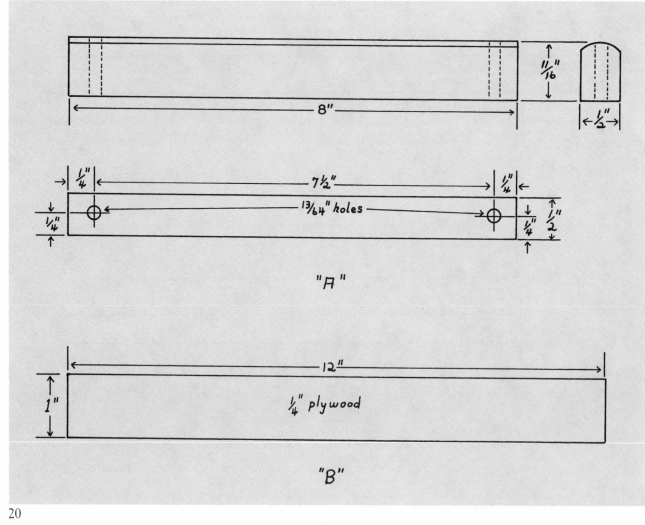

Fig. 26—Bridge slotting jig continued. "A" is the guide rail/depth adjuster and "B" is the backup guide. One of each is needed.

Fig. 27—Bridge slotting jig continued. The basic table set up with legs, plywood backup guide, guide locking pieces, and the guide rail/depth adjuster assembled. Note the height adjustment washers under the guide rail/depth adjuster.

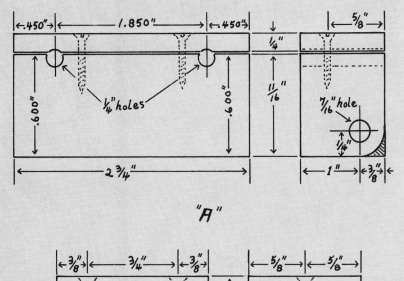

"A"

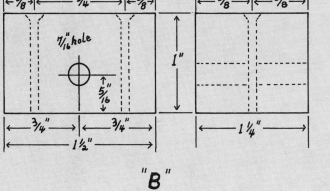

"B"

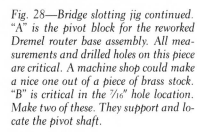

Fig. 28—Bridge slotting jig continued. "A" is the pivot block for the reworked Dremel router base assembly. All measurements and drilled holes on this piece are critical. A machine shop could make a nice one out of a piece of brass stock. "B" is critical in the 7/16" hole location. Make two of these. They support and locate the pivot shaft.

21

Fig. 29—Bridge slotting jig continued. Needed portion of #229 Dremel routing attachment with the excess plastic trimmed away and the bottom sanded flat as compared to an untrimmed piece. The excess material is removed for better visibility while using the jig.

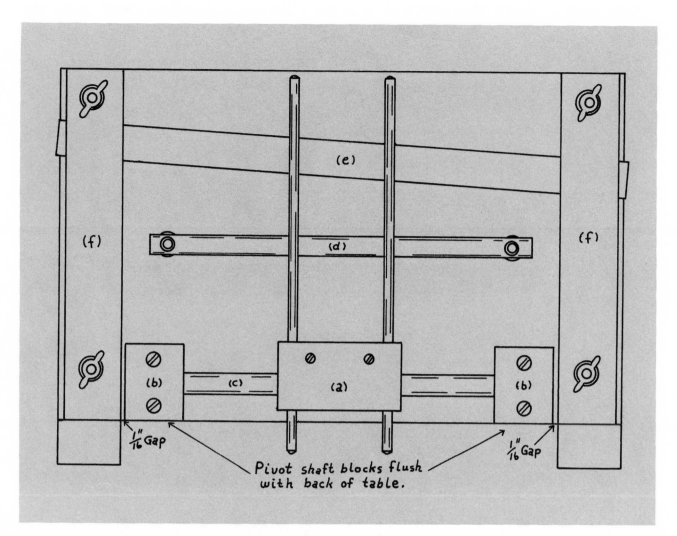

Fig. 30—Bridge slotting jig continued. Location of pivot (a), pivot blocks (b), pivot shaft (c), in place on the basic table with the guide rail/depth adjuster (d), bridge backup guide (e), and backup guide locking pieces (f). The pivot blocks are screwed down flush with the back of the table with 1/16" gaps between them and the backup guide locking pieces. The photograph in Fig. 31 gives a better perspective of the layout.

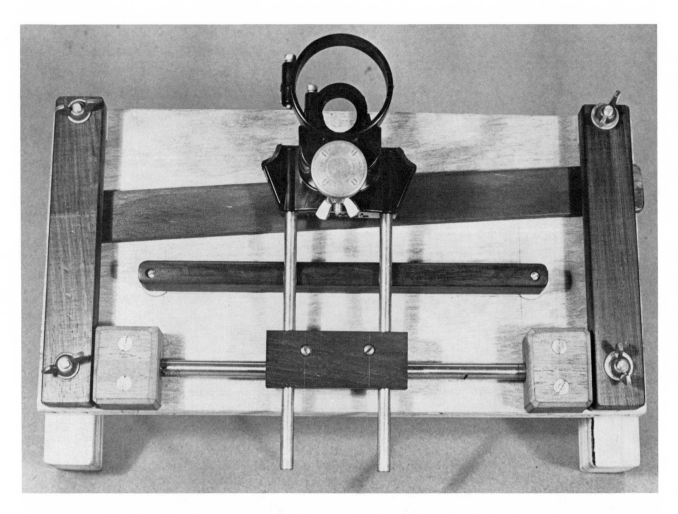

Fig. 31—Bridge slotting jig continued. The pivot and slide assembly is assembled and screwed to the basic table. The Dremel Moto Tool may be set into place and the saddle slotting jig used "as is" by feeding it with your hand. However, the screw feed mechanism is worth the time and effort to make for smoothness and ease of operation. It's also easier on router bits.

Fig. 32—Bridge slotting jig continued. The screw feed mechanism is assembled and screwed to the back of the jig.

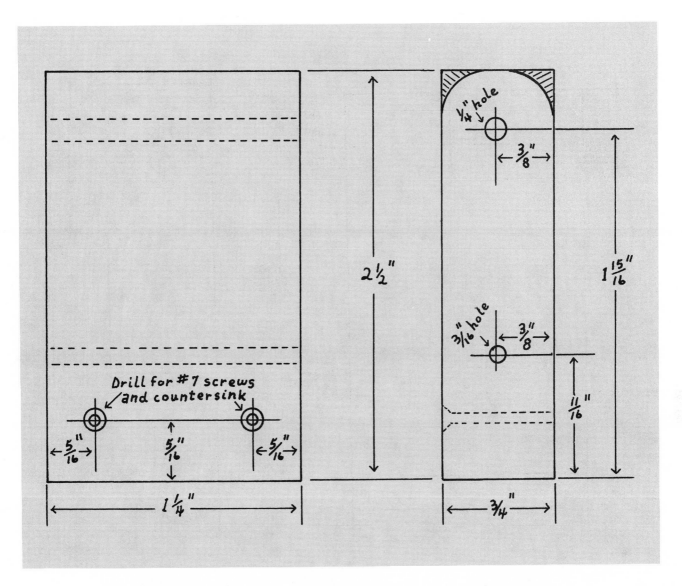

Fig. 33—Bridge slotting jig continued. The screw feed mechanism guides. Two of these pieces are needed and the ¼″ and ³⁄₁₆″ holes must be perfectly in alignment. You might start with a single ¾″ x 2 ½″ x 2 ½″ block and split it into two pieces after drilling the ¼ and ³⁄₁₆″ holes to insure a proper alignment. Shades areas are cut or sanded away.

simple if made a step at a time. It is made from threaded rod, nuts, washers, and scraps of wood.

Parts list for the screw-feed mechanism.

1 piece—¼″ by 13″ threaded, cadmium-plated Ready Rod (available from hardware stores).
6 pieces—¼″ washers.
5 pieces—¼″ plated hexagonal nuts for the Ready Rod.
2 pieces—⅞″ by 1¼″ by 2½″ hardwood (rosewood, maple, etc.).

1 piece—¾″ by 1 ¹⁹⁄₃₂″ by 2¼″ hardwood (the same as above).
1 piece—¼″ by ⅝″ by 2″ hardwood (crank handle).
1 piece—½″ by 1½″ dowel (rest of the crank handle).
4 pieces—#7 by 1½″ flat-head wood screws.
1 piece—#7 by 1½″ round-head wood screw.

The wooden parts are cut, drilled, slotted, and assembled as shown in Figures 33 to 35, then screwed to the back of the basic table assembly (see Figure 32). The center wooden piece should fit snugly between the two ¼″ rods of

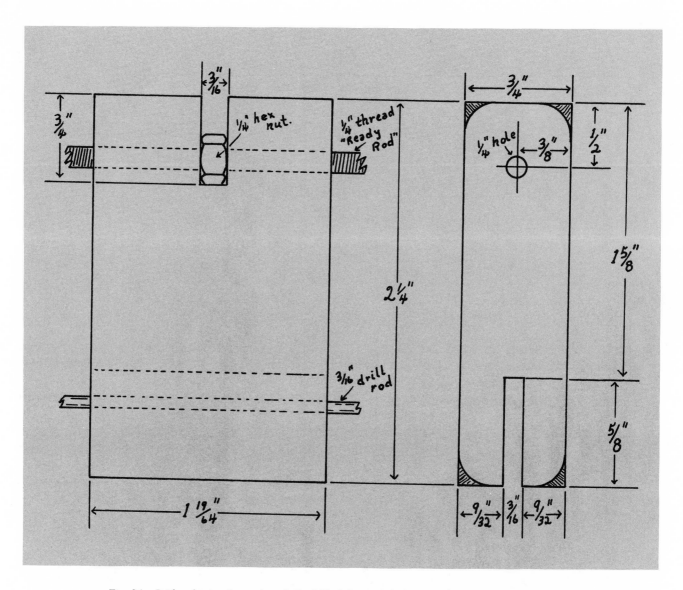

Fig. 34—Bridge slotting jig continued. Feed block for screw feed mechanism. Shaded areas are cut or sanded away.

the router attachment but should have enough clearance so that the router attachment will pivot up and down freely of its own weight. A small amount of sanding and fitting may be necessary if the two holes in the pivot block were drilled off a few thousandths of an inch.

If you want to get fancy—I did—the holes for the ¼" Ready Rod can be drilled larger and sections of ¼" I.D. aluminum or copper tubing can be pressed into the holes for bushings to minimize wear. It's a nice finishing touch, because the sharp threads on the Ready Rod can wear out the wood if unbushed, but a small amount of looseness in the feed rod will not impair the efficiency of the jig.

Using the bridge slotting jig is easy, although I would suggest trying it out on a piece of scrap to get the feel of it (see the photo in the bridging chapter). Set the Moto Tool in place with a ³⁄₃₂" router bit chucked up. Make sure that the spacer–depth-setting washers are in place under each end of the guide rail-depth adjuster. Loosen the four wing nuts on the backup guide locking pieces and slip the ¼" plywood backup guide back out of the way.

Center the laid-out bridge blank on the front of the table and clamp it in place with two large spring clamps (photo in bridging chapter). Loosen the two top screws in the pivot block and slide the router back and forth until the bit is

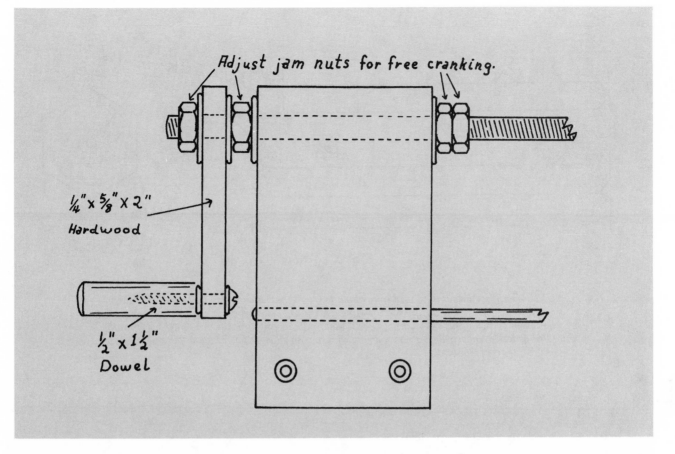

Fig. 35—*Bridge slotting jig continued. Crank and handle assembly for the screw feed mechanism. The handle may be used on either end of the feed rod for right or left–hand usage. The block opposite the feed crank acts simply as an idler to keep the rods aligned.*

roughly centered over the saddle slot layout line and then retighten them.

Crank the router (Dremel) back and forth, shifting the bridge blank as necessary to center the router bit on the saddle slot line and reclamp with the spring clamps. When centered, move the ¼" backup guide up snug against the back of the bridge blank and tighten down the four wing nuts.

Adjust the height adjustment on the *router base* until the tip of the router bit rests lightly on the top of the bridge blank, then lock it. Pivot the router assembly up out of the way, lift out the guide rail-depth adjuster bar and remove the washers, then slip the bar back in place on the studs. I use 1/16" thick washers, which will give me a saddle slot approximately 9/64" to 5/32" deep. A piece of masking tape added to the thickness of the washers will add another 1/64" to 1/32" more depth if you want a deeper saddle slot. You can experiment for the depth you need.

Keep the router pivoted up out of the way and crank it

down to the right end of the required saddle slot (facing the front of the jig) and start the Moto Tool. Lower it gently until the cutter bottoms in the wood. Blow a steady stream of air on the router bit at all times while it is cutting. Start cranking slowly so that the router moves to the *left*. Always *make the first cut from right to left* as the torque of the router pushes the bridge blank back into the backup guide. If you go left to right, the spring clamps will allow the bridge blank to shift out of position and screw up your saddle slot.

When you reach the end of the laid-out saddle slot, *then* you can crank it right to left until the bit is back to its starting point. Shut off the Dremel. Pivot it up out of the way, replace the two spacing washers under the guide rail-depth adjuster (to keep from losing them), remove the spring clamps and bridge blank, and you have a beautifully smooth saddle slot.

On a compensated (wider) saddle slot do not remove the spring clamps or replace the washers yet. Loosen the two

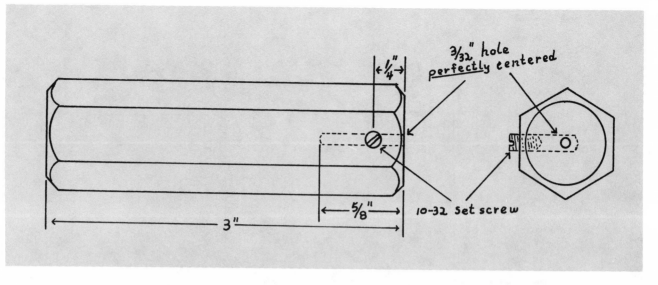

Fig. 36—Drill rod holder to be used in combination with the shaper table and Dremel for making the 3/32" router bits for the bridge saddle slotting jig. I used 5/8" hexagonal brass stock because that's what I had on hand, but 5/8" square stock will work just as well. Note: the 3/32" center hole must be drilled perfectly centered since we are working with such small stock for the router bit and should be bored on a lathe for accuracy.

screws in the top of the pivot block, lift the router bit free of the saddle slot, and slide it back the necessary distance for the wide slot, lock the screws again, turn on the Moto Tool, and make the next cut, again right to left, then back. Repeat if necessary until the slot is the proper width.

Where do you get a 3/32" router bit? See the next section of the special tool chapter.

MAKING A ROUTER BIT FROM SCRATCH; ANOTHER DREMEL JIG.

Double-flute router bits as small as 1/8" are available from any supplier handling the Dremel line, but most bridge saddles are cut for 3/32" saddle slots. Small-shanked, single-flute "veining" bits used to be available for large routers using an adapter, and these would fit the Dremel chucks without the adapter. It may still be possible to find some of these in old stock, but they are unavailable in my area. Nowadays they just grind the small veining bits on a standard 1/4" router shank, and they are useless for our purpose. The single-flute jobs had a tendency to wander anyway if you forced them, and the double-flute bits that I will show you how to make are much better. The following jig and setup are designed to be used in combination with the shaper table described earlier in this chapter.

Parts and tool list for router bits.

1 piece—5/8" by 3" hexagonal or square brass stock.
1 piece—10–32 by 1/4" set screw.
1—#402 Dremel mandrel for cutting wheel.
1—#409 Dremel cutting wheel (pick up a package to have some extras on hand).
Miscellaneous small files. A flat and a three-cornered Swiss needle file will do and may be purchased at your local X-acto dealer individually.
1 stick—3/32" drill rod to be cut into 1¼" lengths for the router bits.

The first step is to make the drill-rod holder (Figure 36). You will have to drill the 3/32" by 5/8"–deep hole in a lathe to get it perfectly centered—and it *must* be perfectly centered. This dimension is critical since we are working with only 3/32" stock and any out-of-roundness will ruin the bits if the hole is off more than two- or three-thousandths inch. A 5/32" hole is then drilled a quarter inch from one end and tapped to a 10/32" thread for the set screw. After tapping, run the 3/32" drill back into the end hole to remove any burrs.

Saw (do not cut with wire cutters) several 1¼" lengths of 3/32" drill rod. *Both* ends of the rod must be perfectly flat and square because the router flutes will be cut on both ends of each section of the drill rod. To square them up nicely, chuck each piece in a drill press, turn it on high speed, and run them down against the side of a fine hone. Why not the bottom or top of the hone? Save that for your knives and chisels, etc.

After squaring up, set a piece of the drill rod into the holder until it bottoms and tighten the set screw.

The next step is done with the #409 Dremel cutting wheel mounted on the #402 mandrel in the Moto Tool. Set the Moto Tool in the shaper table and adjust the height of the cutting wheel so that the *top* of the cutting wheel is perfectly in line with the *center* of the drill-rod holder. Since my holder is of ⅝″ stock, the measurement from the table top to the top surface of the cutting wheel would be exactly ⁵⁄₁₆″.

Next set the depth of the cut. The bit is to be a double-flute tool, and a certain amount of material, slightly less than one-third of the drill rod should be left in the center with slightly over one-third being cut away on each side. Thus approximately one-third of ³⁄₃₂″ would be around .030″ or ¹⁄₃₂″. A piece of material, shim stock, cardboard, etc., not over .035″ thick should be placed against the face of the guide on the right of the cutting wheel, facing the guide fence, and the drill-rod holder with the drill rod in place is set against the shim stock.

Move the fence toward you until you can slide the ³⁄₃₂″ drill rod past the edge of the cutting wheel with a minute amount of drag and lock the fence in place. Double-check your setting and reset if necessary. Remove the shim stock, and the edge of the cutting wheel will grind a slot the depth of the thickness of the shim stock in one side of the ³⁄₃₂″ drill rod.

Before grinding, however, paint the drill rod with Dykem steel bluing dye or India ink. Dykem is available from most industrial suppliers. It is removed as the various metalworking steps take place and makes any unworked area highly visible. The next steps are shown in the drawings.

Put on your safety glasses and turn on the Moto Tool. Slide the drill-rod holder *from right to left* until the cutting wheel makes contact (see Figure 19 for a look at this operation). Work slowly to prevent burning the drill rod. Cut a short distance and quench in water. Continue until the first slot is about ⁵⁄₁₆″ in length. It should resemble "A" in Figure 37 from the end view. Turn the holder *exactly* 180 degrees and cut the same length slot in the opposite side of the drill rod. The end view should now resemble "B" in Figure 37.

Lower the cutting wheel the amount of the wheel's thickness and repeat the grinding process on both slots. The end view should now resemble the drawing "C" in Figure 37. Lower the cutting wheel again and repeat the grinding process as before. The end view should resemble "D" in Figure 37.

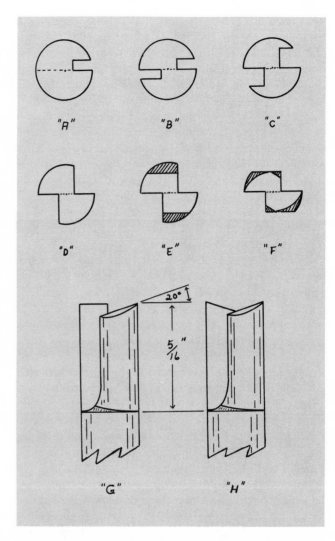

Fig. 37—The eight steps to making a double–flute ³⁄₃₂″ router bit (much enlarged, of course) using the drill rod holder and shaper table with the Dremel Moto Tool and a mandrel-mounted cutting wheel. See the text for the details.

Remove the drill rod from the holder, reverse it to the new, uncut end, lock it in place with the setscrew, blue it with Dykem, and repeat the whole procedure on the opposite end. I find it advantageous to set up and make several bits—usually six—at the same time. Six double-ended router bits give you the equivalent of a dozen bits and should last a year in moderate use. At any rate, one or six, the work with the power tools is done. The rest is done by hand with the flat and three-cornered needle files.

I still use the holder, however, for ease of handling the tiny things during the filing process. File away the shaded area marked in "E" of Figure 37 with the small flat file, working the length of the slots. An eyeglass-type magnifier is handy here if your eyes aren't too sharp. Once this is completed, file off the shaded corners as in "F" of Figure 37, then file the final clearance (shaded area in "F" also) up to the cutting edges. Be very careful here and file only until the Dykem is no longer visible. The only Dykem left will be on the shank past the work area and the flat ends. Both flutes of your new router bit now have side clearance.

The end clearance is the next step. I use the three-cornered needle file for this. Clamp the holder in a vise so that you can use both hands on the file and file a 20-degree bevel on one flute as in "G" of Figure 37. Then bevel the opposite flute. It should now resemble "H" in Figure 37. This end is now ready for heat-treating. First, though, reverse the bit in the holder and file the clearances on the opposite end.

For a better visual check than the drawings, I would suggest doing as I did when I made my first router bit. I bought a larger double-flute bit and studied it closely. It will give you a three-dimensional look at how they are made. The whole process of making a router bit sounds a bit scary until you have made a few, then it's routine.

Hardening the cutting ends sounds scary, too, but is relatively simple. I use Kāsenit hardening powder (available through your industrial supply) and a propane torch. Clamp the router bit lightly in a pair of Visegrips, heat the flutes red-hot, dip the end into the hardening powder, reheat until the powder melts and the whole end is red-hot again. Plunge the end into cold water with a rapid swishing motion and repeat the process on the opposite end. The cutting edges will be case-hardened almost file-hard.

Clean off the residue of melted powder with a wire brush and hone the *flat side* (inside) of the cutting edge with a slipstone, such as the Norton #MS24. Never hone the outside or rounded edge or you will narrow the width of the router bit. Always hone lightly with the slipstone before using or, as I do, after using. This way it's sharp and ready for the next time you need it.

Bridge Slotting Jig (on the Guitar) for the Dremel, an Improvement

Plans for the basic jig are found in Volume I, pages 38 and 39, Figures 30 and 31. Figure 31 shows the jig in use. I have used this jig often and had only one problem with it. You cannot see what the router bit is doing very well—specifically, to see when you are at the beginning and end of your cut. It needed some stops that could be preset so that all that was required was setting the Dremel in place in the guide, butting it up against one stop, then running it down to the next stop and removing it. No hassle about overrunning the original slot. The drawing (Figure 38) shows my solution to the problem, and the photo (Figure 39) shows how it works.

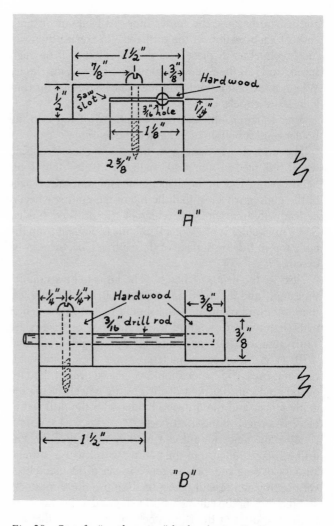

Fig. 38—*Stop for "on the guitar" bridge slotting jig. Two stops are needed. "A" shows the end view while "B" shows the back view. For instructions on building the complete jig, see Volume I, page 38, Figure 30.*

I visited the Martin factory back in 1976, and one of the repairmen took me back to his workbench to show me something. It really made my day to find out that the Martin repair shop liked one of my ideas well enough to use this jig on their repair line. I knocked out a quick sketch of the stop improvement while I was there, and he took it straight to the jig shop to be made. He even had me autograph his copy of my repair book while I was there. As I said before, it really made my day.

Parts and materials for the stops.

2 pieces—½″ by ½″ by 1½″ hardwood.
2 pieces—⅜″ by ⅜″ by ⅜″ hardwood.
2 pieces—2¾″ by ³⁄₁₆″ drill rod or other smooth ³⁄₁₆″ rod.

Fig. 39—Guide stops for the "on the guitar" bridge saddle slotting jig in place. See Figure 38. The Martin shop liked the idea enough to make and use this jig.

I think that the drawings and photograph (Figures 38 and 39) can explain how to make them better than words, so please refer to them. This is the last of the Dremel jigs.

DOVETAIL JIG AND CUSTOM ROUTER BIT

This jig would normally be of little use to the average repair shop unless you are making guitars, but I decided to include it for those of you who might be interested. I did use it once for a repair job you will find mentioned later on in this volume.

If you are occasionally making a guitar using the Euro-

pean and American technique of dovetailing the neck to the body, you know that cutting a close-fitted dovetail joint by hand can be a real problem. Back when I had time to make a few guitars, I would get a perfect fit on about one in five and would end up having to shim the others to fit. One day I got disgusted and decided to attempt to make a jig that would simplify cutting a mating dovetail. It turned into a major project figuring all the dimensions—mostly by hit or miss—but I was finally able to come up with one that worked very well indeed.

Most of the metal parts will have to be farmed out to a machine shop unless you opt to use high-alloy aluminum

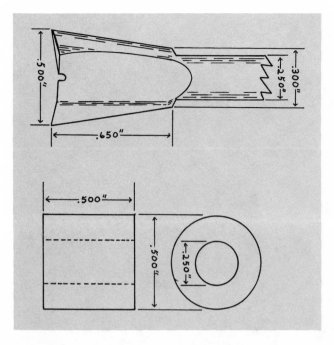

Fig. 40—Guide sleeve and router bit configuration for use with the dovetail jig. These pieces will have to be custom made, the sleeve from ½″ drill rod or bar stock, and the router bit from a straight-sided cutter. See the text.

for the main guides (I did) which can be cut with a bandsaw using a skip-tooth blade at a slow speed. However, if you plan on using the jig often, the main guide plates should be machined from steel for longevity's sake.

One problem is in finding a dovetail cutter for your router. Most of the ¼″-shank dovetail cutters will cut to only a ½″ depth, and you need one that will cut to a ⅝″ depth. It will have to be custom-ground from a large straight-sided cutter. Most industrial or woodworking supply houses can refer you to a shop that specializes in sharpening and re-working router bits, etc. For occasional use a high-speed steel cutter will suffice, but if you plan on a lot of dovetail cutting, the added expense of a carbide cutter (if you can find a shop that will tackle the job) would be worth consideration for they will outlast the high-speed steel cutters by about 10 to 1.

Have the router bit and its guide sleeve made to the exact dimensions of the drawing (Figure 40). If you slip up slightly when making the main guide plates, the router bit sleeve may have to be made a few thousandths of an inch larger or smaller to compensate. More on that later.

The two main guide plates can be laid out on a single piece of metal and sawed or milled so that the male guide is exactly .100″ smaller than the cutout for the female guide. The plate used should be around ⅜″ thick (I used

³⁄₁₆″ high-alloy aluminum glued to ¼″ plywood but would use thicker plate stock if I were making it again).

Note the dotted line 1.500″ from the bottom of the guides (Figure 41). This is the edge to where the ¾″ wooden pieces of the guide are screwed. The sizes and shape of the male and female guide plates can be varied to your individual tastes, but the .100″ difference between the male and female pieces should be maintained exactly. The dimensions in the drawings will give you a dovetail that is 1.700″ maximum width at the top with a 3.125 maximum depth.

Part one of the male guide drawings (Figure 42) shows the added piece that surrounds the male guide itself to support the router base. It may be made of the same metal as the male guide or of plywood the *same thickness* as the male guide. The rest of the guide is made from ¾″ plywood, and the male guide and router support are screwed to the edge as in Figure 43. Gussets can be used in the corners to keep the router support perfectly square with the face piece. The male guide should be lined up with the aforementioned dotted line, flush with the inside edge of the face piece.

Figure 44 shows the positioning of the neck blank in the guide and the positioning of the router, the dovetail cutter, and its guide sleeve. The ½″ hole in the face piece is used to align the jig with the centerline of the neck. Two countersunk screws hold the male guide to the end of the neck blank, and a third screw is used to lock the face piece to the neck blank. Place the whole setup in a woodworker's vise for stability while routing out the dovetail.

Figure 45 shows the female guide screwed to the ¾″ face piece. Again, the aforementioned dotted line is positioned on the inside edge of the face piece. The countersunk screwhole at the tip of the female guide (marked "A" in Figure 45) is to fasten the guide to the guitar. The hole left will be covered by the heel after the neck is set into place. The face piece is clamped to the face of the guitar with a "C" clamp as in Figure 46.

The jig is easy to use once it's completed. Line up the male jig on the center of the neck blank as in Figure 44. The female guide is attached to the guitar's body as shown in Figure 46.

Slip the guide sleeve over the dovetail cutter, chuck it into the router, and set the depth to where it will cut a ⅝″ deep female dovetail into the guitar body's neck block. Reset the router cutter depth ³⁄₃₂″ shallower and rout out the male dovetail on the butt end of the neck. If you wish, you can leave the depth set for a ⅝″-deep cut and saw off a small amount to give a bit of end clearance between the butt of the male dovetail and the neck block. There must be a small gap there for water and a soldering-iron tip should the neck ever need removing.

However, before using the jig on an instrument, you should try it out on some scrap wood for fit. If the male

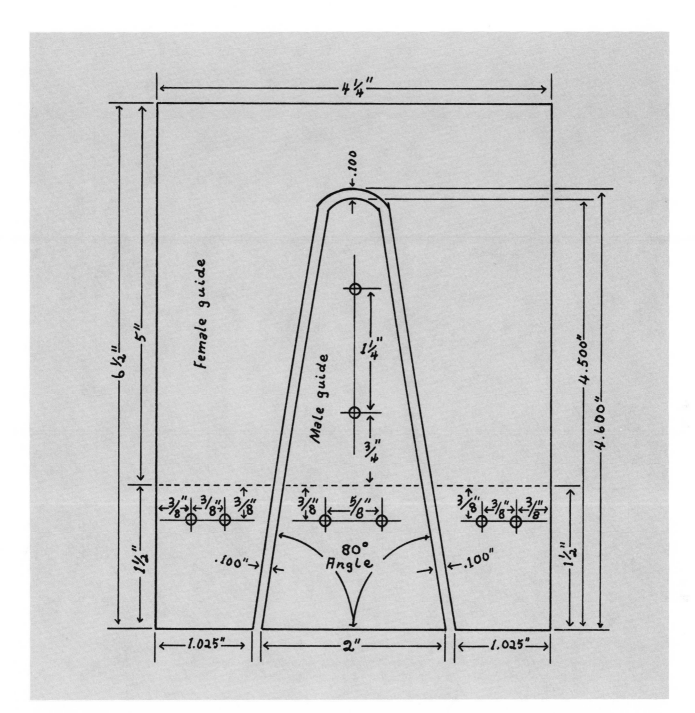

Fig. 41—Dovetail jig main guide plates, male and female. The eight holes are drilled ⁵/₃₂″ and countersunk from the face for #7 wood screws. The dimensions and shape of the guide plates maybe altered for a different length and width dovetail, but the .100″ difference in size between the male and female guide surfaces must be maintained for use with the dovetail cutter and sleeve in Figure 40. The dotted line is scribed on the back side of the two plates for the inside positioning of the ¾″ plywood part of the jig. See the next drawings and the text.

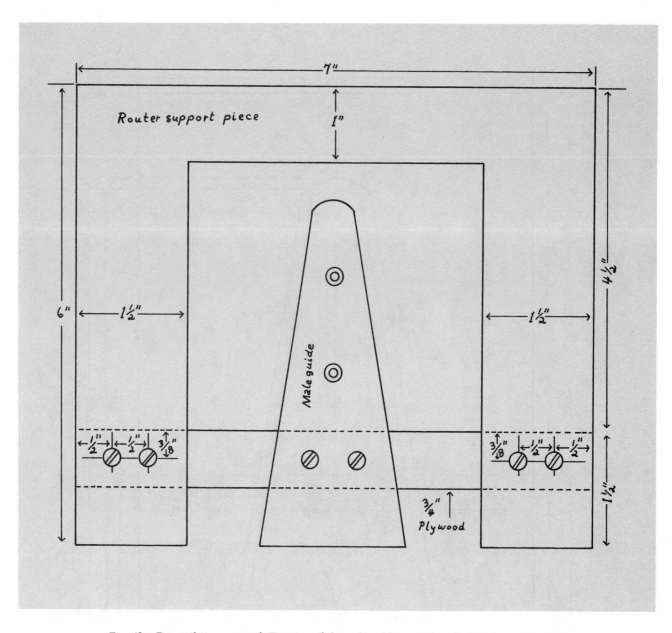

Fig. 42—Dovetail jig continued. Top view of the male guide screwed to the ¾" plywood faceplate with surrounding support piece. The support piece must be exactly the same thickness as the male guide. Only the support dimensions are given in this drawing. See Figure 41 for the male guide dimensions.

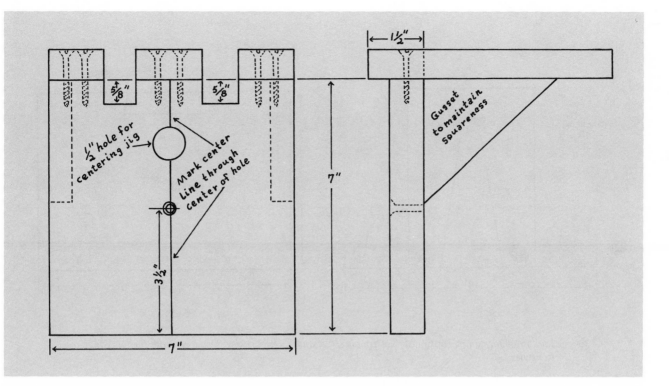

Fig. 43—Dovetail jig continued. Front and side views of the male dovetail jig and support mounted on the ¾" plywood face piece with ½" gussets (use two) in place to maintain squareness.

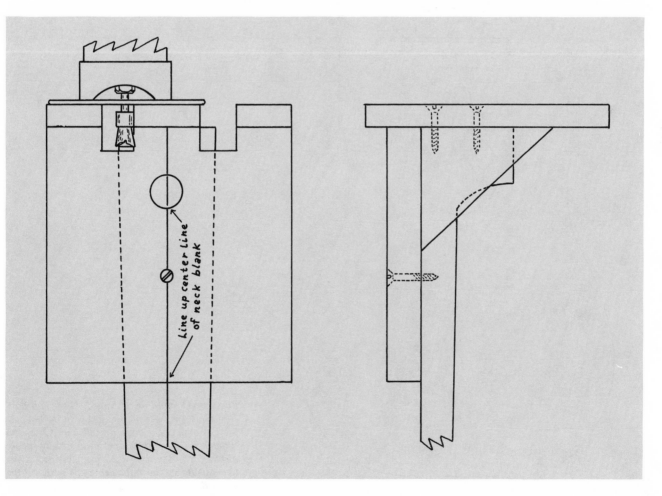

Fig. 44—Dovetail jig continued. Front and side view of the male dovetail jig with a neck blank screwed into place. The dovetail cutter and sleeve is set up in the router and the wood routed out following the male guide for a perfect dovetail.

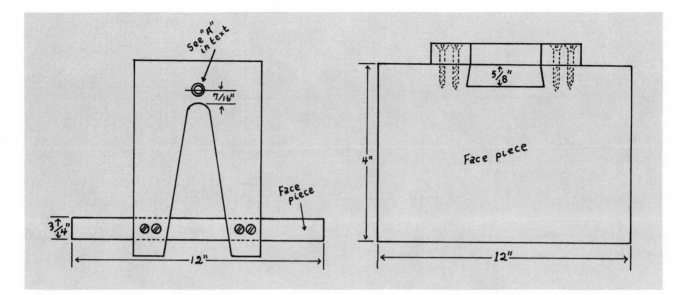

Fig. 45—Dovetail jig continued. The female guide and it's ¼" plywood face piece from the top and front view.

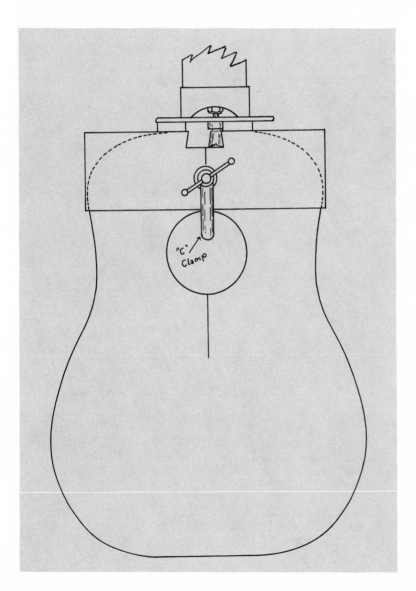

Fig. 46—Dovetail jig continued. The female dovetail jig is lined up and squared with the body at the top and upper bout. Install one "C" clamp through the sound hole and finish locking the jig in place with the screw ("A" in Figure 45) at the upper bout. Set the router depth and route out the dovetail.

Fig. 47—Dovetail jigs, male and female. These are slightly different than in the drawings which are the way I would make them if I had to do them again.

dovetail is too large to fit the female dovetail, take a few thousandths of an inch off the router-bit sleeve. If it's a sloppy fit, have a larger O. D. sleeve made or shim the dovetail to the proper fit.

Figure 47 shows a photograph of my jig. It ended up a little rough after some extensive reworking during the developing process, but it will give you an idea of what the finished jig should look like.

Bridge Plate Heater

In 1965 (I think) C. F. Martin started using larger bridge plates in their dreadnought guitars to minimize "bellying" in the bridge area of the tops, and most other manufacturers followed suit. This was an excellent idea that even seemed to improve the tonal qualities—possibly by stiffening the central area of the top to help it vibrate more as a unit, as well as eliminate the bellying.

Well, almost. There are those people who leave an instrument in the trunk of a car in hot weather or find other ways of exposing the guitar to "heat prostration." The glue softens, and the top pulls loose from the struts or allows the bridge plate to shift. When it cools off, you have a belly like a boat's bottom.

The problem then is removing this larger bridge plate so that the loose struts can be glued, if necessary, and the top can be flattened by reverse clamping and gluing in a new unwarped bridge plate.

In Volume I, pages 29 and 30, Figure 22, and on page 142, Figure 121, I show how to make and use a reworked wood chisel for pulling a standard bridge plate (an idea I got from the Martin factory repair shop). I still use this tool, but with the advent of the modern glues the bridge plates are more tenacious and, with the larger plates, almost impossible to remove by this method without tearing up the top. The grabber, hook, or whatever you want to call it needs some help in the form of the enemy—heat—to soften the glue for ease of removal.

I really pondered over this problem after removing several bridge plates in splinters to keep from damaging the top itself. One method I used with some success was to machine a brass shoe that screwed onto the tip of a small pencil-type soldering iron in lieu of the standard tip. It worked, after a fashion, but was hard to handle and took a long time to heat to a working temperature. Finally I discarded it and went back to the drawing board.

What I needed was something with a fairly large shoe to cover more area and something that would retain heat for

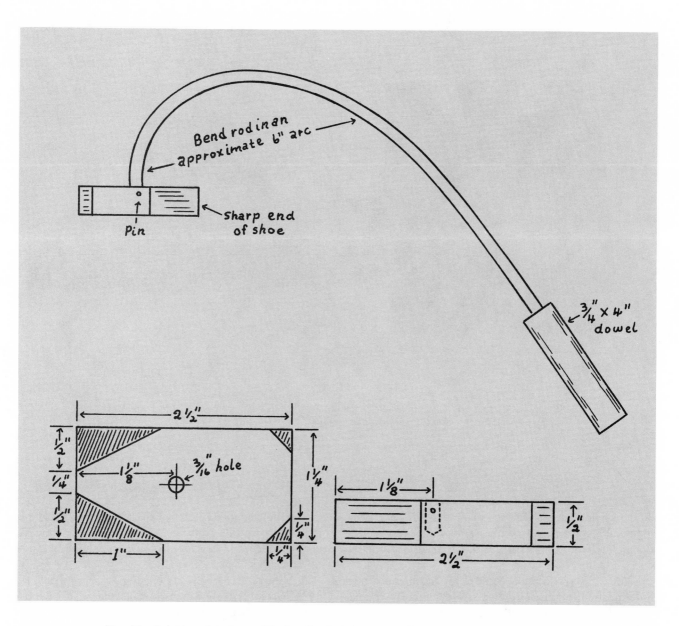

Fig. 48—A bridge plate heater. The heavily shaded areas on the metal shoe are cut away and discarded.

a usable length of time—preferably something with a slender handle so that I could use it and a mirror at the same time through the soundhole and see what I was heating.

The drawings in Figure 48 are the results of several experiments. I tried square, rectangular, round, and triangular shoes of several sizes before settling on the shape and dimensions in the drawings. It fits for maximum area coverage on x-braced tops, as well as ladder or lute-strutted tops, on small or large (with several heatings) bridge plates. For my own usage, it seems to be a happy medium.

I won't bother with a parts list, for only a few parts are needed that will be described as I go. I had some ½" scrap aluminum plate (junkyard stock) lying around that I used for the shoe, but if you have a piece of brass stock, by all means use it. It will retain usable heat much longer than the aluminum.

Cut the shoe to shape with a hacksaw or a bandsaw with a *skip-tooth* blade and smooth off any burrs with a file or belt sander. The handle is simply a piece of ³⁄₁₆" mild steel (I used an old broken tension rod) or brazing rod 15" long and bent in approximately a 6" half circle on one end. Drill a hole three-fourths of the way through the top of the shoe

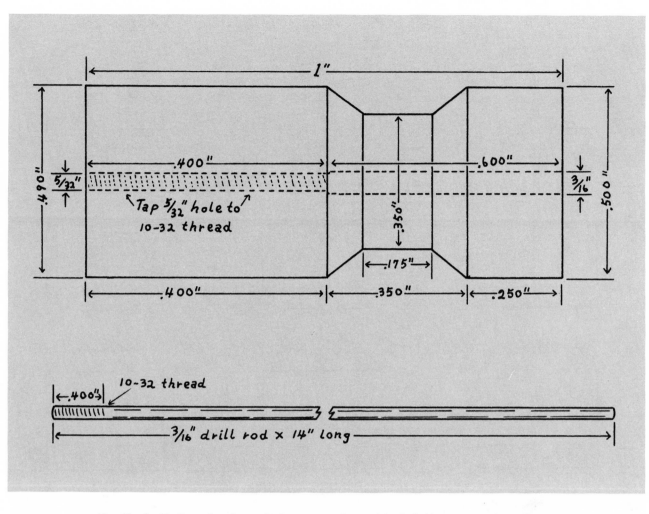

Fig. 49—Profile dimensions for machining a counterbore tool for the hidden tension rod installation.

for a press fit on the end of the rod or, better yet, pin it in place. A smoking-hot shoe loose in a guitar body could blister the finish through the wood if left in place long enough—or fry your fingers when you try to fish it out. Go ahead and pin it.

A piece of wooden dowel drilled to fit, a file handle, or even an old corncob makes a good handle on the end opposite the shoe. I use a propane torch for a heat source, but a blowtorch or gas burner will suffice. It *should not* be heated red-hot—just hot enough to vaporize the moisture from a licked fingertip. The chapter on disassembly and reassembly explains how to use the tool.

COUNTERBORE TOOLS FOR TENSION ROD INSTALLATIONS

I designed and made these tools to simplify installing tension rods, both hidden and standard peghead adjustment styles, in guitars that are not equipped with adjustable tension rods. Since I am an ex-machinist and own a small metal lathe, I was able to do my own machine work, but the average shop will have to farm out at least part of the work in the preliminary stages of construction.

You will notice in the drawings that the cutter ends of both counterbore tools are identical (specifications are marked on the "hidden rod" drawing only) except that the *cutting edges are angled in the opposite direction.* The reason for this is that the short counterbore (hidden rod tool) is threaded onto a length of ³⁄₁₆″ drill rod and works by pulling the counterbore into the workpiece rather than pushing it as in the "head-end" counterbore. In other words, they operate in opposite directions. I will describe the "hidden rod" counterbore first, but will give you a list of materials for both counterbores at the same time.

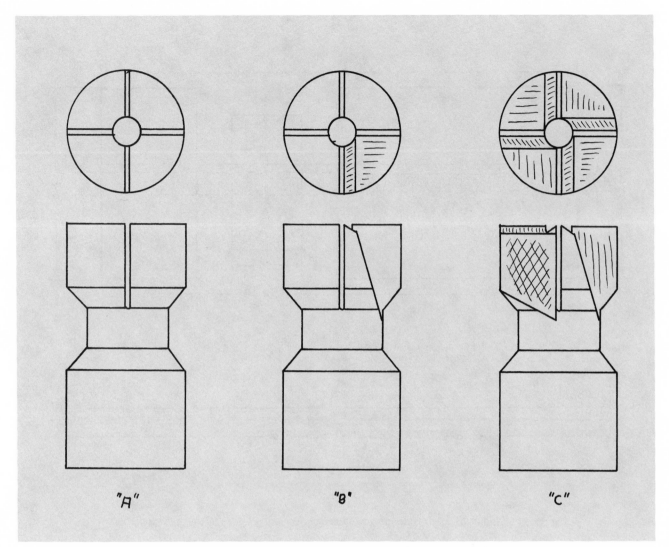

"A"   "B"   "C"

Fig. 50—Hidden rod counterbore tool continued. Saw the "X" slots in the head of the counterbore with a sharp hacksaw as shown in "A". File or grind the bevels and cutting edge as in "B". When all four bevels and cutting edges are finished, your tool should resemble "C".

Materials for the counterbore tools.

1 piece—½″ by 1″ *drill rod.*
1 piece—½″ by 5″ *drill rod.*
1 piece—½″ by 5″ *mild steel.*
2 pieces—³⁄₁₆″ by 14″ drill rod or mild steel.
1 piece—³⁄₁₆″ drill bit (to be brazed on one end of one of the 14″ rods,
1 piece—1¾″ by 1¾″ by 1¾″ hardwood.

The counterbore heads are machined from the ½″ drill rod (available from an industrial supply house). The cutter head itself is left the full ½″ diameter, but the shoulder or guide portion to the rear of the step on the short counter-

bore is machined .010″ smaller to prevent it from binding from wood chips, dust, etc., while in operation. The hole in the center is step-drilled while it's in the lathe for the exterior machine work, to ensure accuracy. Drill the first hole ³⁄₁₆″ by .300″ deep starting from the cutting edge end. Change to a ⁵⁄₃₂″ drill and drill on through, then tap to a 10-32 thread. Cut a piece of ³⁄₁₆″ by 14″-long drill rod and thread one end for ½″ with a 10-32 die. Figure 49 will give you a better look at it.

If you own a bench vise, a hacksaw with a sharp blade, and a sharp file or grinder, you can complete the counterbore tool yourself. Saw two slots through the head down to the machined relief as in drawing "A" of Figure 50. Make the cuts straight and as smooth as possible and try not to

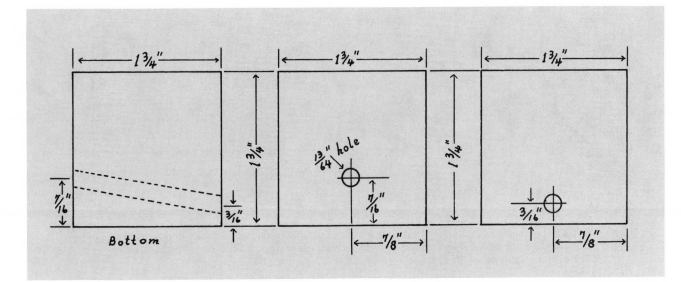

Fig. 51—Guide block for the long–shanked drill and counterbore shaft. Dimensions from the hole centers to the bottom of the guide block must be exact.

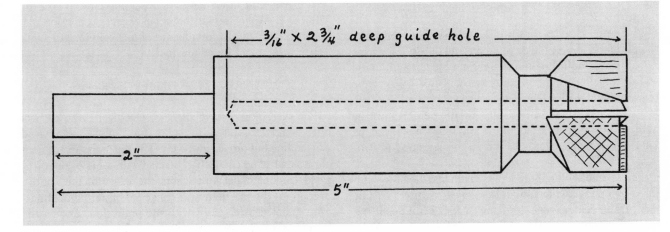

Fig. 52—A counterbore tool for peghead adjustment type tension rods. The diameters and head configuration are the same as for the hidden rod counterbore, but the cutting edges are reversed (see Figure 50) since it cuts while pushing rather than pulling as in the hidden rod tool.

scratch up the end, because this will be the cutting edge when the work is finished.

Grind or file away the metal as shown in "B" of Figure 50. Make the contour exactly as shown in the drawing. It should look like "C" of Figure 50 when finished.

To harden, heat the cutter end to a bright red with a propane torch, dip quickly into Kāsenit surface hardening compound (available from an industrial supplier) until the surface is completely coated with the powder, and reheat to a bright red. The powder should be thoroughly melted and coated. Recoat if necessary for a full coating and plunge immediately into cold water with a swishing motion. The excess compound will come off with a wire brush and leave a silver-colored, file-hard surface that will work for years in wood.

While you're having the machine work done, have a ³⁄₁₆″ by 14″ length of drill rod brazed onto the butt of a ³⁄₁₆″ drill, or try to buy a long-shanked, aircraft-type drill ³⁄₁₆″ by 14″

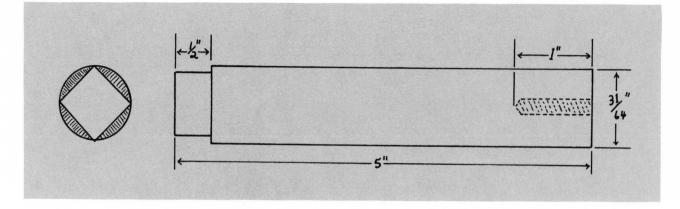

Fig. 53—Temporary tension rod nut to be used while gluing in the rod and fillet to prevent glue from filling the cutout. The 1" deep hole is drilled and tapped to a 10–32 thread. The butt end of the "nut" is squared off (shaded area) for a wrench.

or longer. An alternative is to grind off two sides of a 14" length of ³⁄₁₆" drill rod (see photo in the tension rod chapter) and sharpen the end like a spade bit. Harden it for good measure.

The guide block is shown in Figure 51. Both the long-shanked tools above, the counterbore and the drill, are used in cutting the adjusting nut socket for a hidden tension rod and work better when guided properly. I used a 1¾" cube of walnut and drilled the angled hole as shown in the drawing. The critical point is the angle on the hole. It must be right. If you miss, the bottom of the guide block can be sanded on a belt sander until it is on the ³⁄₁₆" and ⁷⁄₁₆" centers.

The second counterbore tool is made like the other with three exceptions which should be noted (Figure 52). The hole in the center is ³⁄₁₆" in diameter for its full depth (no threads) to ride on a piece of scrap ³⁄₁₆" drill rod (see the tension rod chapter) as its guide. The shank is longer, and the machined step on the butt is for chucking up in an electric drill. Also, since it works by pushing into the workpiece instead of pulling, the rake angle of the cutting edges is filed or ground in the *opposite* direction from on the short counterbore. Study the drawings closely. Don't forget to case-harden the cutter end.

The temporary tension rod nut (Figure 53) is used while gluing in the fillet over the tension rod simply to prevent any glue squeeze-out from filling the adjustment nut socket and coating the threads. It's removed after the glue is set and leaves you with a clean socket ready for the adjustment wrench and brass nut.

This piece may be made from any kind of metal (even hardwood, but the threads won't last long), as shown in Figure 53. It is heavily waxed while using so that the glue

doesn't stick to it. A square area is filed on the butt end so that a wrench can be used to remove it if it does stick.

You will find other tools for installing tension rods in Volume I, in the special tool chapter and the tension rod chapter. The tension rod chapter of this volume will demonstrate the use of these new tools.

Heater for Removing Fingerboards

For years now I have used an electric flatiron to heat fingerboards to soften the glue for removal. The iron worked fine but proved awkward. The top of the instrument always had to be carefully protected with asbestos or corrugated cardboard because where the edges of the flatiron overlapped the top there was danger of blistering the finish from radiated heat. Even with the protection, to heat the fingerboard hot enough to soften the glue the finish would sweat badly and sometimes soften to a certain degree, resulting in minor marring when working the blade of a knife between the top and the fingerboard.

The answer? Why not make an electric heater designed specifically for removing fingerboards, one that would not overhang the edges of a fingerboard? This would eliminate the need for protecting the top and would draw less current than the average electric flatiron.

With this in mind, I started experimenting. I used a single heating element and an aluminum shoe for my first try, but, although it worked, it was slow and did not provide as much heat as was needed.

The second—and successful—experiment utilized two heating elements and a brass shoe covered on the top and sides with asbestos. This one really did the trick without messing up the finish, and the parts are readily available from the local hardware store and junkyard. The brass bar stock can be purchased from most industrial supply houses, but I found mine at a scrapyard where they buy scrap metals of all kinds.

The two soldering irons that I purchased for the electric heating elements can be found at the larger hardware stores or suppliers specializing in air-conditioning ductwork. I found mine at a lumberyard. The copper tubing is stocked by most hardwares, the wiring was salvaged from the soldering irons along with the elements, and you can find the wood in your own shop. For bending the ½″ O.D. tubing, I used a spring with the loop ends ground off.

Parts and materials.

2—model #88 Lenk 75-watt soldering irons.
2 pieces—13″ by ½″ O.D. copper tubes (make them a few inches longer for ease in bending if you like).
1 piece—1″ by 2″ by 4½″ brass bar stock or two pieces of ½″ bar stock drilled, tapped, and screwed together to form a 1″ thick piece.
2—½″ by 1″ by 4½″ pieces of hardwood (for handle).
3 pieces—wood screws or ⅛″ stove bolts and nuts for attaching handle.
Optional materials for shielding (if wanted).
1 piece—asbestos soldering pad or hot pad (to be cut up for shielding).
6 pieces—miscellaneous self-tapping screws (for attaching shielding).

Grasp the tube of the soldering iron with one hand and its wooden handle with the other. Work carefully and the wooden handle will pull off of the tube. The electric pencil-type element will slide from the tube. Cut the electric cord fifteen or sixteen inches from the ceramic element and slide off the wooden handle. Ditto on the second soldering iron and you will have the guts of the fingerboard heater, two 75 watt elements or 150 watts of heating power. Be *very* careful not to crack the insulating material that covers the wires for several inches from the heating elements but do cut or break off the tab you will find clamped to the wire several inches from the element. Otherwise the wire will not feed through the copper tubes once they have been bent.

The next step may be handled by a machine shop if you are leery of tackling it yourself or don't have access to a drill press. Lay out the end of the brass shoe as in Figure 54 and drill two ½″ holes ¾″ deep in the ends. Rather than using cutting oil to cool the drill bit, I find that WD-40 works fantastically well and does not leave an oily mess to clean up (it also works beautifully for tap and die work). Change to the ¹³⁄₃₂″ drill, center in the ½″ holes, and drill them 3¼″ deeper. These smaller holes are for the electric heating

elements. They should slide right in with a couple thousandths of an inch clearance.

One of my elements, however, was not perfectly straight, and I worked it down very carefully on my disk sander until it fit. The brass will mark the high spots on the white ceramic so you will know where material has to come off. *Don't force* the element into the hole as it is fragile. Work it down until it slips in easily. In a pinch, you might drill the holes out ¹⁄₆₄″ larger, but the better the fit, the quicker the iron will heat up. The top or wire end of each element should be flush with the top of the ¹³⁄₃₂″ hole. If not, drill the hole deeper until it fits.

The next step is optional. Asbestos is hard to come by nowadays as it is considered a hazardous material if inhaled, so use a dust mask when working with it. I used an old soldering pad purchased several years back and sawed it into thin pieces. Another source of asbestos would be to cut pieces from the hot pads used over cookstove burners to prevent scorching.

Cut three pieces to fit the top and sides of the brass shoe. Drill a pair of shallow holes for each piece of shielding, making sure you drill them the right size for your self-tapping screws—and that you are not drilling into the holes for the elements—and screw on the shielding. The heater will work fine without the shielding, but with the shielding more heat will be dissipated through the bottom of the shoe into the fingerboard.

There is another optional step not shown on the plans. Most fingerboards are arched on steel string instruments and the majority of fingerboards removed will be from these. To improve the contact area, sand a slight concavity lengthwise on the bottom of the shoe using a belt sander. Work it over the end of the roller of the sander to where it will fit the curvature of a Martin fingerboard down near the body end. The brass shoe will get hot during this sanding process, but the asbestos shielding will protect your hands.

Some of the fingerboards will have more arch than others, but the slight arch will still give more contact area than a flat surface, and the slight concavity will not slow down the heating of a classical or flat fingerboard that much.

Sand out all the scratch marks left by the belt sander by using gradually diminishing grades of emery cloth or Wet-or-dry sandpaper, finishing up with 600–grit or the equivalent, then buff to a mirror finish with a cloth buffing wheel and jeweler's rouge.

Use a ½″ tubing bender, or as I did, the spring with the ends ground off, and bend the two ½″ pieces of copper tubing as per the drawing (Figure 54). They should be matched perfectly as they are pressed into the brass shoe and will carry the wires to the handle. Use a bender so that you won't collapse the tubing while bending. Next you have to slip the wires through the tubes.

Feed each element wire through the copper tube, slip

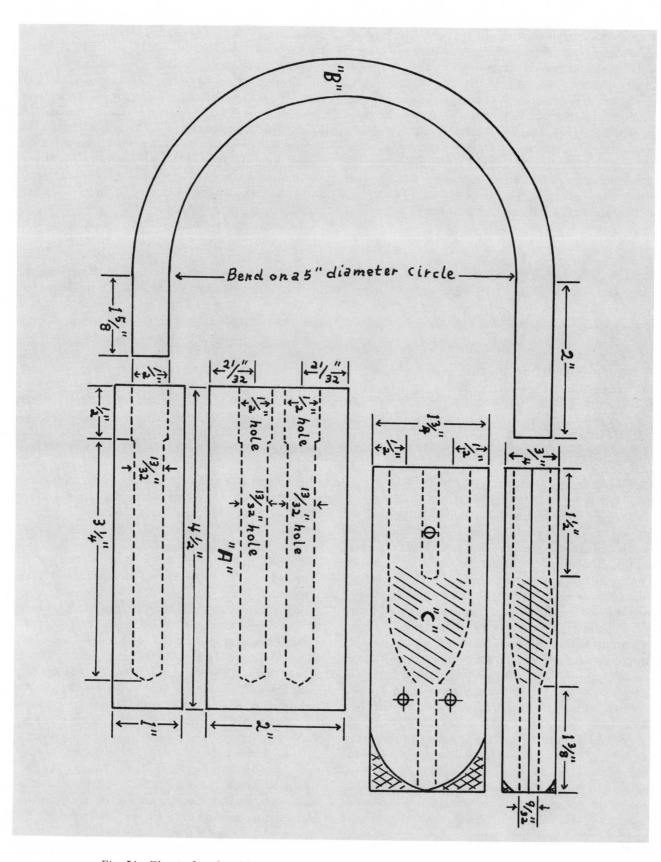

Fig. 54—Electric fingerboard heater. "A" is the brass shoe for the heating elements. "B" is the bending configuration for the ½" O. D. copper tubing. Two pieces are needed. The single–line–shaded area in the handle "C" is hollowed out with a Moto Tool and carving burr for connecting and insulating the wiring. Carve out both halves of the handle. The crosshatch shading represents material cut away.

the elements into the shoe and force the bottom ends of the tubes into the ½″ by ¾″ deep holes. They should be a snug fit. If not, you can deform the end of the copper tubing slightly until the fit is snug. Scratch a mark on the end of each tube so you will know when it's in all the way. The hard part is over.

Screw or bolt the two pieces of hardwood together and drill the two ½″ holes and the one ⁹⁄₃₂″ hole as per Figure 54. Remove the screws or bolts and gouge out the cavity connecting the three holes. I used a Dremel Moto Tool and ball cutter, but it can be done with a chisel or carving gouge. This connecting cavity is where the wires from each element and the single pair of wires for the plug-in are joined.

Trim off the excess wire, strip the ends, twist together properly, and *solder* the two connections. Use plenty of plastic electrician's tape to cover the soldered joints. Lay the bottom of the handle under the two tubes, and line up the tubes and wires. Lay the top half of the handle in place and screw or bolt together.

You are now ready to plug it in. The handle curved over the top of the shoe gives you a perfect balance for the heavy brass shoe and you can hang the iron over the edge of a workbench to heat to a working temperature where it's out of the way. It will take twenty to thirty minutes to heat that hunk of brass to a working temperature (slower than an electric flatiron) but it draws only 150 watts, whereas the electric flatiron draws approximately 1,500 watts. The brass shoe also takes a long time to cool off. You could use aluminum for the shoe for faster heating and cooling, but the weight of the brass gives you a very stable tool.

The iron actually gets hot enough that spit on a finger does not sizzle. It vaporizes instantly, and there is no need to remove the frets to heat the glue hot enough to remove the fingerboard. The frets conduct plenty of heat into the wood and it takes only minutes to remove a fingerboard once the iron has reached working temperature.

See the disassembly and reassembly chapter for the assembled fingerboard heater at work.

The String Tension Simulation Jig

This string tension simulation jig idea may sound a little "farfetched" at first, but it actually works and works very well indeed. You can take a guitar with the screwiest of necks and duplicate all the humps, dips, and twists on this jig with the strings and frets removed so that they may be planed or sanded true under the actual working tension instead of sanding on a relaxed neck.

You can even allow for the proper amount of forward bow in the neck with your calculations which is invaluable in a plane and fret job on an instrument such as the Martin guitar which does not have an adjustable tension rod.

The proper use of this jig takes all the guesswork out of refretting as the results are nearly 100 percent predictable, if you use my system of gluing in the frets rather than driving them in. I won't vouch for the results of a "drive–in" fret job as it is almost impossible to calculate the expansion of a given fingerboard owing to the varying densities of different woods, so I never drive in frets when using this jig. That's not to say that the jig cannot be used with the drive–in method, and you're welcome to experiment if you wish.

Primarily, the jig works by suspending the instrument at the butt and nut area of the neck. Then downward stress is applied at the upper bout of the instrument to simulate the tension of the strings. The use of the jig is explained thoroughly in the refretting chapter of this volume so I won't get into the operation further here.

One of the initial problems I had to overcome in making proper measurements was handling the settling of the bridge and top when the string tension was relaxed. Any measurement made from the bridge itself or from the top of the instrument in the immediate area of the bridge would be worthless when the strings were removed because of this settling factor.

Of course, you could always use a 36″ straightedge and set a block at the butt end of the top to rest one end of the straightedge on, but my straightedge is only a 30 incher and I chose to make a bridge elimination gauge which rested across the top immediately behind the bridge and is supported by hardwood blocks at the very edge of the instrument. A good tight fit is essential for an accurate measurement and I can hook rubber bands over one end of the gauge, pass them under the instrument, then hook the other end of the rubber bands over the opposite end of the gauge. This insures a firm contact between the gauge and the instrument's top.

Before proceeding any further, I will give you a list of the parts that must be purchased to make the jig. I will add the wooden parts which may be constructed of various scrap hardwood and plywood as needed during the actual instructions on making it.

Parts and materials for the string tension simulation jig.

1 piece—2″ by 4″ by 50″ extruded aluminum rectangular tubing.
2 pieces—2″ by 4″ by 6″ aluminum tubing (same as above).
1 piece—17″ by ⅜″ drill rod (preferably) or smooth cold–rolled steel.
2 pieces—½″ by 9″ threaded Ready Rod.
4 pieces—½″ hexagonal nuts for the Ready Rod.
6 pieces—½″ washers for the above rod.

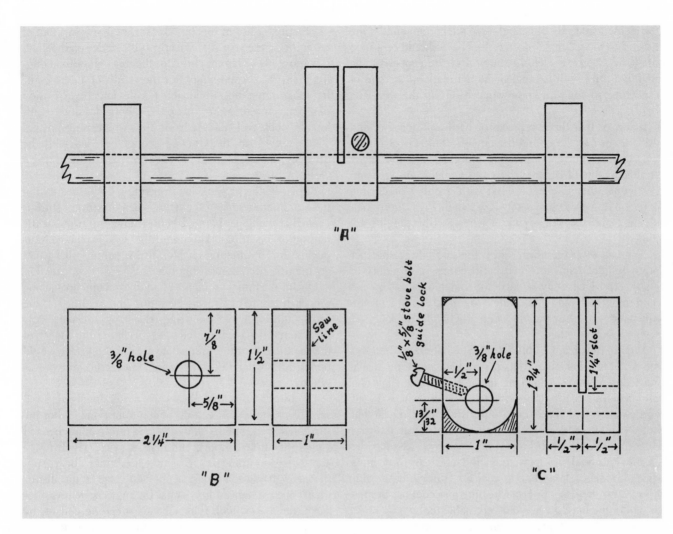

Fig. 55—The string tension simulation jig bridge elimination gauge. "A" shows the assembled gauge. "B" is the end support blocks. They are made of hardwood (rosewood, etc.) as one piece, then split into two pieces. "C" is also hardwood and is the straightedge guide. The ⅛" x ⅝" stove bolt is to lock it in place once positioned. The 1 ¼" slot is sawn only wide enough to fit your individual straightedge and the shaded areas are sawn or sanded away.

1 piece—⅜" by 1" carriage bolt with washer and wing nut.

1 piece—⅜" by 2" carriage bolt with washer and hexagonal nut.

1 piece—⅜" by 3½" carriage bolt with washer and hexagonal nut.

1 piece—1½" by 1½" by 1½" angle-iron clip.

1 piece—12" by 12" by 1/16" cork for padding.

1 piece—3/16" by ¾" round-head stove bolt with washer and wing nut.

Miscellaneous screws and hardwood, etc., to be listed as needed.

Some of these materials can be obtained at a hardware store, such as the bolts, washers, nuts, etc. The extruded aluminum and drill rod may be found at most industrial suppliers or check your local scrap yard. The cork can be purchased from almost any gasket company, and you may have to buy a large sheet, but it's inexpensive and can be used for various other purposes, padding clamp faces, clamping blocks, etc.

The bridge elimination gauge is simple to make. Study Figure 55. It consists of one piece of hardwood (ebony, rosewood, walnut, etc.) laid out and drilled according to the dimensions in Figure 55, drawing "B." This piece is

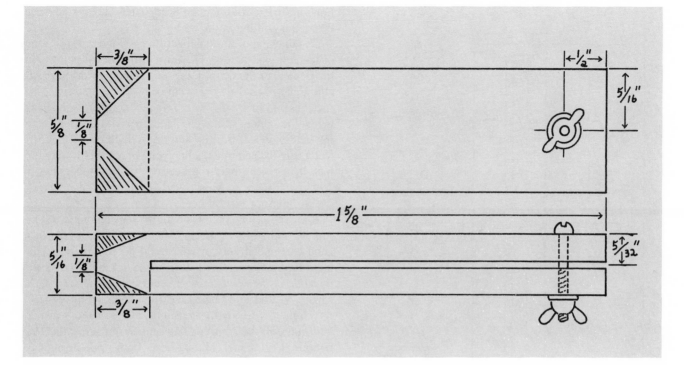

Fig. 56—String tension simulation jig continued. Fingerboard pointer for the nut end of the straightedge. The dimensions are for my straightedge and will have to be adjusted to fit yours. Retain the ⅜" measurement from the bottom of the straightedge to the bottom of the pointer, however.

split into two pieces after drilling, to ensure that each piece is identical. These are slipped over each end of the ⅜" by 17" drill rod for the edge supports. The hole is drilled off center so that you have several different heights depending on which edge of the blocks is set on the instrument. This is necessary for clearing the bridges on various types of guitars, flattops, *f*-holes, etc., with their different heights and designs of bridges.

Hardwood is also used for the moveable straightedge guide (part "C" of Figure 55) so that you can thread the wood for a stove bolt to lock it into place. The slot is cut to fit your particular straightedge and must be cut deep enough so that the straightedge will rest on the drill rod rather than the wood when making your stress measurement.

A word on the gauge rod diameter. I used the ⅜" rod to ensure no flexibility in the gauge and would recommend not using anything smaller.

I used a scrap of ebony to make my nut-end pointer, but this piece could be made of aluminum if you want to get fancy. The dimensions in Figure 56 may have to be changed somewhat to fit your particular straightedge, but the dimensions on the fingerboard contact end should be

retained as is. The shaded areas represent material to be removed.

Now that the bridge elimination gauge is out of the way, we can get into the meat of the jig. Unless you have access to and the knowhow to operate machine shop tools and heliarc equipment, this will have to be farmed out to a machine shop.

The 6" pieces of extruded aluminum should be heliarced to the 50" piece and the welds ground flat. You could use aluminum channel for the skeleton of the jig rather than rectangular tubing, but the tubing looks much neater—and the scrapyard just happened to have the tubing on hand.

For neatness and accuracy, the two ⅜" and two ½" slots in the beam (Figure 57) may be machined on a Bridgeport mill while it's in the machine shop for the welding. If you have a good sabre saw with a metal cutting blade and an accurate guide, the tubing may be slotted before taking it in for the heliarcing. Drill a ⅜" starting and finishing hole at each end of the main beam slots—½" holes for the two short slots in the short beams—and saw out, using an edge guide on the sabre saw to ensure straight cuts. The ragged edges left by the saw blade can be smoothed out with a file, but don't widen the slots so much that the square corners

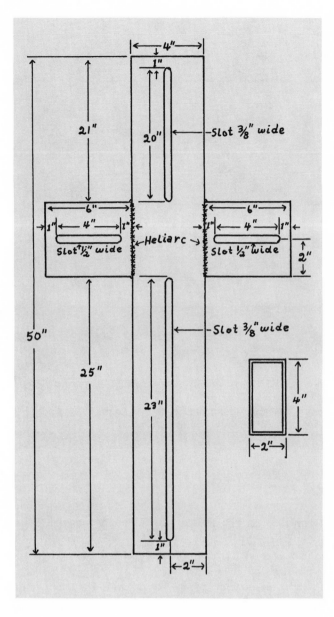

Fig. 57—*String tension simulation jig continued. The main beam layout. The slots may be milled or cut with a guided metal cutting sabre saw. The two 6" side beams are to be heliarched to the main beam and the welds ground smooth.*

on the carriage bolt heads will turn in the slots. A little file work might have to be done on the carriage bolt shoulders or slot so that they will slide freely the length of the beam slots. Ditto on the ½" Ready Rod fit for the two short slots in the short beams.

For those of you with plenty of room in your shops, this part of the jig could conceivably be built into a tabletop or workbench for a permanent installation. My own shop is rather small and cluttered (to put it mildly), so I drilled a

hole in the back of the main beam where it could be hung up on the wall out of the way.

The drawing of the stabilizer wedge (Figure 58) is more or less self-explanatory. The only really critical point is in the flatness of the contact area on the bottom of the metal clip and wedge. I used a scrap of mahogany, screwed the metal clip to the wedge with a small amount of wood lying below the bottom of the clip, and dressed it down true on my belt sander. If the clip and wedge bottoms are not perfectly true to each other, when you tighten the wing nut to lock it in place under the heel of the instrument, it will "cock" and screw up your calculations for the planing procedure. Be supercritical here.

Use good, tough hardwood for the tension brackets (Figure 59) and adjusting knobs. Maple or walnut would be a good choice. Hickory or oak would do just as well. One *important factor* to note before laying out the pieces is the *direction of the wood grain*. It is marked on the drawing in Figure 59 and *must* be made with the grain in the right direction to prevent the tension brackets from breaking. The grain on the adjusting knobs must run across the 1½" measurement to prevent the threads from stripping out easily also.

Drill the ½" holes in the tension brackets, saw out the pieces to the dimensions in the drawings, and glue on the cork padding. An alternative to cork for the padding would be thin leather. Smooth or round the corners for a neat, professional appearance and seal with a good paste wax or polyurethane plastic finish.

Drill a $^{27}/_{64}$" hole in the centers of the two blocks for the adjustment knobs and thread with a ½" 13 tap to match the threads on the ½" Ready Rod. If you like, you may drill the holes out to ½" and sink a nut into the knobs for the threads. This is unnecessary, however, as it takes little pressure for the tension brackets to work. I've been using the thread-in-the-wood knobs for the past three years with little wear. A little beeswax on the threads will ensure longevity and ease in adjusting.

Cut off the corners and bevel the edges on a belt or disk sander for a pair of nice-appearing, grippable knobs, and assemble the pieces on the ½" by 9" Ready Rod and on the short beams of the jig. See Figure 60.

The neck support assembly is relatively simple to make. I used a piece of scrap redwood (or what have you) 1¾" thick by 4" wide by 4½" long with the grain running across the 4" dimension to make the base rider. Saw a ¾" by ¾" slot across the same dimension as shown in the drawing in Figure 61 and drill the ⅜" hole behind it. Two pieces of ⅜" plywood are used for the guides on each end of the block and are screwed to the base rider. It should ride freely up and down the main beam without too much looseness, and the ⅜" hole should line up with the slot for the full length. If the rider is too tight, a thin shim of paper between

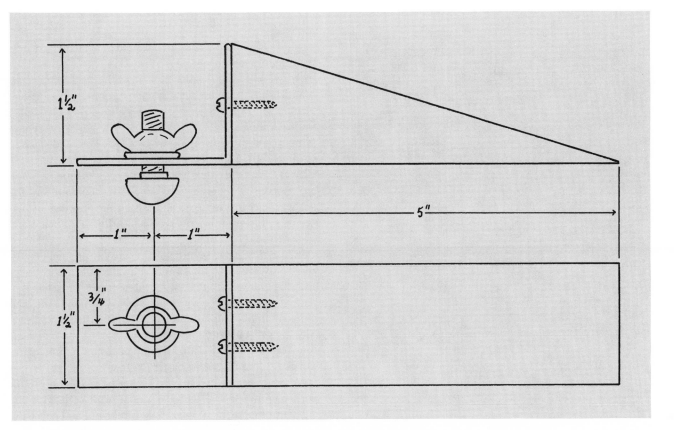

Fig. 58—*String tension simulation jig continued. The stabilizer wedge consists of an angle bracket, a ⅜" x 1" carriage bolt with wing nut and washer, and a hardwood wedge.*

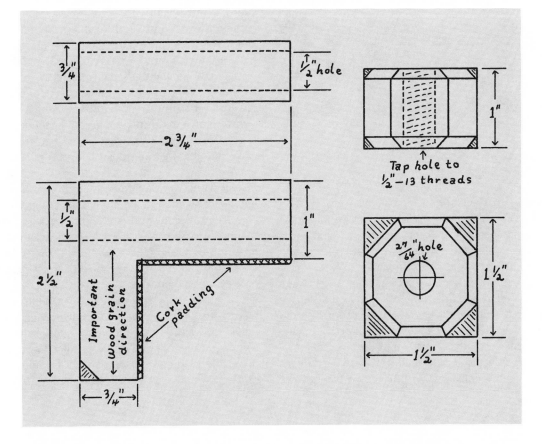

Fig. 59—*String tension simulation jig continued. Tension brackets and adjustment knobs. Two of each are needed and are made of hardwood. The threads in the two knobs are tapped directly into the wood.*

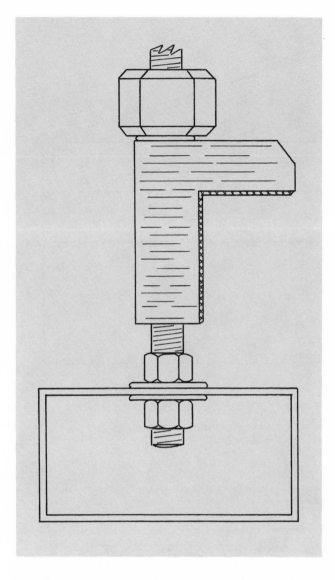

Fig. 60—String tension simulation jig continued. Tension bracket pieces assembled on the short side beam.

the plywood guides and the main block will give a little more clearance. If the fit is satisfactory, remove the guide screws and guides, apply a few drops of Titebond, and screw back into place. The base is ready for sealing or waxing, and you can move on to the neck supports.

The neck supports (Figure 62) are made of ¾" plywood and should be fitted into the base block with as little looseness as possible, but should be loose enough for easy removal. I use two different neck supports as shown in Figure 62, the tall one for flattop guitars, and the short one for solid and shallow-bodied electric guitars. Cut to the dimensions shown in the drawings and line the v-notches with

cork or leather to prevent any possible finish damage to the instrument's neck.

A final drawing (Figure 63) shows the neck support assembled and in place on the main beam. I use a regular hex nut on the carriage bolt here because it is located under the neck and locked into place after the guitar is set into position and the neck support is positioned properly. It's easier to use a wrench on the nut, for there isn't much room.

At last we get to the final assembly, the butt support. You are perhaps wondering why the fancy contour on the pusher block in Figure 66 and not on the drawings in Figure 64. This assembly rides on top of the main beam and pivots around the single ⅜" by 3½" carriage bolt. I've tried to make this jig as adjustable as possible to handle just about any kind of guitar. You will encounter many sizes and shapes of instruments with different sizes and shapes of butts. In fact, I've used my jig on several mandolins, and the pivotability and contours of the pusher block will fit a wide range of instruments. However, the "V" arrangement shown in Figure 64 is much simpler to make and should work just as well, and it's easier to draw.

I used 1¾" redwood for the pusher part of the butt support. Cut it out and face the v-edge with cork, glue the pusher to the ⅜" by 8" by 12" plywood base, and cover the exposed part of the plywood with cork. The butt end of the instrument back will rest on this, and the cork-covered *v* portion pushes against the butt itself.

The locking knob is made as shown in Figure 64 with the ⅜" nut for the carriage bolt sunk into the top side of the knob. Threads in the wood are not advisable for this knob because there is quite a bit of strain when it is tightened, and it will strip out quickly. The butt support sets on the main beam as shown in Figure 65.

Assemble all the parts, and the jig is ready to use. In Figures 66 and 67 you will find a couple of electric guitars set up in the finished jig. Instructions for setting up an acoustic guitar and using the jig will be found in the refretting chapter. I jig 99 percent of the fret jobs I do just to make sure that the fingerboards are accurate before I refret them.

Personally, you couldn't pay me to go back to the old traditional method of refretting after using this system. It eliminates all guesswork and after working a few "impossible" jobs with this system, you practically have to beat refretting customers off with a club. To see a customer's eyes light up after finishing a job on one of the really screwy ones can make your day.

For those shops specializing in mandolins, a smaller, more compact string tension simulation jig could be designed by scaling down the dimensions given here in this volume. Mandolins don't need as much forward bow in the neck with the shorter scales they use. I would suggest .004" to .006", whereas the guitar can use from .010" to .015".

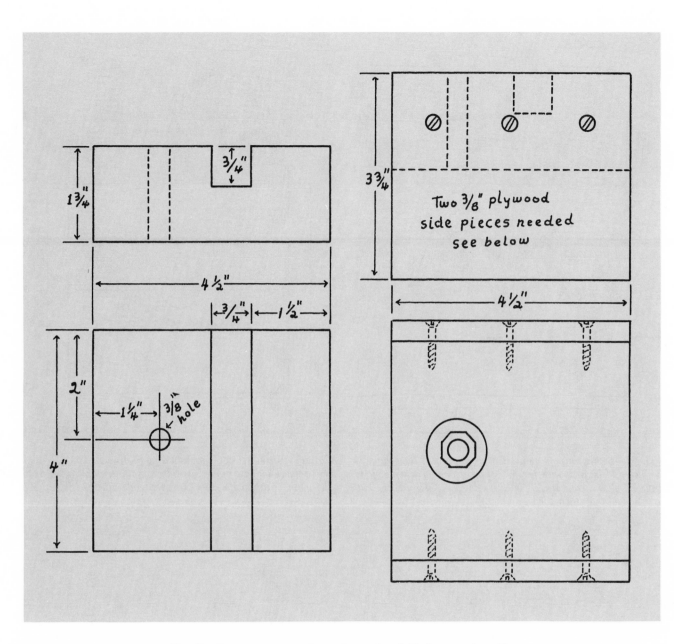

Fig. 61—String tension simulation jig continued. Neck support base rider.

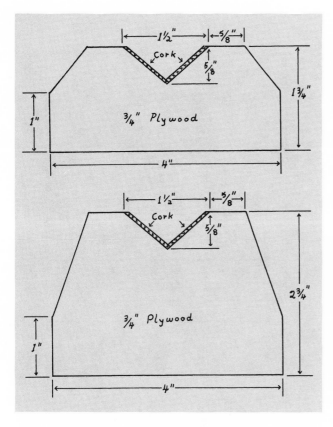

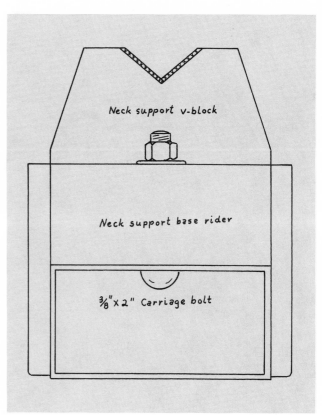

Fig. 62—String tension simulation jig continued. Neck support V–blocks to be used with the neck support base. These are made from ¾" plywood and the "V" of each v–block is corklined. The two sizes are all that are needed.

Fig. 63—String tension simulation jig continued. The neck support v–block in place in the base rider and the assembly is bolted to the main beam on the upper (shorter) end with the ⅜" carriage bolt.

Banjos? Now that's a whole new ball of wax. So many of them have the fingerboard surface level with the skin or plastic head which would make it impossible to dress out with the sanding block. I've never attempted to set one up in the jig, but I guess a system could be devised, perhaps bolting the neck up on a dummy pot. The pot could have a solid wooden head set below the level of the fingerboard.

It wouldn't have to be elaborate. An f-hole adjustable bridge and any kind of a crude tailpiece to which the strings could be hooked would work. The main thing would be to tune the strings up to pitch to properly stress the neck for the straightedge measurements. It would entail more work, but I've seen some pretty weird necks on some fine banjos,

and the extra time and effort might be worth experimenting with if you work on many banjos. I'm lucky. I have a banjo maker here in town to refer the banjo work to.

GAUGE FOR SETTING BLOCK PLANE AND JOINTER-PLANER BLADES

Accurately setting newly sharpened block plane or jointer-planer blades can be a real hassle. A block plane is not so bad since you have to contend with only one blade, but setting the three jointer-planer blades to exactly the same height, and getting them level with the back table, is an impossibility without a gauge of some kind.

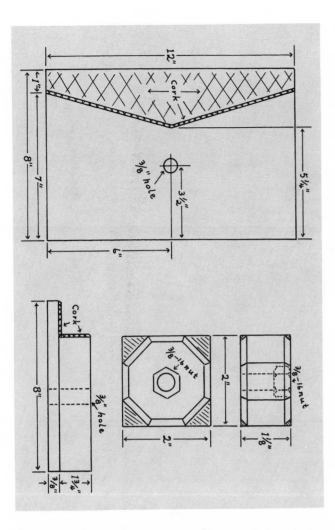

Fig. 64—String tension simulation jig continued. Butt support base rider. The x–shaded area is cork-faced. The regular line shading on the adjustment knob is area to be removed.

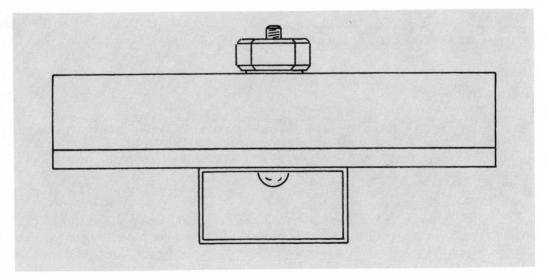

Fig. 65—String tension simulation jig continued. End view of the butt support base rider bolted to the main beam on the lower (longer) end with a ⅜" carriage bolt.

Fig. 66—*Fender electric bass in the string tension simulation jig. Note the positioning of the stress bracket posts and the swiveled butt support block to allow for the irregularly shaped body. The V–shaped butt block in the drawings works just as well as the fancy shape in the photo. The fingerboard on this one has to be refinished after planing. See the refretting chapter.*

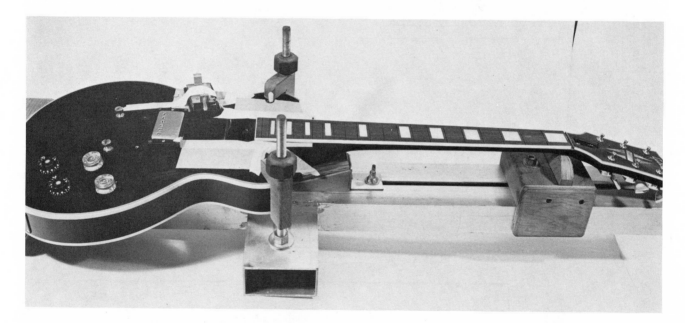

Fig. 67—*A Les Paul Gibson electric guitar in the jig. Note the extra block on top of the stabilization wedge to insure a firm contact and the short neck support piece in the nut-end support block. The fingerboard has been dressed true and the instrument is ready to be removed.*

The only problem with the block plane is setting the cutting edge level with the plane's base from one side to the other so that you have a uniform cut. The dial indicator (Figures 68 and 69) mounted in the block makes this an easy task. Clean off any dust or chips from the bottom of the plane and the dial indicator block, press the block against the plane's bottom behind the blade, and zero the dial indicator. Carefully slide the block toward the blade until the dial-indicator button rests on the blade's cutting edge and remember the reading. Take a second reading

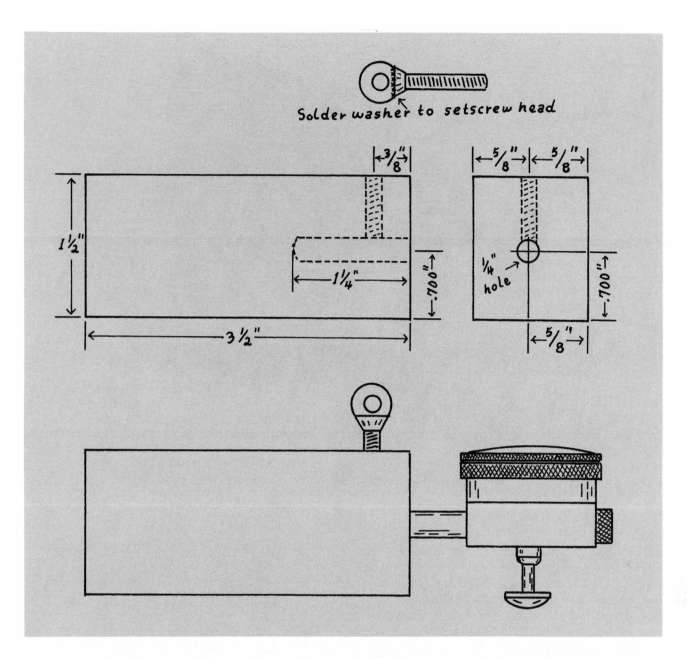

Solder washer to setscrew head

Fig. 68—A gauge to set the depth and to level block plane and jointer/planer blades. The bottom drawing shows the assembled gauge. A second longer block could be made for setting the jointer/ planer blades for ease of use. Note: the dial indicator button should extend slightly below the level of the base.

near each end of the cutting edge. They should be the same. If not, tap the opposite end (top of the plane) of the blade to one side or the other with a *plastic* hammer until you have an identical dial-indicator reading near each end of the blade's cutting edge. The blade is now true to the plane's base, and you can adjust the cutting depth normally and go to work with a true-cutting plane.

Setting the blades on a jointer-planer is a bit more complicated, to say the least. Not only do the blades have to be set accurately from side to side but the height must be the same on all three blades, and they *must be flush* with the back (nonadjustable) table.

Actually the dial-indicator block would probably work better in setting a jointer-planer if the block were made from a heavy metal, such as brass, and were 10 or 12″ long instead of 3½″ as for setting the block plane.

Wipe the back table and the bottom of the dial indicator block perfectly clean. Press the gauge in place on the back

Fig. 69—*Dial indicator and block being used to set the squareness of a block plane's blade. See the text for setting the jointer/planer's blades.*

table and zero the dial indicator's pointer. Slide the gauge forward until the dial indicator's button contacts the cutting edge of the first blade. Rotate the cutter drum *counterclockwise* and note any discrepancy. The dial indicator should read zero as each blade passes under the button. Take a reading on each end of the three cutting blades and recheck the zero setting on the table often to make sure your gauge setting hasn't slipped.

Loosen the blade's locking screws only enough to be able to shift the blades with a *light tap* from a *plastic* hammer. If the blades are too low, a small wedge (I use the pointed end of a scribe) may be tapped in under the back of the blade to lift it. Set each end of each blade until it zeros exactly with the back table *after the locking screws are tightened*. Tightening the locking screws may vary the blade setting and you may have to compensate accordingly, but all three blades *must* be perfectly level with the back table.

Parts and materials.

1 piece—Lufkin #399 dial indicator or the equivalent.

1 piece—1¼″ by 1½″ by 3½″ brass or very hard wood.
1 piece—³⁄₁₆″ by 1″ flat head stove bolt.
1 piece—³⁄₁₆″ washer (to be soldered to the head of the stove bolt).

Drill the ¼″ hole as shown in Figure 68. Drill and tap the set-screw hole for the ³⁄₁₆″ stove bolt.

Solder the washer in the slot in the head of the stove bolt. You may use a round-head stove bolt or a regular set screw and adjust it with a screwdriver or Allen wrench, but don't overtighten or you will distort the shaft on the dial indicator. This is why I prefer the soldered-on washer. It doesn't give you as much leverage.

If you used wood for the block (or blocks), sand the bottom smooth with 600-grit Wetordry sandpaper laid on a flat saw table, then wax heavily and burn it in by vigorous rubbing against the tabletop. Assembly the parts as shown in Figure 68, and you are ready to use the gauge. Figure 69 shows the gauge being used to set a block plane.

56

3

More on Stocking Materials and Hardware and Comments on Taxes and Business Problems with a Small Shop

The materials, hardware, and other supplies you keep on hand depend on your individual shop requirements and circumstances. Some shops specialize, while others will work on just about any instrument the customer can carry, or haul, in. For instance, I try to repair any of the fretted instruments with the exception of banjos. As noted earlier, there is a full-time banjo maker in my town. He refers guitar repairs to me, and I reciprocate with the banjos. There are also three shops to which I can refer instruments of the violin family, so I shy away from those.

Many, perhaps most, repair shops work in partnership or are subsidiaries of music stores. Under such an arrangement, you would, of course, have on tap any of the vast array of strings, machine heads, etc., that a well-stocked music store handles. Of course, you would have to stock specialty items such as the various types of woods needed, fret wire, finishing and refinishing materials, various bindings and purflings, perhaps a few types of precut mother-of-pearl inlay pieces, rough mother-of-pearl in both white and abalone for custom work and cutting of missing fingerboard inlays (primarily, white mother-of-pearl dots of various sizes). Occasionally, if you're so privileged, you might get an old 45-series Martin (I just finished a 1934 000-45 that you will find pictured in the front of this volume) or one of the old Washburns that require the duplication of a little more complicated piece of inlay, and the rough pearl would be necessary to cut the pieces.

If you are a small, one-man or woman shop or working out of a converted garage (as I do) or other similar situation and specialize only in repair, you have to stock most of the items yourself. I handle very little retail merchandise and work as an independent. In other words, I'm not tied in with any store, although I am an authorized warranty repair station for a guitar manufacturer. I handle only a few lines of strings and fast-moving parts. Under such circumstances if you tried to stock every line of strings available today, your inventory would eat your bank account alive unless you were independently wealthy. I'm not. Ditto on the machine heads, guitar straps, picks, capos, and the multitude of other guitar accessories flooding the markets nowadays.

And that's not to mention the tremendous outlay required to venture into the electric-guitar field.

This is especially true in the field of electric-guitar strings. There must be twenty-five or thirty different brands on the market—possibly even more that I've never heard of. And it seems as though every performer has his or her own ideas concerning the particular brand and gauge of string required to satisfy individual tastes in sound, feel, etc.

Since I specialize in acoustic instrument repair but also handle many kinds of repair jobs on electrics (excluding electronic work—and refinishing, which I shall discuss further in a rehash of the finishing chapter), I am directly involved in this "can of worms" controversy. I have, however, arrived at a simple solution: stay out of it. To keep my overhead at a reasonable level, I no longer stock electric-guitar strings. I merely ask my customer to furnish a new set of the particular "flavor" and gauge of strings to which he or she happens to be partial.

In a way this can be worked out to your advantage if there happens to be a well-stocked music store or two in your area. Make sure that they are aware that you are not trying to cut into their business, and they will, in most instances, be more than happy to send you their repair business or refer customers your way. And they will usually give you discounts on parts and supplies.

This kind of arrangement should be cultivated, for some manufacturers will sell parts only to franchised dealers, and the only way an independent has access to the parts is through such a dealer.

I do stock a limited line of acoustic-guitar strings for both six- and twelve-string guitars in bronze-wound and silk and steel, as well as a few sets of strings for classical guitars, mandolins, and banjos.

My stock of machine heads remains basically the same as outlined in Volume I of my repair book: Grover Rotomatics, Grover Slimlines for twelve-string guitars, Kluson Deluxe in both individual and three-to-a-plate for original equipment replacement on Gibsons, an excellent set of classical-guitar machine heads with enclosed gears (the

Schaller MK6), usually a set of Five Star planet pegs for banjos, and a set or two of mandolin machine heads. You can tie up a lot of cash purchasing quality machine heads. Most music supply houses give one-week to ten-day delivery, so unless you are moving quite a few machine heads, or other hard parts, a large supply is unnecessary. Experience and time will tell you what is moving well in your particular area, and you can manage your stock purchases accordingly.

As mentioned in Volume I, humidity or rather the lack of humidity is a tremendous problem in many areas. Any shop or music store should stock a line of instrument-case humidifiers and really push them through the low-humidity winter months, or "crack season," as I call it.

Of course, I am referring primarily to the quality instruments constructed of single-thickness veneers. Plywood instruments are seldom damaged—except by excessive heat—by these seasonal climatic changes; however, there is often a noticeable change in their tonal quality during extremely dry periods, and they, too, can benefit from the use of a humidifier.

Speaking of humidity or the lack of it: all music stores and shops in areas where the humidity is high during the summer months and low with the dry and cold through the winters should have a system of shop humidification to prevent cracking of the instruments. The system doesn't have to be anything elaborate. I use a couple of pans of water sitting on top of my gas heater and have two humidity gauges in two different spots in my shop. I keep the pans full of water when the shop humidity reaches 45 percent, and I don't let it get below that level. Commercial humidifiers are available in many different price ranges. Some system of humidification should be used to prevent the level from dropping below 40 percent.

Woods: They are a real problem nowadays. Tone woods and the selection thereof were pretty thoroughly covered in Volume I, but problems in availability of certain woods have cropped up in the past few years. Owing to overcutting of some species, the tremendous demand for guitar-making materials, and the political situations in many countries supplying instrument tone woods, the supplies of some of the old standbys are limited or nonexistent. When you do stumble onto a supply, the prices are usually exorbitant. For instance, most rosewood coming out of Brazil nowadays is in plywood form, and nearly all of the class (nonplywood) instrument manufacturers have switched to East Indian rosewood. If you are so lucky as to have a supply of Brazilian rosewood on hand, guard it with your life and be extremely stingy with it.

I have a small quantity which I purchased rough-sawed and nearly green back in the late sixties. I cured it naturally and use it strictly for repair purposes. I've accumulated several small boxes of scraps of a multitude of figuring, color-ing, and grain patterns from my guitar-making days which are invaluable in repairing the old Brazilian instruments. When that is gone, I guess I'm up the proverbial creek without a paddle.

Don't get me wrong: East Indian rosewood is an excellent tone wood although rather difficult to finish at times. One of the men at the Martin factory said that in some areas it is actually superior to Brazilian rosewood. From their repair records it appears that East Indian rosewood is quite a bit more resistant to cracking when exposed to climatic changes. And when properly finished, it is a beautiful wood. The tonal qualities of the East Indian rosewood compare very favorably with the qualities of Brazilian rosewood. Comparison is like the old adage of six of one and a half a dozen of the other.

Another wood nearing the vanishing point is Gaboon ebony. This is the dense, nearly jet-black wood that is so prized for fingerboards and bridges of the more expensive instruments. Again, however, there is a satisfactory substitute. There seems to be a barely adequate supply of Maccassar or black-and-white ebony, sometimes called marblewood. It's nearly as hard as Gaboon ebony, but most pieces have streaks of tan (or white) running through the grain, and it is somewhat more porous than Gaboon ebony.

Some people—I for one—find beauty in this patterning, but for your customers who find the tan streaks objectional and demand the jet-black color of the traditional Gaboon ebony, the streaks can be stained with an aniline dye and either waxed heavily in the case of fingerboards and bridges or finished over for peghead facings. Let's face it: it's a problem that has to be dealt with, and we have to improvise, to make do with what is available for us to work with or do without.

You will want to stock a selection of bindings and purflings for repair purposes. These may be purchased from most instrument makers' supply houses in both wood and plastic. Of course, you can cut your own wood bindings if you prefer. White holly or maple are excellent for lighter trim and can be dyed various colors. Maple is rather hard to bend.

I've heard of an instrument maker who uses white holly (very flexible when wet) and an old pressure cooker formerly used in canning food with water-soluble dyes such as those used for dyeing clothes. The steam pressure forces the dye throughout the grain for an excellent uniform color. Some sort of pressure dyeing is necessary on thicker purfling pieces to ensure full penetration of the color. For darker, natural-colored wood bindings you can use the darker woods such as rosewood and black walnut and bend them by soaking in water and heating with a bending iron.

There are many purfling patterns commercially available from simple multilayers of contrasting woods to complicated patterns such as the ever-popular herringbone pattern

Fig. 70—Hot knife attachment for separating wooden purflings.

used on the old prewar Martins (and also the new HD-28 Martin). One supplier, Gurian Guitars Ltd., Inc. (address in the back of this volume) even lists half strips of herringbone, which should simplify the bending to fit the curvatures of a particular body shape. He also stocks a herringbone soundhole purfling already bent in a circle.

In Volume I, I used a technique (page 45, Figure 36) for separating purfling strips with heated knives to facilitate bending fancy purfling strips, but I have discovered an easier method. Some hobby shops stock a screw-on tip to fit the quarter-inch threads of a pencil-type soldering iron that will accept the common X-acto knife blades. This setup is actually designed for heat-cutting plastics, but I honed a blade very thin, and it really does a job on the glue in wooden purflings—and it's constantly hot. You don't have to keep heating it as you do the reworked putty knives. If you can't find one, you might slot a stock copper soldering tip with a razor saw and rivet an X-acto blade in the slot as a substitute.

One of the most frequently recurring jobs in my shop these days is refretting. Finding a reliable supply of various sizes of fret wire for partial fret jobs has been a problem. Many times I've ordered fret wire by catalog numbers, and many times I've received different sizes of wire although the catalog number remained the same. The crown width, height, or both would be different from order to order. This is exasperating to say the least, unless you are refretting the entire fingerboard, when it doesn't really matter that much. I don't know how many times I've wished that I could obtain consistent sizes of fret wire without ordering from half a dozen different sources.

Now there is such a source. The Jim Dunlop Company (of capo fame—address in the back of this volume) is offering a cabinet of twelve different gauge sizes of fret wire in precut 2⅜″ lengths with replacements available. He also offers 24-inch lengths in around two dozen sizes and a couple of different hardnesses. A complete statistical chart is available listing all these sizes with complete profile measurements of each individual size in both thousandths of an inch and "Mickey Mouses" (millimeters for those of you who are into metrics). It is possible to order a given size of wire and know exactly what you will be receiving.

Another serious problem today is the shortage of quality materials for nuts and bridge saddles. Traditionally, ivory is by far the favorite material. It has strength and longevity and is an excellent conductor of sound. But the supply of ivory is critically short—as is the remaining world population of elephants. Owing to rampant poaching, the population is on the downswing, and legal, registered ivory is becoming almost prohibitively expensive.

Most suppliers nowadays are stocking supplies of bleached bone which is almost identical to ivory in looks and performance, and the raw material from slaughterhouses is almost endless. I use bone almost exclusively except in circumstances where I cannot purchase pieces large or thick enough for certain applications. Even then pieces of bone can sometimes be laminated to meet the size requirements, such as for compensated bridge saddles. I lap the contact surfaces of each piece on fine sandpaper laid over a hard, flat surface—sandpaper file, saw table, etc.—wash with alcohol and dry, then bond them with cyanoacrylate glue.

Of course, there is always the ever-increasing abundance of plastic nuts and bridge saddles. In many instances, particularly on the foreign imports, the quality and performance of the plastics is woefully inadequate. Most of them gum up or melt when worked down on a power disk sander. I've had some of these instruments in my shop—victims of "heat prostration"—on which the plastic actually melted and allowed the strings to embed all the way down to the wood surface of the fingerboard or bridge. The nuts and saddles had to be broken into pieces to free the strings. Some of the injection-molded nuts are actually hollow (see the plywood guitar chapter). Talk about junk.

I have also used good dense ebony as a nut replacement, and in my opinion using ebony for nuts is far superior to using most of the plastics. It wears better than the cheap plastics, and it doesn't melt. Ebony for bridge saddles is out for the average bridge saddle, however; it is just not structurally strong enough in thin pieces. It will usually break when used in pieces under ⅛″ thick.

Martin is now using a synthetic material that seems to be working rather well. It is a product called Micarta that is close to the hardness of bone and ivory. It has a light-yellow cast, resembling antique ivory, and powders off when power-sanded instead of melting as most plastics do. Martin literature describes it as an epoxy resin, which I guess would be a type of plastic, and it sure does have a peculiar stench while it is being worked. In fact, it smells a lot like Bakelite.

A new product that is finding many applications in many different fields is resin-impregnated graphite. One guitar maker is even using it for guitar tops, and it is hard enough to work for nuts and bridge saddles. Of course, there might be some objection to the black color, but if it will do the job, surely some way of coloring it, perhaps painting it, can be found. One of these days maybe I'll get my hands on a piece of it and experiment with it.

Another alternative being pushed nowadays is brass, but I'm not too enthusiastic about this for bridge saddles. It should be excellent in longevity, structural strength, and sound conduction, but it seems to add a slightly harsh, metallic quality to the sound, especially to the treble strings. And brass bridge saddles add unnecessary weight to the top of an acoustic guitar with resultant loss (although minor in most cases) of volume.

I have no objection to the use of brass on an electric instrument, except for the extra time required to fit it and set it up properly. Extra care must be used in cutting the string slots, because the slightest discrepancy can cause string binding with the resultant tuning problems or, in the instance of too wide a string notch, strange, buzzing noises.

To satisfy my own curiosity about comparisons in hardness of the various available nut and bridge saddle materials, I checked around town for someone with a Brinnel or Rockwell hardness tester I could use. They all had scales for steel and hard metals but nothing that I could use for the softer stuff. I was forced to conduct my own tests, such as they were. I used a weighted steel spur and a dial indicator to measure penetration, and I ran each test six times on each material for consistency. The results may not be as scientific as they would be with standardized test equipment, but the results were pretty much as I had expected.

Brass, of course, came out on top with a .002″ spur penetration. Ivory and bone were next, identical with a .004″ penetration, or half as hard as brass. Micarta—now used by Martin—had a .005″ penetration, a respectable 80 percent as hard as ivory or bone.

The various cheap plastic nuts and saddles made very poor showings ranging from .011″ to .015″. In other words, bone and ivory appear to be two to three times harder than cheap plastics.

I also tested some hard, dense ebony and rosewood and came up with an .008″ to .010″ penetration. This would compare in hardness with the harder of the cheap plastics, but the wood would have an advantage in a heat situation and, I would guess, better abrasion resistance. Some of the old Martin 15 and 17 series used ebony nuts, and they take years to wear down to a replacement situation.

Last I tested several pieces of well-cured Elmer's brand epoxy glue for a reason you will find discussed in the refretting chapter. The penetration was .008″ to .010″ or identical to that of ebony and rosewood.

Keeping track of retail stock can be a problem in a small, cramped shop such as mine. I've found a solution to the problem by using metal filing cabinets. Of course, if you have a large retail stock and push retail sales, it's a good idea to have a display area, preferably glassed-in display cases to keep out the dust, sticky fingers, etc.

Filing cabinets are also handy for small tools that are used only occasionally. Good metal cabinets cost an arm and a leg new, but by shopping around used office-supply outlets and watching the want ads, you can usually find them at a reasonable price.

If you stock a large amount of retail merchandise, a card system for keeping track of your stock is a good investment. When you add new stock, make a card for it. Check off the items sold at the end of the day or week, and you will have it down in black and white exactly what stock is moving and how much. You can figure percentages and know how much of a given item you are selling during a given time period and can restock accordingly. If kept up to date, these cards are invaluable at inventory time. And a periodic check of the cards against your stock can tell you if there has been any pilfering at work.

As discussed in Volume I, keep a complete and thorough set of books for sales and income-tax purposes. Use an outside accountant to handle this end if you have little knowledge in the field. So many changes in the tax laws are thrown our way by both the state and federal governments that I find a good accountant a necessity—and their charges are deductible as a business expense. They can be worth their weight in gold when it comes to dealing with these matters, and I am speaking from experience. I'll give you a "fer-instance."

Several years ago I turned in my quarterly sales-tax reports in accordance with our state's tax laws for a small business with limited retail sales. I started moving a bit more merchandise, and the sales-tax people informed me that I was to start turning in my taxes monthly. Sure, I agreed, and turned the matter over to my accountant. She set things up on the monthly basis as instructed, and things rocked along for several months. Then the tax commission's computer spit out the information that I hadn't paid my *quarterly* sales tax. They had evidently forgotten to inform the computer about the new setup. Confusing? And how!

My accountant took over and went through the tax department. She ended up going all the way to the top and straightened everything out (we thought) after leaving a few out-of-joint noses in her wake.

A few weeks later who should show up at my door to do an audit of my sales-tax receipts but an accountant from the tax commission. He insisted on doing an audit for the preceding three years. He spent two whole days wading through my receipts. Then he audited my accountant's books for the same three years. The net results? A discrepancy of around seven cents, much to the auditor's chagrin! Was my accountant worth the expense? You bet your best "G" string she was—and still is. I had a follow-up visit a few months ago, the same fellow who visited me last time, but he chickened out when I referred him to my accountant. He just shook his head, muttering to himself, and left. He evidently remembered the last time, too.

My thoughts on the subject are this: I'm the expert when it involves instrument repair, and I plan to leave my accounting and tax work to an expert in that field. Nuff said?

My thinking on glue has changed to a certain degree since 1972, when I completed the manuscript for Volume I. I still use Elmer's Epoxy exclusively in my system of refretting and "Q & D" (quick and dirty) repairs on loose necks of inexpensive instruments. It is still one of the best sealers around for spruce tops when mixed with alcohol (see the refinishing chapter of Volume I), but I seldom use it for anything else except maybe as a filler for pearl inlay work when mixed with dye or wood sanding dust.

Some applications, such as installing a transducer pickup under the face of an instrument, call for a hard-setting glue with around a five-minute curing time. You can hand-hold the transducer in locations too awkward to clamp, and a five-minute setting time is not fatiguing. For this purpose I use the Archer brand of quick-setting epoxy available from the local Radio Shack. It comes in a twin-tube dispenser and sets in approximately four to seven minutes at room temperature. Its quick-setting properties, however, severely limit its uses in instrument repair; in many instances it would set up before you could get your clamps in position.

I have discontinued the use of white glue (polyvinyl resin) altogether in favor of the aliphatic resins. My personal preference is Franklin's Titebond, but there are several other excellent brands on the market: Wilhold, Borden's, Elmer's Professional Carpenter's, and many others. The aliphatics are fairly easy to distinguish from the polyvinyls: the polyvinyls are white whereas the aliphatics have a noticeable light-yellow cast. The aliphatics sand clean and will not lift to any degree under a lacquer finish as the white glues will.

Both these glues dry clear or relatively so, but in my experience the aliphatics seem to dry harder (an asset in sound conduction) and seem to be stronger and more heat-resistant. This last factor is another asset because people *will* leave their instruments in hot cars. Don't get me wrong: this aliphatic resin will still turn loose under this kind of treatment, just not as soon as the white or polyvinyls will. Judging from the hardness of cured aliphatic resin, its sound conduction should easily equal that of the more traditional hide glue without the hide glue's vulnerability to

humidity, heat, and mold. All this and the aliphatic's resistance to lifting under finishes make it perhaps the best all-around glue for use in guitar repair, and Titebond is one of the mainstays in my shop.

I used to use a liquid hide glue for hairline cracks in top and body repair because its thin consistency gave better penetration in a tight crack, where it would be next to impossible to work in the thicker synthetic glue. Also the aliphatic resins had a tendency to darken the spruce along the crack, whereas the hide glue was nearly invisible.

There is now a glue on the market with the penetrating ability of solvents such as alcohol or lacquer thinner that greatly simplifies the repairing of hairline cracks in much less time. The capillary action of this glue is fantastic. It will actually flow into and solidify a hairline crack that has not penetrated all the way through the wood, an impossibility for most glues.

You have perhaps guessed that I am referring to the cyanoacrylates or so-called superglues. Before proceeding any further, I think that a frank discussion of the cyanoacrylate's dangers and peculiarities is in order. There is no doubt about it: these glues are extremely dangerous in the wrong hands (children's for instance) or when used carelessly. They contain a strong eye irritant, and the fumes, while not toxic, may cause problems for those with allergies or respiratory problems, so *use with adequate ventilation.* Anything, a small fan, the breeze from an air conditioner, etc., will do the trick.

This glue will also *bond human skin in seconds*, so avoid any unnecessary contact with your fingers. It would be rather embarrassing if a customer walked in to find you with a guitar glued to your hand. If you use this glue regularly as I do, however, not only is it bound to happen, it will happen. Just don't panic and try to jerk your hand free. To do so will only result in leaving part of your hide glued to the workpiece and you with a bloody finger.

If the workpiece is unfinished, try a little acetone. If this doesn't do the trick or the workpiece is finished, try rolling a wooden matchstick, a round toothpick, a round needle file, etc., between your finger and the workpiece while pulling away gently. Still doesn't work? Wait a while, or move your hand close enough to a heat source to promote sweating, and the body oils will eventually cause it to turn loose. In your eyes? Flush liberally with water and get immediate medical attention.

I will mention no names, but to give you an idea of what can happen if you are careless with this stuff, I will tell you what happened to a friend of mine and his first experience with cyanoacrylate. He purchased a tube of superglue and removed it from the card. He was familiar with its skin-bonding properties from my experiences with it—up to a point.

When he was finished with it, he screwed the cap on tight, and since there was a young child in the house, he slipped it into his jeans pocket until he had a chance to hide it in a safe place. Yes, you guessed it. He forgot all about it. Now he was wearing rather tight pants, and the first time he sat down, the tube ruptured. He managed to pull the pants away from his leg a split second before it solidified, and he telephoned me in a panic. I told him to try as hot a shower as he could stand and plenty of soap, but he still lost all the hair from the contact area in removing the pants. Please be careful in handling this very useful but dangerous glue.

There are many brands of cyanoacrylates available, varying in consistency from a thin syrup to the water-thin types with the super capillary action. Some of these are designed to be used only with nonporous materials, but some are designed and formulated especially for model building such as assembling radio-controlled model airplanes. They work very well with plastics, nylon, ivory, bone, metal, glass, balsa, and hardwoods. In fact, they will stick to nearly any *clean* surface except the polyethylene plastics and waxed paper.

Any model or hobby shop that handles RC airplanes will usually have a brand in stock. The three particular brands that I am familiar with and have used with excellent results are Jet, Zap, and Hot Stuff. All three are formulated to *work with woods* as well as with nonporous materials. If you find the Hot Stuff brand, check to see if it is labeled Blue Line. If so, forget it. Blue Line means exactly that. It contains a blue dye so that you can determine the depth of penetration, and it is useless for gluing light-colored woods. Purchase only the clear types. New brands are coming on the market all the time, but remember, for repairing of hairline cracks, be sure that it is formulated for use on wood. Read the label to be sure of this.

I also use some of the thicker brands because of the slightly slower drying characteristics. I use it primarily as a sealer over repaired areas and for sealing down aged fingerboard surfaces, as will be discussed in future chapters. You can get by with just about any of the cyanoacrylates for this type of job, whether it's formulated for woods or not.

The various applications I have discovered for cyanoacrylate glues have been tremendous time savers, and when you work with the volume of repairs that circulate through my shop, any time saver that will do the job faster with no sacrifice in quality is welcome. Of course, there will be those who will scoff at the use of any other than "traditional" glues, but who cares? After all, this is the twentieth century, and there are advances in every field, including guitar repair.

One final word on cyanoacrylates. They should be stored in a refrigerator when not in use. Unopened, the shelf life is around six months at room temperature, somewhat shorter after they have been opened. The life is extended two or three times under refrigeration.

5.

Some of the Same and More on Cracks

Cracks—the guitar repairman's headache. Sometimes I even have nightmares about them. And the thing that irks me the most is that many of the cracks are caused by simple neglect or sheer carelessness and could be prevented by using a little care and common sense.

As I mentioned in Volume I, and should, I believe, rehash here, the factors that cause cracks are many and varied. Some can be compensated for, and there are others that seem to happen regardless of how one babies an instrument.

An example of the latter are cracks caused by the difference in expansion and contraction or the coefficient of expansion between some of the various materials normally used in instrument construction.

To be more specific, we have the crack that forms at the top edge, or occasionally at the bottom edge, of some pickguards that are glued directly to the bare wood of a guitar top. The plastic tends to shrink slightly through the years, apparently through a loss of volatiles in the chemical com-

position of the material. The old celluloid material used by most instrument makers in the past was particularly bad about this. I have actually seen celluloid pickguards curl up like a potato chip, leaving a gaping crack in the wood at one edge of the pickguard (see Figure 71). Sometimes the stress created is enough to pull the top away from the strut beneath the face of the instrument in this area.

My solution to this problem is to insert carefully a thin, sharp-edged spatula (Volume I, page 64) under the pickguard and remove it completely. This will relieve the stress. Lay the instrument out of the way for a few hours—a day or two if there is no particular rush for the instrument. You will find that if the crack hasn't developed to the aforementioned potato-chip state before the customer got around to bringing it in, it will close up almost completely with the relaxation of the stress.

If the top has pulled away from one of the struts, I use a hypodermic syringe (Volume I, page 38, Figure 117) loaded with Titebond to squirt glue under the strut, then I

Fig. 71—Bad top crack caused by a shrinking pickguard. (1943 D–18 Martin). This guitar had been overheated which worsened the crack. The neck had pulled loose among other heat-related problems.

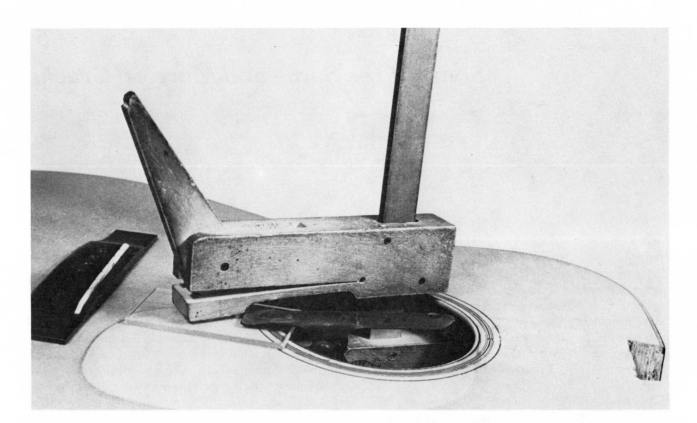

Fig. 72—Clamping setup used to pull face back down to the strut underneath where the shrinking pickguard had pulled it loose. A piece of Plexiglas is used here for the clamping pad.

Fig. 73—Top cracked by the pickguard stress is glued back to the strut. The crack has closed almost completely after removing the pickguard to relieve the stress (1943 D–18).

lay a clamping pad in place with a piece of waxed paper separating the pad and the top and clamp with a wooden cam clamp.

A variation is to use a piece of ¼″ Plexiglas in lieu of a wooden pad and waxed paper, but be certain that the Plexiglas pad is fairly large and lies perfectly flat when clamped (Figure 72). The spruce top wood is soft enough for a small Plexiglas pad to compress and permanently mark the wood. I use Plexiglas part of the time when I want to be able to see through it to tell what is happening when I apply the clamp, but I prefer to use redwood and waxed paper for most applications.

66

Fig. 74—Cam clamp with small redwood block taped into place to clear the struts while clamping the cross–patch in place. Note the masking tape folded back on itself to provide stickum for holding the cross–patch. Double–stick tape may be used in lieu of the masking tape.

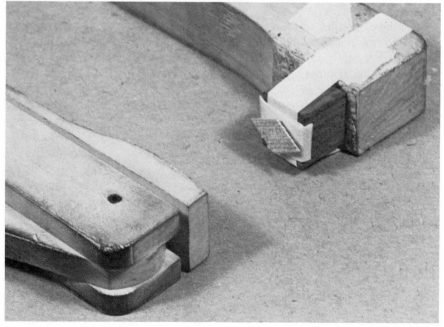

Fig. 75—The diamond–shaped cross–patch is stuck to the tape and ready for gluing into place.

Fig. 76—The pickguard area has been taped off and contact cement applied to both contact surfaces. On bare wood, apply one coat of cement, let dry for an hour, then apply a second coat to the wood and the first coat to the guard. Let dry for 15 minutes and press carefully into place.

The next step is to glue in a small cross-patch under the crack for further reinforcement. The pickguard cracks are within easy reach of a small cam clamp. I tape a small block of wood (Figures 74 and 75) to the lower jaw of the cam clamp so that it will clear any struts in the area, then apply a piece of double-stick tape or masking tape folded back on itself with the sticky side out. Either method will serve the purpose.

Stick the cross-patch to the top of the block, slip a mechanic's mirror into the soundhole so that you can see what you are doing, apply Titebond to the contact surface of the cross-patch, and clamp into position. Again, use the outside clamping pad over the crack.

A couple of hours later remove the clamp, block, and tape, and there should be only a hairline crack left to contend with if you're lucky. You are asking perhaps why I didn't work glue into the crack itself before clamping in the cross-patch? I often do, particularly if the crack is something more than a hairline or is in a location that will be concealed when the pickguard is replaced. If the crack is only a hairline and exposed, I use a slightly different technique.

If you have already glued the crack, however, tape off the perimeter of the pickguard area (Figure 76) and reglue the pickguard with contact cement, as discussed in the disassembly and reassembly chapter of Volume I, and touch up.

Now we get into preventable cracks. Lack of humidity is probably far and away the worst offender in causing body cracks. People who live in humid regions and travel to the high country or desert areas where the humidity is very low without some provision for humidifying their instruments are often in for a rude shock when they suddenly find old cracks expanding or new cracks developing.

Why? Again, we are dealing with our dubious old friend coefficient of expansion. Different types of wood with their variations in density, composition, etc., "breathe" at different rates. A soft wood such as spruce will lose and absorb moisture more rapidly than, say, mahogany, maple, or a resiny wood such as the various rosewoods. With the differences in shrinkage rates in these woods cracks will happen.

Cold weather is particularly hard on an instrument when heating systems are in constant use. The average heated household without a humidification system, either external or incorporated into the heating system, may drop to as low as 10 or 12 percent relative humidity. These desertlike conditions can and will cause loose joints in your furniture, dry-skin problems, intensify head and chest cold symptoms—and cracks in your musical instruments. I usually

Fig. 77—The pickguard crack is glued and the pickguard replaced on the 1943 D–18 Martin. It's ready for touchup. Grime from years of playing after the crack first developed makes it impossible to hide the repair.

Fig. 78—These cracks appeared at the bottom edge of the pickguard instead of the top edge of this old 000–45. Of the pickguard cracks, approximately 10% will show up in this location. The repair procedure is the same for both.

have to contend with at least 50 percent more cracks in winter than any other season and even higher in extremely cold winters.

Besides the lack of humidity the most common cause of cracks is sheer carelessness and stupidity. I had one ten-year-old Martin in my shop with seventeen—yes, *seventeen*—cracks in the top, back, sides, and fingerboard. The finish almost wasn't. Upon questioning the poor owner—I had accused him of taking a shower with the instrument or using it as a canoe paddle—I found that he had actually been using it in a sky-diving routine, subjecting the guitar to around 100 degrees of temperature on the ground, to the abrupt change in temperature and atmospheric pressure of jumping from an airplane where the temperature was around freezing, then back to the heat at ground level. And he wondered why the instrument cracked—and why I refused to repair the cracks under the warranty.

Other, perhaps less dramatic but just as disastrous causes

are from impact damage or just about any kind of accident imaginable, from car wrecks, being run over by cars, buses, campers—once by an army tank—to less spectacular incidents such as falls and bumping into furniture or other objects. One Martin was neatly removed from a trailer house by an Oklahoma tornado and was found floating merrily down a creek. It was repairable, but the hard-shell case was a total loss. Others I have repaired have had bullet holes, had been in fights, and had been hit by various flying objects. I repaired one, a complete retop job, that was hit by a flying boondocker (heavy boot) thrown at a guy who dodged. He should have let it hit him. It would have hurt less than the blow to his pocketbook.

Then we have cracks caused by people sitting on instruments left lying on chairs, sofas, and beds instead of in the cases where they belong. Others lean on instruments, inadvertently perhaps, but an elbow leaned a little too hard on the side of a slab-sided or dreadnought guitar will result in the horrifying sound of wood grain splitting.

Let's face it: a guitar is a highly stressed work of art and will not tolerate such treatment. Individually, the thin pieces of veneer, usually ³⁄₃₂" plus or minus a few thousandths of an inch, that make up the tops, sides, and backs of musical instruments are very fragile (except plywood, which we will get into later). When it is assembled into a single unit, a musical instrument, the curvature of the sides and the braces or struts of the tops and backs do give the thin veneers tremendous unit strength.

Then we add the tension of the strings. The guitar body is now highly stressed, and any impact to the unit in the right ("wrong" might be a better word) place can cause the instrument literally to explode if the impact is great enough or, at the least, cause cracks of all descriptions. I restrutted the face of a twelve-string guitar one time that had collapsed when the owner's mother (angry at the racket at 3:00 A.M.) cut the strings with a pair of sheet-metal shears.

Now we finally get down to the new technique that I use in gluing that I mentioned a few paragraphs earlier after getting a few gripes out of the way. Most of the cracks, if brought into the shop for repair soon enough after they occur, are hairline cracks, or small ones that can be easily aligned and clamped to where they amount to little more than hairlines. These are the easy ones.

On longer cracks (Figure 79) I use the cross-patching gadgets (thoroughly described in Volume I, pages 51 to 61 with accompanying illustrations) to pull cross-patches into place from the inside and to correct any stress-related misalignment problems. When the glue on the cross-patches has dried (two to three hours for Titebond at normal room temperature) and the gadgets are removed, you should be left with the tiny holes drilled for the guitar string used to lock the patches in place and a hairline crack.

Shave a sliver of matching wood down to a point, add a drop of glue, press into the hole, and lightly tap the glue-

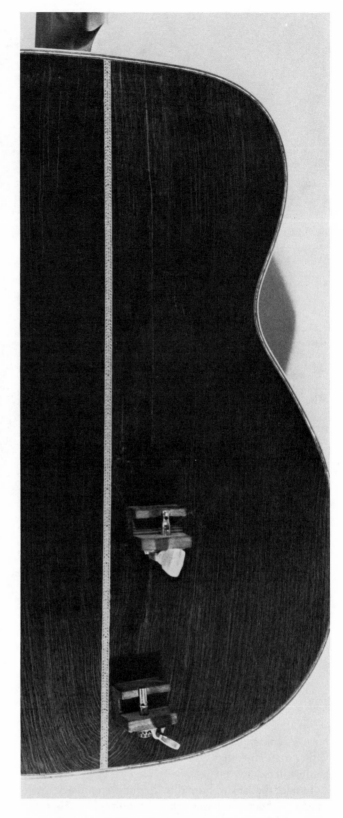

Fig. 79—This 1934 000–45 Martin has been badly dried out. The back crack runs the full length of the back and had to be realigned in one place with the cross–patching gadgets. See Volume I, Chapter 6.

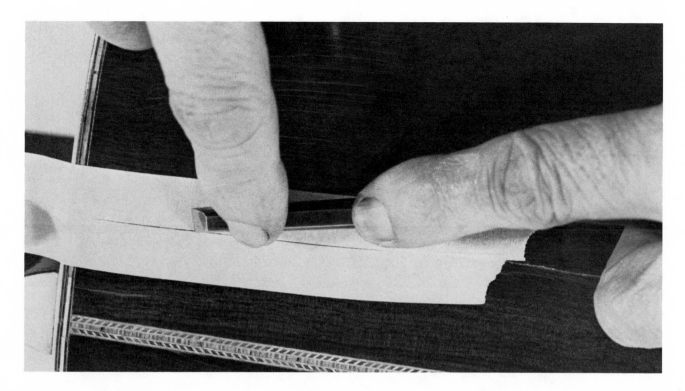

Fig. 80—*When using cyanoacrylate glue for repairing hairline cracks, work with one short section at a time. I am using the bottom of a ¼″ chisel to very carefully flatten the wrinkles in the masking tape. Note the overlapped ends of the tape to prevent the glue from spreading. However, if you are planning on refinishing the instrument, the taping job may be omitted (000–45 Martin).*

coated sliver into the hole. Trim it off flush, and there are no more holes.

To glue the hairline crack remaining, I use one of the cyanoacrylates or so-called superglues described earlier in the chapter on glues. Before using this glue, please read again all the precautions outlined in the glue chapter—and the instruction sheet supplied with the glue—*very carefully*. My present favorite in hairline-crack repair is Hot Stuff, but any of the water-thin cyanoacrylates mentioned in the glue chapter or those *expressly formulated for use on wood* will suffice. Cyanoacrylate, by the way, seems to darken spruce little more than hide glue does, so it is an excellent subsitute for repairing light-colored woods.

Now for the next step—taping off the crack. *This must be done with extreme care.* The capillary action of the water-thin cyanoacrylate glue is so powerful that it can and will penetrate under the wrinkles of masking tape instantaneously if improperly applied. I use half-inch tape for the job because it is easier to use when there are slight curvatures to the crack. This is the reason for the wrinkles in the masking tape—so that it can be used to follow a flat curve.

Lay a strip of the tape along one edge of the crack and make a mark on the tape with a soft-lead pencil at each end of the crack. Use an oblique light if necessary so that you can see to apply the edge of the tape as close as possible to the edge of the crack without covering it. Next lay the tape on the opposite side of the crack and try to leave a gap no more than a few thousandths of an inch between the two pieces of tape. Stretch each end of the second strip of tape over the first just past the pencil marks so that you have a slight overlap. This will tend to act as a miniature dam to prevent the glue from flowing onto the uncracked area, because this glue actually bonds into most finishes. As a point of interest, I prefer to work a short section of a long crack at a time, usually four to six inches.

Now, take a ¼″ chisel (Figure 80) and, using the flat side, mash the tape down carefully. Use the same angle you would normally use when making a cut, only *drag the chisel backward*. Flatten the area where the overlaps are located at each end of the tape with special care, so that the damming effect is complete. Take your time and go over the tape several times with the chisel. One little gap left under the tape will leave you with a mess to clean up as shown in the macrophoto in Figure 81. This poor taping

Fig. 81—This is what happens with cyanoacrylate glue when the tape is not properly pressed down (scrap back for demonstration purposes). The capillary action of this glue is tremendous and has penetrated nearly the width of the tape, following the wrinkles. This means trouble as cyanoacrylate glue will bond to the finish rather well.

job was done deliberately on a scrap back to show what happens when the tape is not properly applied. The area would have to be sanded down and spot-finished.

If the technique scares you, perhaps it would be wise to experiment on an instrument that is destined to be stripped for refinishing or on a piece of junk. Confidence comes with practice. As a matter of fact, I always work the tape down with the back of the chisel regardless of the type of glue I use. It becomes automatic after a few repair jobs.

Now the tape is in place and mashed down good. Another precaution is advisable. The thin cyanoacrylates are sold with Teflon capillary tubes for application purposes and are prone to dribble. You can spot-tape a couple of pieces of waxed paper or cardboard on the instrument to protect the finish until you have used the stuff long enough to handle it without dribbling it everywhere. Flow a bead of cyanoacrylate along the gap between the two pieces of tape. The first application will usually sink out of sight, but run a small spatula (I make mine from worn-out X-acto razor saw blades) along the tape. Work fast because this glue kicks off (hardens) in seconds. Apply a second bead of glue in fifteen or twenty seconds. If this also sinks out of sight, give it a minute or so this time, then hit it again with more glue. Two applications are usually enough, however.

At this point, I will tell you how I often break one of the rules in handling cyanoacrylate that I so carefully stressed earlier. You have to work fast to prevent gluing your finger to the guitar, so if you decide to do this, you have been warned. Instead of using the small spatula, I use my finger and work rapidly in small circular motions to work the glue into the crack. *Do not*—and I repeat, *do not*—stop this motion at any time while your finger is in contact with the tape—or *touch the glue-coated fingertip to any other surface for several seconds.*

I hate to keep harping on this subject, but I speak from experience. This glue will bond skin almost instantaneously. Often when you set the bottle down (in a safe place) a few drops of glue will bleed out and run down the outside of the Teflon tube onto the bottle or drip onto your fingers. The natural tendency is to rub your fingers together. *Don't!*

Acetone will ususally remove the glue, but it is toxic, whereas the glue is not. A piece of sandpaper will remove the glue from your skin (I'm not kidding), or wait awhile. Body oils and sweat will build up under the dried glue on your skin after a half hour or so, and it will simply peel off or can be removed with grit soap and water.

If you like, you can cut a finger from a thin plastic glove to slip over the finger used to work the glue into the crack and discard it when finished.

All of this must sound pretty complicated. Really, it's not. After using the cyanoacrylate a few times, you can repair a small hairline crack that is not out of alignment in minutes instead of hours. You can have the job cleaned up, touched up, and ready to go while standard glue is still drying. And, after all, time is money.

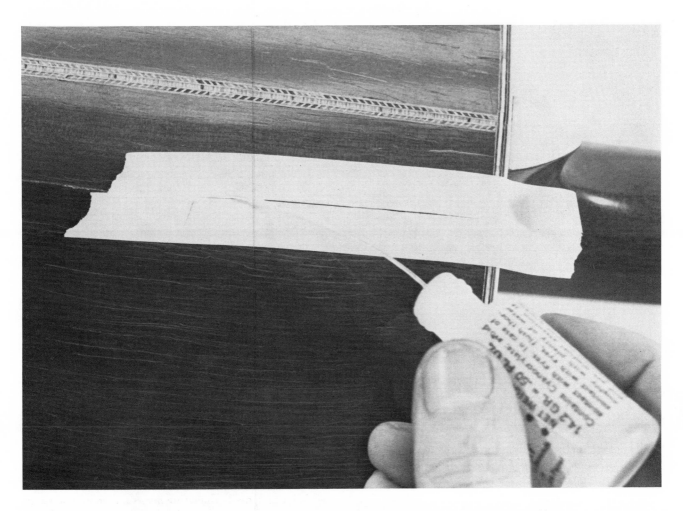

Fig. 82—*After careful taping, flow the water–thin cyanoacrylate glue into the hairline crack as per instructions in the text.*

No, I have not forgotten the cleaning-up process. After the second—or third, if necessary—application of cyanoacrylate kicks off, the gap between the tape should be filled with glue. Remove the tape immediately and trim the ridge off level with the finish. I use a razor-sharp ¼″ wood chisel for this purpose. Hold the cutting edge at an angle to the ridge of the glue and use a shearing action. I run a corner of the blade down one side, then the other, rather than trying to trim all the way through from one side. This will prevent chipping and give a neater line for touching up. A small curved "riffler" file will take the line slightly below the finish, and you can then hit it with an artist's brush and lacquer immediately—no waiting for the glue to cure. Cyanoacrylate, by the way, will not shrink under a lacquer finish. More on this characteristic in the finishing chapter.

If you will check inside the instrument with a mirror after gluing, you will see where the cyanoacrylate has penetrated (Figure 83). Instead of forming a ridge or "bead" as most glues do, it has flowed out to where the surface is almost flat.

Unless cross-patching is necessary (on long or misaligned cracks or done before the gluing), you are finished except for the touch-up. Any crack, if located in a high-stress location, should be cross-patched regardless of the glue used.

Do not use this glue unless the crack pulls together perfectly. Use Titebond or an epoxy if there is a slight gap. Cyanoacrylate glue *must* have a tight-fitting joint to work properly. If an area is to be refinished, though, and you have a splinter missing, reinforce behind the missing piece, sand dust from the surrounding area into the crack, and hit it with cyanoacrylate. It will give you a nonshrink wood filler that sets up almost instantly. *Do not* try this on light colored woods such as spruce, for it will show. I have, however, used it on maple fingerboards such as certain models of Fenders which will be explained in the refretting chapter.

Fig. 83—Macrophotograph showing the penetration of cyanoacrylate glue, "Hot Stuff", on a hairline crack. Diamond cross–patches may be glued in place with little sanding as it flows out on the underside of the crack rather than "beading up".

Do not attempt to use this glue if you have to *apply the clamps after applying the glue.* You will not have time to set them into place before the cyanoacrylate sets up. Use Titebond on such jobs.

Cyanoacrylate can be used successfully in a gaping crack where you cut and insert a piece of wood grain (Volume I, page 55, Figures 41 to 45) to fill a top crack. Follow the instructions outlined there, but with a few changes. Be sure to remember to work out the wrinkles in the tape as instructed for the hairline cracks. *Do not,* however, apply the glue before inserting the piece of grain into the crack. Press it in dry and work it down into place. *Then,* and only then, flow the cyanoacrylate along each side of the grain. Instead of pulling the tape and cleaning up immediately as you do in working with the harder woods, give it several minutes to cure and then pull the tape and trim flush. There will be little or no discoloration of the wood, and if the whole top is to be refinished, the repair will be nearly invisible if the job was brought in before body oils and polishes had a chance to seep into the crack. Of course, any repair to light-colored wood will show to a certain extent unless you are very lucky.

Sand off the underside of the repair and cross-patch any wide areas of unsupported wood (Figure 83) between the struts. If the gaping crack was misaligned, you should cross-patch before inserting the grain using the cross-patching gadgets. If not, the patches can be applied with the method demonstrated in Volume I, page 52, Figure 39.

Cedar or quarter-sawed redwood is becoming more frequently used for instrument tops. This wood poses a different problem from that of repairing a spruce top. It has a bad habit of actually shattering *across* the grain when subjected to an impact, as well as cracking with the grain. Break a common lead pencil and look closely at the break. Most pencils are made of redwood or cedar. This is the type of break that you will have to contend with. Nasty-looking isn't it? Believe me, it can be a real woolly-booger.

Cyanoacrylate can be a real lifesaver here if the pieces can be worked back into position. If not, a piece will have to be cut and grafted to replace the shattered area, or the whole top may have to be replaced. Try to save the original top first, if possible.

If a place is pushed in, try using a strut jack (Volume I, page 139, Figure 118) with a piece of polyethylene plastic taped to the head to see if the shattered pieces can be jacked back into place. If not, try the cross-patching gadgets with a spruce cross-patch and Titebond. One of these two methods should do the trick. Remove the cross-patch gadgets after the glue has cured and study the surface. If the top was shattered, the whole damaged area will have to be spot-finished, so I don't bother with taping it off.

Dig out your water-thin cyanoacrylate (it should be kept in the refrigerator when not in use) and flow it into the cracks. It will penetrate into every tiny broken cross-grain and stress crack, and you are in business. Allow the cyanoacrylate several minutes to cure thoroughly. If you have

74

used the strut jack and plastic to level things, remove it, clean up with sandpaper, and reinforce the cracked area from underneath. If you forgot to use the polyethylene plastic between the head of the jack and the wood, you're in trouble. It will be bonded to the wood and it's good-by jack. *Use the plastic.* Waxed paper can be used in a pinch, but if it should tear when you are applying pressure, you can still end up with a jack bonded in place. Of course, you could break the jack loose, but you might destroy what you have attempted to repair. Cyanoacrylate is a very tenacious glue.

With all jacks and gadgets out of the way and all rein-

forcing pieces glued in place and cured, your surface should be ready for finish-sanding and spot-finishing.

Do not attempt to repair cracks such as a split and gaping crack on a bridge. You will get most of these back if you do. Make a new bridge.

Some repairmen attempt to repair broken or cracked pegheads with cyanoacrylate glue. I prefer to use Titebond applied with a hypodermic needle in such a crack so that I have plenty of time to apply the proper clamps. This is well covered in the miscellaneous chapter of Volume I.

6

Disassembly and Reassembly of Acoustic Guitars

I really don't have much material to add to this chapter since I still use most of the basic techniques described in Volume I. There are, however, a few changes, primarily in tooling, that I have made to make things faster and easier.

One of these changes is in the removal of fingerboards. The original system used is found in Volume I with the text and illustrations starting on page 66. I used an electric flatiron for my heat source, but there were certain problems involved. Electric flatirons are much too wide for the fingerboards and hang over the edges. This is no problem once you clear the body, but when you are removing the fingerboard from the face of the instrument, the top finish must be protected or it will blister. I've used pieces of asbestos or corrugated cardboard to protect the top, but it seems that, no matter how careful you are, the finish is softened to a certain degree and will be marred when you remove the fingerboard. There's just too much heat required to soften the glue. Frustrating.

The fingerboard heater found in the special-tool chapter of this volume is a product of this frustration. I have used this heater on six or seven fingerboards, and it does a bang-up job. In using the common electric flatiron, particularly if I chose not to remove the frets before removing the fingerboard, I usually ended up with a certain amount of wood slivers stuck to the glue surface of the fingerboard or the neck itself. This new heater softens the glue to the extent that the fingerboard invariably comes off perfectly clean.

A word of caution, however, that I neglected to mention in Volume I; any plastic or celluloid fingerboard bindings or mother-of-toilet-seat (celluloid) inlay pieces *must be removed before heating*, or they will be destroyed. Celluloid has an extremely low flash point and will practically explode from the heat generated, even if the frets are left in place.

This fingerboard heater is slower in reaching a working temperature than an electric flatiron, so it must be plugged in about thirty minutes before you plan to use it. It works faster, though, once the working temperature is reached. I've designed it where it can be hung over the edge of a workbench with the hot shoe out of the way during the heating and cooling cycle.

While the heater is warming up, I drill six $\frac{1}{16}''$ holes in the fingerboard, two between the nut and first fret, two between the fifth and sixth frets, and two between the eleventh and twelfth frets. These holes are for alignment pins when the fingerboard is reglued, and are drilled from each side of the fingerboard surface. I usually drill each one $\frac{1}{2}''$ from the edge of the fingerboard and angle the bottom of the hole toward the center of the back of the neck (see Volume I, page 86, Figure 71).

Of course, if you remove all the frets first, the alignment pin holes can be drilled in the fret slots so that they won't have to be plugged after the fingerboard is reglued. And if I remove only the end of the fingerboard over the face, I use only four alignment pin holes. The two alignment pin holes at the end of the fingerboard on a partial removal should be drilled to where they go into the heavy cross-strut immediately under the top by the soundhole.

The fingerboard heater will get so hot that a moistened fingertip touched to the brass shoe will not sizzle. The moisture vaporizes instantly, and if it is preheated long enough, the heater will even melt solder. After all, the heating elements were scavenged from a pair of soldering irons.

Set the heater's shoe (Figure 84) in place over the face end of the fingerboard and slip your hand through the soundhole of the instrument with your fingertips touching the face wood under the area being heated. You will notice in Figure 84 that I now don't have to bother with protecting the top. When the wood under the face becomes hot to the touch, remove the heater, hang it over the edge of the workbench out of the way, and work your knife blade under the fingerboard as described in Volume I, page 68 and 69. The glue seam should part almost immediately.

The knife will begin to stick after a few moments, so set the heater back on the fingerboard to heat the next section. In a few minutes you can work the knife farther. Work a section at a time until the fingerboard is off. On page 69 of

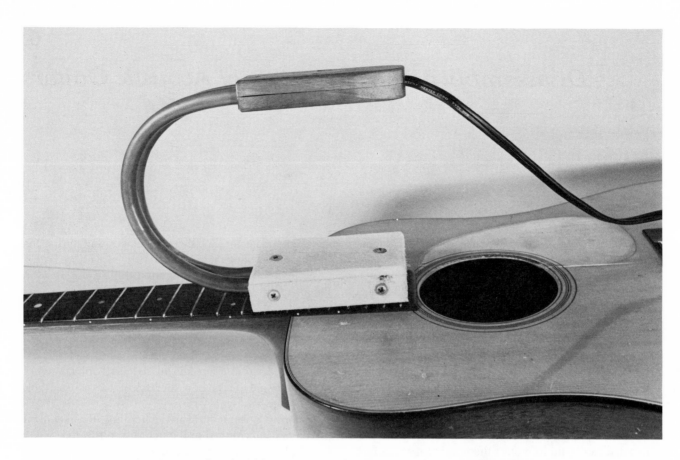

Fig. 84—My new fingerboard heater (see special tool chapter) in use. The fingerboard is being removed from the face to expose the neck's dovetail joint so that the neck may be removed and reset.

Volume I, I mention straightening the fingerboard with heat after removal, but with the new heater it will come off straight and clean. None of the fingerboards I have removed with the new heater—all with the frets left in place—have required straightening, and there have been no slivers or splinters to reglue. It's worth the time and effort to add this heater to your tool inventory.

Another change in this chapter is in regard to the use of the Dremel Moto Tool, the router attachment, and the #115 Dremel cutter for cleaning up and cutting new binding and purfling grooves. This #115 cutter works fine but is prone to rapid wear, particularly when you are working with a hard, resinous wood such as rosewood. Dremel now offers a double-flute router bit in the ¼″ size (Figure 13) which is far superior for the purpose and, unlike the #115 cutter, can be resharpened with a slip when it gets dull. It will outlast several of the aforementioned cutters. The router bit cuts cleaner and faster, too. A nice time and money saver.

I've changed my technique in removing necks to a certain degree also. Basically, it is the same as described in

Volume I, pages 81 to 85, Figures 67 to 70 with a few small but important changes which I will describe. The end of the fingerboard is removed to expose the dovetail joint. As much of the old glue is removed between the end of the neck's dovetail and the neck block to make room for water and the heating tool.

Now take a length of plastic electrician's tape or other rubberized tape (no wrinkles as in masking tape) and carefully tape off the neck-to-body joint (see Figure 85) to prevent any water leakage. Tape the clamping blocks in place on the face of the instrument (Volume I, page 81, Figure 67) and fill the dovetail joint with water. Allow to soak for a half-hour or so.

In Volume I, I used a propane torch and a thin-bladed stainless-steel table knife for heating the water, but Michael Holmes of *Mugwumps* magazine suggested the use of an electric soldering iron instead. He's right. It works much better (Figure 86) and faster than the table knife.

Add more water after presoaking, if necessary, until the water level in the dovetail joint is about ¼″ below the surface of the wood. Another tip here. If you are removing a

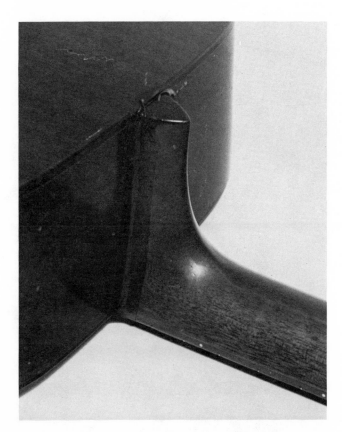

Fig. 85—Plastic electrician's tape had been applied to cover the neck–to–body joint to prevent water leakage while removing the neck. The tape is nearly the same color as the guitar and you will have to look closely to see it. Electrician's tape works much better than masking tape for this job as it has no wrinkles.

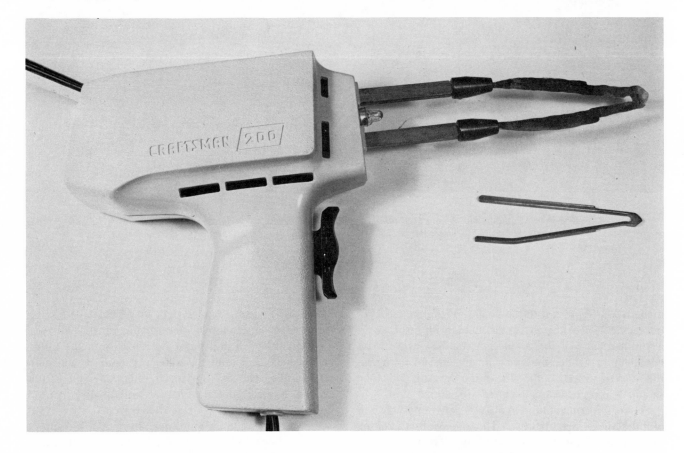

Fig. 86—A flattened tip compared to a new one for use in neck removal with the soldering iron. The tip should be heated with a propane torch and hammered flat to where it is only about 3/64" thick.

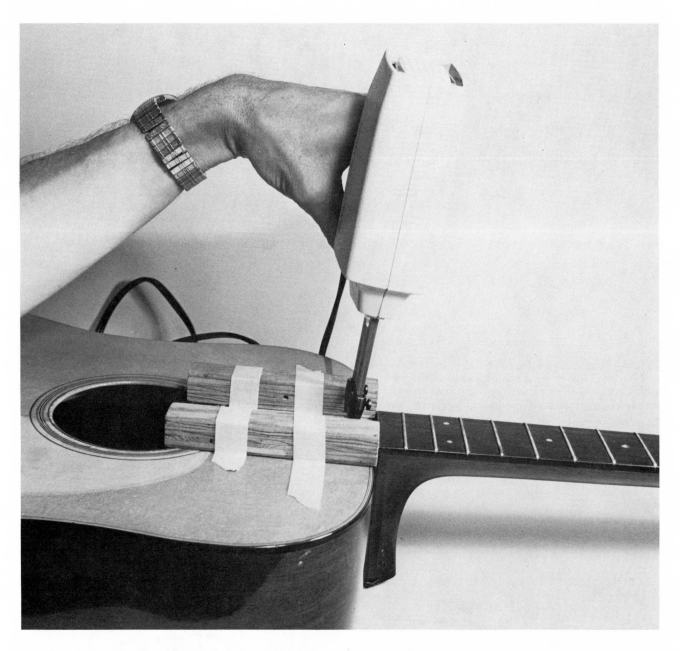

Fig. 87—Clamping blocks have been taped into place and the electric soldering iron with the flattened tip is being used to heat water poured into the dovetail joint to soften the glue for neck removal.

modern Martin neck with the square steel-tubing neck reinforcement, pack the end of the tubing with tissue paper, a trimmed piece of cork, wood, or what-have-you. If you don't, you may soften the glue of the fingerboard down near the nut end as well as the glue in the dovetail. This tube should be plugged before the presoaking cycle.

Set the soldering-gun tip in place as deep as possible and pull the trigger. See Figure 87. The water will start boiling in moments. I use a Sears dual-temperature gun and use the high-temperature range until the water starts boiling, then switch over to the low-temperature range. Otherwise the high heat will boil the water out all over the instrument's face. Boil until the water is vaporized, add more water and repeat. Try working the neck after the second boiling. It should have some give to it. If not, try more water and a third boiling. That should do it.

Remove the soldering gun, invert the guitar, and apply a clamp as shown in Volume I, page 82, Figure 68. The neck

Fig. 88—A miniature wire brush (Dremel catalog #424) mounted in a variable–speed Dremel Moto Tool is excellent for removing old glue. Be sure to wear goggles or safety glasses when using this or any wire brush.

should slide out easily with the glue as soft and alive as the moment the neck was originally slipped into place.

Now is a good time to scrape off most of the old glue while it's still soft. Then the parts will have to be dried thoroughly before you proceed any farther. The end grain of the neck and neck block will have soaked up a lot of water, and the heat needed to soften the glue helps to cause further swelling of the parts. Allow a couple of days—preferably, a week—for the wood to shrink back to normal.

When you're ready to work on it again, check the neck-block area of the body carefully. If the boiling treatment has loosened the top-to-neck-block joint or a side-to-neck-block joint, reglue these before trying to fit the neck.

All the old glue should be removed to the bare wood. You can use a chisel or scrapers, but I have a pet trick that

I like to use: the Dremel Moto Tool with a #424 or #442 miniature wire brush shown in Figure 88. A variable-speed control for the standard Dremel or the Model 380 Moto Tool with the built-in variable-speed control should be used to cut the rpm by about half. Otherwise, 30,000 rpm can throw a lot of "whiskers" from the tiny wire brush. The brush eats old glue and takes only moments to clean up a dovetail joint. *Of course, safety glasses or goggles are a must.*

Regluing the neck is thoroughly discussed in Volume I, pages 84 and 85, but I use a trick now that tends to simplify the fitting process when you have an ill-fitting dovetail or someone has reset it previously using soft wood or cardboard for shims. Yes, you read me right, cardboard. Several times I have found cardboard shims in a dovetail joint, and the owner wondered why the neck came loose again. The cardboard works fine for a while, but it eventually compresses, and the neck shifts again.

However, I've found that cardboard shims are very useful when used properly. Some necks that have been previously shimmed have to be shimmed again, and the original shims are almost invariably destroyed or mutilated beyond reuse during the neck removal—and were probably not the right size to start with or the neck wouldn't have shifted again. Cutting and fitting new wooden shims of various dimensions is a time-consuming task.

All kinds and thicknesses of cardboard are readily available. I merely whack up a few pieces of cardboard in several thicknesses and use them in place of wooden shims while prefitting the neck. When you achieve a fit, then all you have to do is measure the thickness of the cardboard with a micrometer or vernier calipers and duplicate the measurements with *hardwood*—mahogany is fine—and you're in business.

Please do not yield to temptation and use the cardboard shims to reset the neck because of the aforementioned reasons. Besides, you might be the one who has to reset the neck again.

It's amazing—or disgusting—to see the shoddy work on some of the neck resets that I've had to do. I won't go into all of them, but one that I had to salvage really sticks in my mind. It was a real challenge, and I'll use it as a "fer-instance." It was an old Gibson B25–12 that belongs to Luther Wilson, the editor of the University of Oklahoma Press. He took it to some turkey in New York City to have the neck reset before he moved to Oklahoma.

He brought it in to me with the neck out of whack again, primarily a ⅛″ gap where the bottom of the heel had pulled away from the body. Luther had some time to kill and we were hashing over the idea of doing Volume II of my guitar-repair book, so I decided to have a good look at it while he was here. I took the strings off, lifted the fingerboard from the face, and the neck fell out in my hands! This repairman (?) had run a saw between the body and the heel of the neck, sawing through all but ³⁄₁₆″ of the dovetail under the finger board, and filled the slot with glue and clamped it. Of course, with the equivalent of a butt joint and the tension of twelve strings, it broke loose within a week, just long enough for Luther to make the move to Oklahoma. It was a little late to take it back.

I racked my brains trying to figure out some method of permanently grafting a new piece of wood to the butt of the neck so that I could cut a new dovetail to fit the neck right. It had to be something that would stand up to the stress of twelve strings. I could have tried doweling a piece to the heel, but I was afraid that it wouldn't last, and I didn't want my editor mad at me. It had to be something better. A good friend of mine, Wally Foulkes, from Tacoma, Washington,

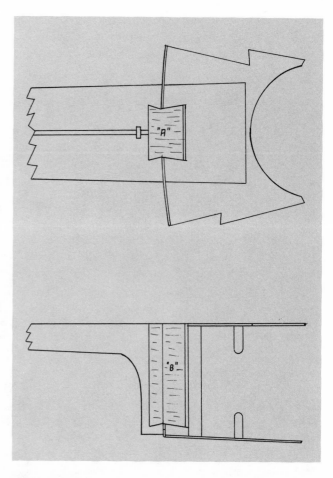

Fig. 89—Top view "A" and side view "B" of a double–dovetail or "butterfly" joint I used to graft a new dovetail onto the stub of an old Gibson 12 string neck. The shaded area is the new piece of wood.

dropped in for a visit while I was pondering the thing, took one look, and suggested a dovetail joint since the Gibson twelve-string neck has a rather "fat" heel.

It sounded like a good idea—if I could figure out how to cut the female dovetail in the stub-of-a-heel. I sawed through the fingerboard at the thirteenth fret (it had a fourteen-frets-to-the-body neck) and removed the end of the fingerboard for access to the stub.

Some years ago I used to make a few guitars, and I designed and built a male and female dovetail jig for occasional use (see the special tool chapter of this volume). There was just enough meat on the Gibson neck for a shallow jigged dovetail. I cut the dovetail using the jig and router and cut a matching male dovetail from a scrap of mahogany, cutting the male dovetail so that there was no gap. In other words, the fit was snug on the beveled edges and on the end of the stub when fitted into the female dovetail joint on the neck. I epoxied it in place for a solid joint. After the glue cured, I hand-cut a dovetail on the new piece of wood to match the original Gibson dovetail and reset the neck with Titebond.

The instrument was reassembled and strung up to pitch, measurements were made, and a plane-and-fret was done using the string tension simulation jig. So far the guitar is doing fine and has taken nine months of hard playing. I don't know what you would call this kind of a joint formally—perhaps a double dovetail or a butterfly joint (see Figure 89 for a drawing). It's the only time I've ever had to use this technique in the many years I've been in the business, but I decided to include the technique and the plans for the dovetail jig in this volume in case you might need it someday.

Another neck problem you may encounter that's not quite so rough is the Netherlands-built Vega neck situation. Quite a few of these were imported while the Martin factory was closed by a strike. Don't get me wrong; the ones that I've worked on were fine-sounding instruments, and they were not the typical imported plywood jobs. In fact, there was no plywood in the ones that I've worked on. The only problem I've had with them is in the neck-to-body joint.

The fingerboard was glued to the face of the instrument in a normal manner, but the neck itself was joined to the body with a butt joint, secured only by three longitudinally grooved $\frac{5}{16}''$ dowels (Figure 90). The glue appeared to be one of the common white glues, and that was part of the problem. Two of the three dowels were in the fatter part of the heel just below the fingerboard, but only a single dowel was used at the point of highest stress, the lower part of the heel. If you get a Vega in your shop with the bottom of the heel pulled away from the body, the neck will have to be removed and reset.

Use the fingerboard heater and lift the fingerboard free of the top. Lay the guitar on its side and give the neck a sharp sideways rap with the palm of your hand. Don't go overboard and really whack it—just a good sharp rap. You should hear a snap as the glue turns loose around one of the paired dowels. Turn the guitar over on the opposite side and repeat the process. You may have to try more than once, but the dowels have turned loose on the four I've worked on so far. The neck should now have some sideways movement.

Push the neck sideways and slip a cardboard shim in the gap. Push the neck to the opposite side. A wider gap should appear on the opposite side. Double up on the shims in the wider gap and then push the neck back the other way. Keep doing this, adding thicker shims in the gaps each time, until the dowels pull out and the neck is free from the body. You may have to use a tapered wedge under the lower part of the heel in combination with the other shims, but a few minutes work should free the neck.

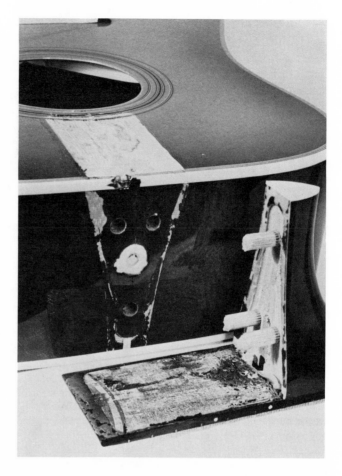

Fig. 90—The three–dowel method used in joining the neck to the body of the Netherlands–built Vega. The bottom dowel has a bad habit of pulling loose, allowing the neck to separate from the body.

Cut the lower (single) dowel off flush with the neck—or body, depending on which end turned loose. Center-punch the dowel with an awl or scriber and drill it out with a $\frac{1}{4}''$ drill. Clean out the remainder of the dowel with a small chisel and clean out the glue from both the body (neck-block hole) and the heel with a $\frac{5}{16}''$ drill.

Check the top two dowels. If one should be cracked during the neck removal, replace it and clean out the mating holes with the $\frac{5}{16}''$ drill bit. Slip the neck back on the body. It should slide right into place. If not, sand the upper dowels lightly until it does.

Now to the problem area, the lower dowel. We need some system that will handle more stress than the common grooved dowel. My solution is a piece of $\frac{3}{8}''$ cadmium-plated, prethreaded Ready Rod cut to the same length as the original dowel. The $\frac{5}{16}''$ dowel hole in the heel is of the proper size for a $\frac{3}{8}$-16 tap. Tap out the hole in the heel

Fig. 91—A workable substitute for threading a hole in wood if you don't have a tap for a particular thread. Simply grind a sharp–edged notch in a piece of rod or bolt with the right thread and chase out the burrs with a three–cornered file. Works with coarse threads on ⅜" and larger rods.

Fig. 92—I remove the bottom dowel, tap the neck for a ⅜" piece of "Ready Rod", drill the bottom body hole out to ⅜" plus, and reseat in epoxy. See the text.

with the standard tap and then finish the threads with a ⅜-16 bottom tap. A Q&D (quick-and-dirty) bottom tap can be made from a piece of the ⅜" Ready Rod ground out as shown in Figure 91. It can also be used to thread the entire hole in a pinch. Whichever method you use, the rod dowel should screw in the full depth of the hole. A few drops of Titebond on the threads and in the hole will lock it into place.

The mating hole in the body will have to be drilled out so that the ⅜" threaded rod will *slide* in. I use the step-drilling method, drilling out the hole ¹⁄₃₂" larger with each succeeding drill until I have a ⅜" diameter hole, then use a ²⁵⁄₆₄ drill for a few thousandths glue clearance and an easy fit. The step-drilling process prevents drilling the hole off to one side, which can easily happen if you try to use a single larger drill.

Slip the neck into place. If you did get the drilled hole off slightly, you may have to drill the hole out to ¹³⁄₃₂" before the neck will fit. Don't worry about a little extra clearance; the upper two dowels and the fingerboard will align the neck properly. While you have the neck on the body—assuming that everything fits properly—tape off everything to catch the glue squeeze-out.

After taping, remove the neck and break out the Titebond and the Elmer's epoxy (not the five-minute glue). Use

the epoxy for the threaded-rod dowel. It will fill the threads and any discrepancy surrounding it. Use Titebond on the upper dowels and for gluing the fingerboard back to the top. You could use epoxy for the whole glue setup if you like, but it's essential for the threaded rod. Clamp into place and let cure for eight hours, clean it up, touch it up, and you're ready to restring the instrument.

I've used this technique on both six- and twelve-string Vegas, and so far no problems.

In Volume I, pages 141 to 146, Figures 121 to 126, I show the Martin-type technique for flattening a badly bellied top. Since I completed Volume I, many guitar manufacturers have begun using the larger bridge plates a la Martin. This is great, for it has reduced the incidence of the bellied top tremendously.

Fig. 93—A victim of "heat prostration". Note the top seam parted, strings of melted and reset glue (a dead giveaway to heat exposure), and the shifted bridge. The customer was lucky that the bridge pulled loose rather than the neck. A candidate for reverse clamping and a new bridge plate.

However, when a guitar has been severely "heat-treated" as in Figure 93, it will still belly up from slippage of the softened glue. The removal of the large bridge plates for the reverse-clamping technique is very touchy.

One way is to use the hook (Volume I, page 142, Figure 121) and remove the bridge plate splinter by splinter, but some of these modern glues are tenacious, and you can take some of the top wood with it.

On the other hand, a simple tool can be made to ease the task. I've tried several methods of preheating these large bridge plates, even to the extent of trying to design an electric heater, but the one I ended up with (Figure 48 in the special tool chapter and Figure 94 in this chapter) is heated with a propane torch and works better than anything I was able to design.

First, the bridge is removed, then the shoe of the bridge plate heater is heated with the torch. It should be hot enough to sizzle when touched with a moistened finger, but not red-hot, for you don't want to start any fires inside the guitar. Insert the hot shoe through the sound hole—very carefully, and press it up against the bridge plate. You can tell by rocking it slightly whether you have it flat, and a mechanic's mirror through the sound hole will give you a visual location.

Start at the back edge of the bridge plate and try to keep the hot shoe from touching any of the struts. Lay the palm of your hand on the surface of the top, and when it feels hot, move the shoe to a new location for a minute or two. Remove the heater and go to work with the hook. Don't try to heat or remove a large plate in one operation, for one

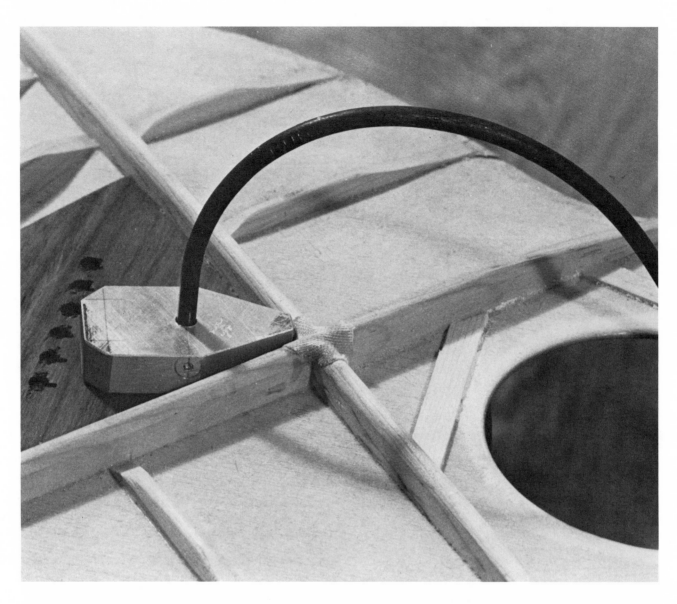

Fig. 94—Bridge plate remover in use (simulated) to soften the glue in preparation to removing a large bridge plate. The metal shoe is heated with a propane torch previous to inserting through the sound hole.

heated area will cool off too much for the glue to stay soft while you're heating another area. When the glue stiffens, remove the hook, slip in a wedge good and snug, reheat the heater's shoe, and cook the area immediately in front of the loosened area. Remove the heater and use the hook again. If you prefer, you can split off the loosened area of the bridge plate before reheating. I usually do because it's easier to get the hook under the part that hasn't pulled loose. Five or ten minutes of alternating with the hot shoe and the

hook, and it should be out and ready to clean up for the reverse clamping technique with a new bridge plate.

The heater works just as well on the smaller bridge plates and is about the only easy way to remove some of the Mickey Mouse plywood bridge plates found under the bellies of imported plywood instruments. You have to be very careful not to heat the plywood tops too much, or you can separate the top plies.

7

More on String Actions and Less on Tension Rod Adjustments

I'm not going to get very deep into tension rod adjustments in this volume; it was thoroughly covered in Volume I. However, I still get many instruments in my shop with problems along this line.

Without a doubt the main problem is from changing gauges of strings without readjusting the tension rods. Say that an instrument has been set up for a medium-gauge string and the owner decides to change to a set of light or extralight gauge strings. Of course, the neck is going to straighten out to a certain degree with less tension on it. The owner ends up with a modulated rattle and wonders why. The rod has to be slacked off until the neck has the proper amount of forward bow. This can be particularly touchy if the owner is already playing with a low action. Sometimes a simple adjustment of the string action will take care of the problem, but more often it entails a combination of action adjustment and rod adjustment or, in the case of an electric guitar, readjusting the bridge pieces to compensate for the different strings.

Changing gauges can bring up another problem. Many times I have slacked off on a tension rod until there is no tension at all, and the neck is still too straight. Many of the electrics equipped with Super Slinkys actually have a backward bow. When an instrument is brought in with the strings rattling on the first half-dozen frets, the problem in almost invariably a perfectly straight neck or one with a backward bow. Here in Oklahoma I have a rash of instruments needing adjustments in the late spring and again in the early fall, particularly the lead rock-and-roll guitarists with their superlow actions.

The increasing humidity of the spring is absorbed by the wood of the fingerboard which expands slightly, and the neck straightens out, thus lowering the string action. The tension rod has to be relaxed to compensate for this.

Exactly the opposite occurs in the fall. People start using their heating systems, and the humidity drops dramatically. The fingerboards lose moisture and shrink. The necks bow up, and up comes the string action along with the necks. This problem can be alleviated somewhat by the use of a room humidifier or, better yet, a humidifier in the guitar case.

Then we have the problem of nonadjustable necks. One of these with a backward bow—or too much forward bow for that matter—is bad news. Ditto the aforementioned necks with the tension rod slacked off all the way that still have a backward bow.

Some shops use a special electrically powered heater which clamps on the full length of the fingerboard and heat-softens the glue between the fingerboard surface and the neck. This is supposed to allow a certain amount of slippage between the neck and fingerboard, and when the glue rehardens after the neck and heater cool off, the neck should be straight. I wouldn't object to the use of the heat on an inexpensive instrument, but I'm a bit leery of glue that has been heated and reset. With most of the better-quality instruments selling in the $600 or $1,000 range nowadays, I worry about the use of heat for something like that.

Another objection to using this heater is that most of the inexpensive guitars, and some of the more expensive ones, use mother-of-toilet-seat (pearl–grained celluloid) fingerboard position markers, and the amount of heat needed to soften the glue may destroy the celluloid unless they are removed before the heating process.

Another objection to the heat-straightening is that, once warped, the wood tends to develop a "memory" and may eventually revert back to the original bow or warp. I prefer to use the string tension simulation jig and do a controlled plane and fret for correction, as described in the refretting chapter of this volume.

On guitars with a really bad forward bow and no neck adjustment, an adjustable tension rod may be installed (see the tension rod chapters of Volumes I and II) to handle the problem.

Say that the neck is correct, with no warpage, with proper bow, etc., and the action is still off. What now? I described setting a string action thoroughly in Volume I, but I've changed my technique enough that, to avoid confusion, I will go over it again in this volume.

My first step is to check the instrument's nut height (reversed from the technique in Volume I). Many intonation and playing difficulties can be corrected by a simple reworking of the nut. It's amazing how many instruments come into my shop with high nuts, many times with only one or two strings high. This can cause the first two or three notes on that particular string to sharp out tremendously while the notes on down the neck will be within tolerences. It will also throw the tuning of the whole instrument out of balance.

A quick check for a too-high nut clearance on a steel-string instrument is to hold each string down individually between the third and fourth frets and slide a .010″ piece of shim stock (Figure 98) or hard plastic between the string and the top of the first fret. You should feel some drag on at least the first three strings. If not, the action is probably off and should be checked out further. Of course, this will vary somewhat depending on the particular instrument's requirements; folk-style fingerpicking, light flatpicking, heavy bluegrass flatpicking, classical nylon strings, etc.

It can be really confusing to set the right height for the individual style of playing, so I have put together a table of the approximate nut-height clearances that I use in my shop.

Remember, all these measurements are taken between the top of the first fret and the string involved with the string held down between the third and fourth fret. On few of the more sensitive instruments it might be possible to set a thousandth of an inch lower, or one with a stiffer top may have to be set a thousandth of an inch or so higher. A set of machinist's or mechanic's shims can be used for checking these clearances. They can be purchased at nearly any industrial or auto supply. I use several pieces of hard plastic in various thicknesses.

To cut down the nut's string slots, you will need a set of needle files (available from a hobby shop or Brookstone Hard-To-Find-Tools) or a set of special nut files. My nut files were purchased from C. Bruno & Son, Inc., under the Ibánez brand (Figure 95), but they are handled by other suppliers under other brand names.

Press down a string between the third and fourth frets, check the clearance between the string and the top of the first fret with the proper shim. If it's too much, it will have to be worked down. Select the proper-size file, lift the string from its notch with a hook-end scribe (you don't have to

String	Electric Jazz, Rock and Roll	Folk	Light Flat-Picking	Bluegrass	Classic
First	.006	.007	.008	.009	.010
Second	.007	.008	.009	.010	.011
Third	.008 Wound—.009 Plain	.009	.010	.011	.012
Fourth	.010	.010	.011	.012	.013
Fifth	.011	.011	.012	.013	.014
Sixth	.012	.012	.013	.014	.015

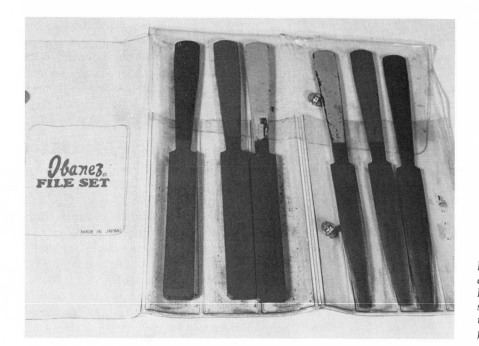

Fig. 95—Fret and nut file set. These are available from C. Bruno & Son, Inc., under the Ibanez line and other suppliers under various other brand names. The nut files are great, the fret files so–so.

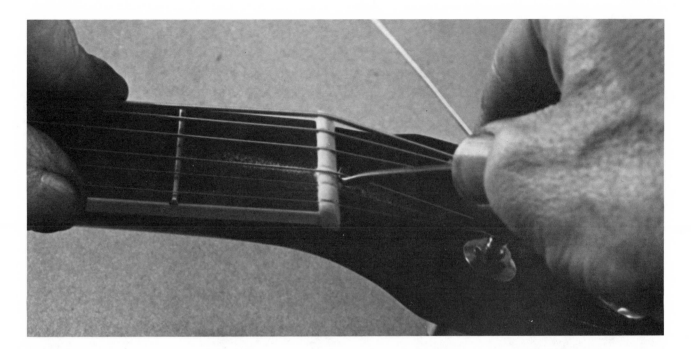

Fig. 96—*The hook on a hook–end scribe (#J–1939 from Bookstone, Hard–To–Find–Tools) is ideal for lifting strings from fret notches without detuning the string. This saves both time and money, and strings as tuning them up and down promotes string breakage.*

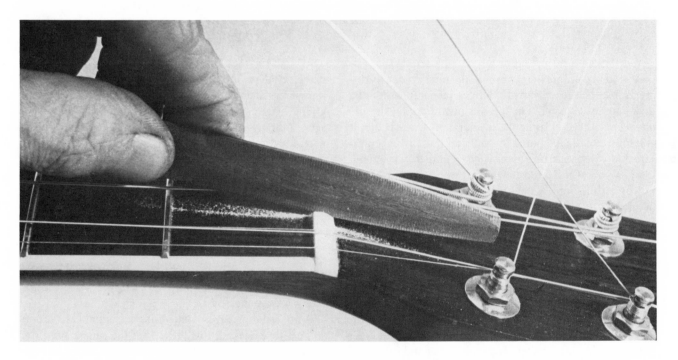

Fig. 97—*Using a nut file to cut the nut's string seat down to the proper height. Small needle files may be used for this job, but the nut files are handier.*

detune for this, See Figure 96), and remove a small amount of material (Figure 97). Lift and set the string back in place with the scribe and recheck the clearance. Repeat the procedure until the clearance is correct.

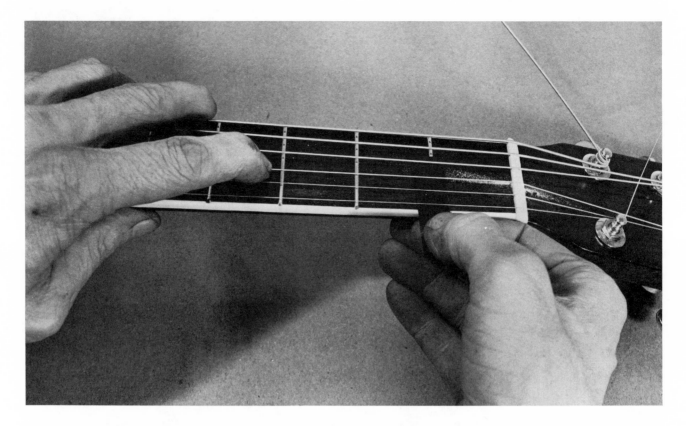

Fig. 98—Using a piece of shim stock to check the string action height at the nut end of the scale.

A word of warning here. Many of the modern-day instruments use plastic of varying degrees of hardness for the nuts—some very soft. On the soft nuts dragging the file *backward* instead of using the file normally works better. If you must use the file normally on these, use *very light* pressure and *check your clearances often* (Figure 98). It's much too easy to cut these too low, which would require a new nut or a shim job. A new bone nut would be preferable because of its durability, and you might notice a slight improvement in sound and tonal quality.

Speaking of shimming nuts, I am definitely in favor of it when the original nut is bone or ivory and in reasonably good condition. With the availability and expense of ivory and bone what they are, a shim of *proper* material to correct a low nut action is perfectly acceptable. I've found everything from tissue and cigarette papers and cardboard (unacceptable) to wood and plastic (acceptable if hard) under old nuts. The softer materials such as paper and cardboard can have a muting effect on the strings and should not be used. They can also compress and screw up the action.

Very seldom does a nut require more than .010" shimming, and you can find many kinds of hard plastics in this thickness range. Try your telephone book for your local plastics dealers. You might try a photographic supply for the transparent sleeves used to protect photographic prints. In a pinch you could use the plastic from guitar-string packages, although the compressibility of these might be suspect. I get my plastic shim stock from Cope Plastics, a distributor in Oklahoma City. Of course, when you shim a nut, you will have to check and correct the nut's string action all over again.

Should you have to make a nut from scratch, save the old nut for a pattern. Shape the contact area of the new blank the same as on the original nut, but leave .015" to .020" extra material on the nut top, and leave it rough until you have the nut string action set. Most of the nuts use a square contact area on their bases, but the Martin instruments use an angled base.

A small sliding bevel square using the old nut as a pattern is ideal for checking this angle. Set the square from the old nut and sand or file the same angle on the new blank. Take it easy if you are using a power disk or belt sander for this job. It's better to make several small cuts to achieve the proper angle than to ruin the new blank.

The nut should fit snugly into place on the instrument without any gaps between it and the fingerboard and the bottom where it contacts the neck. To achieve this fit, any old glue left on the contact surfaces when you knocked the old nut out should be removed with a sharp chisel so that you have a clean area to fit the new nut. *Do not* glue the new nut in place yet.

As for spacing the strings on the new nut, there are three ways to go. One way is to use the old nut for a pattern and file shallow notches accordingly. String the guitar up and set the height as previously detailed. However, many factory or previously installed nuts are spaced off. I've seen brand-new instruments with the spaces between the strings varying as much as .020″ to .030″. In Volume I, page 93, I give a formula for spacing the strings but this is just a rough spacing. I hate to admit that I blew it, but we can't all be perfect. I neglected to figure for the differences in the different string diameters, and using the center-to-center measurements outlined there would make the larger diameter or bass strings closer to each other than the smaller treble strings.

If you figure the spacing strictly mathmatically, the procedure has to be changed somewhat. Take the diameter measurements of the strings you plan to use. Write each one down separately and to one side of each number; also include one-half the string's diameter. I will explain later.

Step 1. Use a long straightedge and mark the location of the first and sixth string on top of the roughed-out nut. Measure the distance from mark to mark with vernier calipers. I prefer the dial verniers for ease of reading. I will continue to do this formula in numbered steps to help prevent confusion. Record this measurement.

Step 2. Add *one half* the diameter of the first and sixth strings plus the *total* diameter of the second, third, fourth, and fifth strings. Record this measurement.

Step 3. Subtract the sum of the string diameter measurements of Step 2 from the mark-to-mark measurement recorded in Step 1. Record this measurement.

Step 4. The answer to the problem in Step 3 is the actual total air space between all six strings. Now is the time to divide by five. This will give us the actual air space needed between each string—also the constant we will be using for the rest of the figuring.

Step 5. The mark for the number-one string will be our constant measuring spot. Each string location will be measured from there, and if done right, the last measurement should fall exactly on the mark for the sixth string. Now for the actual measurements.

Step 6. The second string. Add one-half the string diameters of the first and second string plus the air space constant arrived at in Step 4. Set this measurement on the caliper and lay out the second string's location. Record this measurement for the next step.

Step 7. The third string. Add the measurement arrived at in Step 6 plus one-half the diameters of the second and third strings plus Step 4's constant. This total will give you the distance from the first-string mark to the location of the third string's center. Record this total for the next step. Are you beginning to get the picture?

Step 8. The fourth string. Add the total from Step 7 plus one-half the diameters of the third and fourth string plus Step 4's constant. This is the distance from the first to the fourth string. Again, record the total for the next step.

Step 9. The fifth string. Add the total from Step 8 plus one-half the diameters of the fourth and fifth strings plus Step 4's constant and lay out on the nut. Record the total.

Step 10. The sixth string. This is a double-check on your measurements since it is already laid out. Add the total of Step 9 plus one-half the diameters of the fifth and sixth strings plus Step 4's constant and set it on the calipers. If you haven't blown it, the caliper's pointer should span the first and sixth string center marks exactly. If not, go back and start over again.

Step 11. If you came out on the mark in Step 10, notch out each of the marks just enough to hold the strings in position and string up the instrument. The space between each string should be exactly the same, and you can finish cutting the string notches for the proper nut action.

Sound complicated? Just wait until you start figuring the spacing for a twelve-string nut with pure mathematics. Here you also have to figure the string pair's spacing plus the course spacing (distance between the pairs). "Surely," you say, "there must be an easier, simpler method for an exact nut spacing!"

Luckily there is. The above method gives you your location by pure mathematics, but I find it easier and less confusing to measure the string's position and install the strings at the same time. It's much easier to handle a twelve-string job, too, which I will describe after giving you the technique for a six string. This method also employs the use of vernier calipers, but without all the complicated addition. Again, I will give you the technique in numbered steps.

Step 1. Set the roughed-out nut in place (no glue) and install the first and sixth strings. Sharpen a pencil to a knife edge on a scrap of sandpaper, shift each string to where it is located about ³⁄₃₂″ from where the top of the fret crown is rounded down on the end of the fret, and scratch a fine pencil mark on each side of the two strings. File a shallow notch in the center between each pair of pencil marks only deep enough to hold the strings in position and set the two strings into the notches.

Step 2. Measure the distance between the first and sixth strings with the calipers and record this measurement.

Step 3. Add the total diameters of the second, third, fourth, and fifth strings and record this measurement.

Step 4. Subtract the total of Step 3 (string diameters) from the total of Step 2 and record.

Step 5. Divide the answer from Step 4 by five and you will have the correct air spacing measurement or constant to use in spacing the rest of the strings. Sound familiar? It is, but the next step is where this third technique differs from the previous one, and to me, simplified things.

Step 6. Lock this measurement or constant on your vernier calipers and install the second string, turning it up to where there is a fair amount of tension on it. Set the caliper's inside measurement jaws between the first and second string to space them and scratch a fine pencil mark on either side of the second string on top of the nut. Remove the calipers and cut a tiny notch. Then check the spacing again with the calipers. Adjust by filing the notch to one side or the other until the calipers are a snug fit between the first and second string.

Step 7. Continue installing one string at a time using Step 6 as a guide for the rest of the strings, and they should be perfectly spaced when you install the fifth string, ready to set the proper nut string action. A lot simpler. A lot faster, too, unless you're a glutton for punishment or want the experience of doing it mathematically.

Now for the twelve-string nut. This may be done similarly, but we have six more strings and the small air space between the individual pairs to factor in.

Step 1. Install the first and twelfth string as in Step 1 of the previous method. Make a pair of shims (to keep from having to reset the calipers all the time), one ⁵⁄₆₄″ (.078″) and the other ³⁄₃₂″ (.094″) thick. I use the ⁵⁄₆₄″ shim to space the first and second pairs (between the gap separating the paired strings) and the ³⁄₃₂″ shim to space the pairs with the octave strings. Install the second string with the ⁵⁄₆₄″ spacer, mark and notch the nut. Ditto on spacing the eleventh or octave string to the twelfth string but use the ³⁄₃₂″ spacer.

Step 2. Now we measure the distance between the second and eleventh strings and record this measurement.

Step 3. Add the total diameters of the third and fourth strings plus .078″ (⁵⁄₆₄″), the diameters of the fifth and sixth strings plus .094″ (³⁄₃₂″), the diameters of the seventh and eighth strings plus .094″, and the diameters of the ninth and tenth strings plus .094″. Record this measurement.

Step 4. Subtract the recorded measurements of Step 3 from Step 2 and divide by five. This gives us the constant or air spacing between each course. Lock this measurement on the calipers.

Step 5. Install the third string and apply a small amount of tension, space it with the set calipers and mark, notch lightly, and recheck the spacing, adjusting the notching until the calipers are a snug fit. Install the fourth string, snug up, and use the ⁵⁄₆₄″ shim to space it to its mate. Notch accordingly.

Step 6. Install the fifth string, again using the constant

Fig. 99—Improper. The strings are setting much too deep in the nut notches and can cause tuning problems due to the string binding in the grooves.

set on the calipers for spacing, and notch. To set the sixth, or high, octave string, we now use the ³⁄₃₂″ spacer.

Step 7. The rest of the pairs are installed in the same manner using the ³⁄₃₂″ spacer to separate the octave strings from their mates, but with the constant set on the calipers to space each course.

You may have to make some minor adjustments to get each spacing exact, and this is why I always allow a little extra height on the rough nut blank. When the nut action is worked down to the correct height, set the same fret-to-string action on the octave string as its mate for a twelve-string guitar unless using a compensated bridge, then set them lower as compared to the equivalent diameter string in the nut action table. The roughed-out nut should be removed and the excess material removed until the strings set approximately one-half their diameter into the nut notches on the wound strings and the full diameter on the plain strings. See Figures 99 and 100 for the proper setting. Put a drop or two of Titebond on the bottom of the finished nut, set into place, and tune it up.

Of course, this all sounds very complicated, and you can use the hit-or-miss method of spacing the strings, but with

Fig. 100—Proper. The nut's top had been worked down to where the wound strings set only half their diameter in the nut notches. Set the unwound strings their full depth.

a bit of care in your measurements and calculations—and the experience of three or four nut jobs under your belt—I think you will find it faster and more convenient to use one of the listed techniques for nut spacings.

Any of the above formulas can also be used to space the strings accurately when building a bridge from scratch.

After gluing the nut in place and tuning up to pitch, it is preferable to give the instrument a chance to settle down—

thirty minutes to an hour minimum if you're working on a solid-body electric, several hours for a flattop steel string, and overnight for a classic. This allows the stress to set up fully after detuning for making a nut, etc., so that you can get an accurate measurement for the bridge height.

If the customer is in a hurry, however, you can go ahead and set the bridge action, but the top may (or may not, depending on the individual instrument) pull up a little more during the settling process, and the action may end up slightly higher than what you set on it.

Since I now set the nut action first (reversing the technique from the one described in Volume I), all final action measurements are made at the twelfth or octave fret. As also mentioned, any discrepancy here must be *doubled* when adding to or subtracting bridge saddle heights. In other words, should the height from the *top* of the twelfth fret to the *bottom* of a given string be, say, 1/32″ too high, 1/16″ or *twice* this amount must be removed from the total bridge height to correct the discrepancy. The reason is explained in Volume I, and I won't go into it here.

As for the proper heights for a given type of instrument and playing styles, I've made up a table which gives "happy medium" measurements to work from. This table gives the clearances on the first and sixth strings only. For instance, when I give you the measurement 3/32″ by 1/8″, the smaller number or 3/32″ is the first-string height, and the 1/8″ or larger number is for the sixth string. The heights of the strings in between the first and sixth are graduated higher from the second to the fifth string. None of the in-between strings should be lower than the first string or higher than the sixth string.

To clear up a possible point of confusion—if you're still with me—in reading the table, the short-scale steel string measurements apply to instruments with under a 25″ scale, and long-scale over 25″ (your Martin dreadnoughts etc.).

On the classical or nylon-strung guitars the short scale refers to those under 25½″ and the long scale over 25½″.

ROCK & ROLL, JAZZ, OTHER ELECTRICS
1/16″ by 3/32″ to 5/64″ by 7/64″
Short-scale steel string
5/64″ by 3/32″

BLUEGRASS	
Light action	Heavy action
3/32″ by 1/8″	7/64″ by 5/32″
Long-scale steel string	
3/32″ by 1/8″	

SHORT-SCALE CLASSIC	
Light action	Heavy action
3/32″ by 1/8″	7/64″ by 5/32″

LONG-SCALE CLASSIC	
Light action	Heavy action
7/64″ by 5/32″	1/8″ by 11/64″

As mentioned earlier, these are "happy medium" action settings and should be judged as such. Some of the more sensitive instruments may be adjusted a few thousandths of an inch lower, and others might have to be set higher.

The individual customer's playing style, gauge and brand of strings used, and particular instrument "personality" all have to be taken into consideration when setting a string action. I've found that the best system is to have the customer sit down and play the guitar after you have it tentatively set up and make any minor remaining adjustments at that time to satisfy the customer. In fact, I inform them that if they tell me that it's all right when they pick it up and they bring it back in a few days, a week, etc., saying that it's not, they will be charged again for any time involved resetting things. This way, if the customer changes his mind and wants something different, you'll at least get paid for the trouble.

Lowering bridge saddles. Ninety percent of your action jobs will entail lowering the strings at the bridge along with adjusting the neck's tension rod, nut height, etc. In 50 to 60 percent of the jobs the bridge saddle will be high enough for you to be able to remove the required amount of material with little or no trouble.

The main thing here is to maintain the same contour on the top of the bridge saddle if you chose to cut down the top. If the saddle is clean and smooth on the top with no string wear notches, you can take the material off the bottom of the saddle, but in most jobs the top of the saddle will be worn.

I use a small pair of draftsman's dividers with pencil lead on one end and a metal pointer on the other. Set the metal pointer ³⁄₁₆″ longer than the lead, lay the pointer on the top of the saddle (off the guitar) with the pencil lead marking the contour as you drag it across the saddle. Double-check the pencil mark to make sure you have measured off the right amount to be removed, and sand or file the material down to the mark. Round the top so that the string take-off point is near the center of the saddle, set back in place, and string it up. If your calculations were correct, the action will be right.

But suppose that you have to cut the saddle down to or below the wood of the bridge to achieve the correct height.

This can lead to problems. I tape cardboard over the top around the bridge to protect the top finish from scratches and use a small, razor-sharp block plane to cut the wood down below the level of the required saddle height. In most cases you will have to ream and rechamfer the bridge pin holes so that the pins will sit down deep enough and perhaps even deepen the bridge saddle slot (Volume I, page 39, Figure 31). After planing down the wood, you should also recontour the top of the wood to blend in with the bridge curvatures and go over the bare wood with a good paste wax.

Another problem encountered when cutting the bridge too low is that the ball-end string windings will pull up and ride over the bridge saddle, causing chipping of the bridge saddle, action problems, and rapid string breakage at this point. One way, the Q&D way, is to slip the ball from an old string over the new string before installation, but the best way is to add a new piece of veneer to the bridge plate beneath the top (see the bridging chapter of this volume). Either way will pull the string farther down in the pin hole to prevent the ball winding from mutilating the bridge saddle.

One more problem: string tension over the bridge saddle. Radius the string slot toward the saddle (Volume I, page 134, Figure 115) to give at least a thirty-degree angle of attack between the string and saddle. A shallow angle lessens the tension of contact, which in turn will allow the string to "work." This sideways movement while playing will wear notches in the bridge saddle and cause premature string breakage and odd-sounding buzzes and rattles.

And should the bridge saddle be made of a soft plastic, replace it with a piece of bone or Micarta using the old saddle as a pattern to shape the contour on the top of the new one.

Don't expect even the best of materials to last forever on bridge saddles. Even they will wear to where they will have to be replaced after a few years of steady use.

If everything is right, the neck adjusted properly, the nut action correct, the bridge set to the proper height, and the intonation is still bad, see the bridging chapters of Volume I and II on how to correct this.

8

Refretting and the String Tension Simulation Jig

How many times has an instrument been brought into your shop with a really squirrely neck? I'm talking about one with maybe a twist or two, a hump, and maybe a dip thrown in for good measure, and then the whole screwy mess straightens out beautifully when you relax the string tension. These are the ones that make you want to pull your hair out by the roots and run screaming naked through the streets.

I had such an instrument about four years ago, a Gibson ES-335 electric guitar that the poor owner was trying to use for jazz. It has been back to the factory twice and in three other shops scattered over the nation, and no one had been able to do anything with it. The action was about as high as a flattop bluegrass instrument and still rattled. The man was willing to spend quite a few dollars on it if I could arrive at a solution on how to true up the neck properly.

The main problem seemed to lie in the wood of the neck itself. The piece had evidently been cut from a board that had several knots in it. We found several sworl patterns near each irregularity where the wood grain ran in different directions. However, my customer liked the feel of the neck and didn't want to replace it except as a last resort.

Could I do anything with it? Well, I had been kicking an idea around in the back of my head for some time, and since he was willing to pay for the time and materials it would take to perform the experiment, with no guarantee that it would work, I agreed to take a crack at it.

What I had to do was to design a stress jig that would simulate the tension of the strings in the hope that I could duplicate the irregularities in the fingerboard with the strings and frets removed. Then I could sand or plane out these irregularities while under this simulated tension. The irregularities would then be there when the stress was removed instead of while it was under playing tension.

Sound like a real challenge? Believe me, it was. But I was able to do exactly that. I developed a workable string tension simulation jig. It was crude, mind you, but the customer almost cried when he picked up his guitar with a beautiful whisper-soft jazz action. He was so happy that he referred four more jobs to me that same week.

Since then I have refined it into the jig you will find detailed in the special-tool chapter of this volume. I don't know how this system would work if used with the traditional hammered-in fretting technique because of the varying densities of the fingerboards involved, but when used with my epoxied-in fretting technique, it works beautifully. With this system the results are almost completely predictable, and as a direct result my refret workload now occupies about 50 to 60 percent of my shop time. I now use this jig in all my guitar refret work.

Basically the instrument is suspended at the butt and under the nut area of the neck, and stress is applied to the upper bouts of the instrument. Since we are working with a downward stress instead of the longitudinal stress of the strings, it doesn't require much tension to duplicate even a severe neck bow.

The simulation jig is pretty thoroughly described in the special-tool chapter of this book, so I will get right down to how to use the thing step by step.

Step 1. Study the neck thoroughly. Does it have an adjustable tension rod or a simple, nonadjustable, steel-reinforced neck such as the Martin guitar? Is the instrument strung with the particular gauge of string that the owner plans to use? I insist on a new set of strings of the proper gauge before even starting to work on it. The instrument should be strung up and tuned to pitch.

If the instrument has an adjustable tension rod, it should have some tension on it. If not, tighten it up until it does, even if it imparts a slight backward bow to the neck. If there is a "kick-up" or high point to the body end of the fingerboard, I sometimes deliberately bow the neck backward with the rod. The kick-up and slight hump will be planed out during the truing process. When the instrument has a kick-up, it usually means that the neck has shifted slightly from what it was when the instrument was new and the action is usually too high. By pulling the hump into the middle of the fingerboard, you are dropping the nut and will probably end up near where it was set originally, thus dropping the action when the hump and kick-up are dressed off.

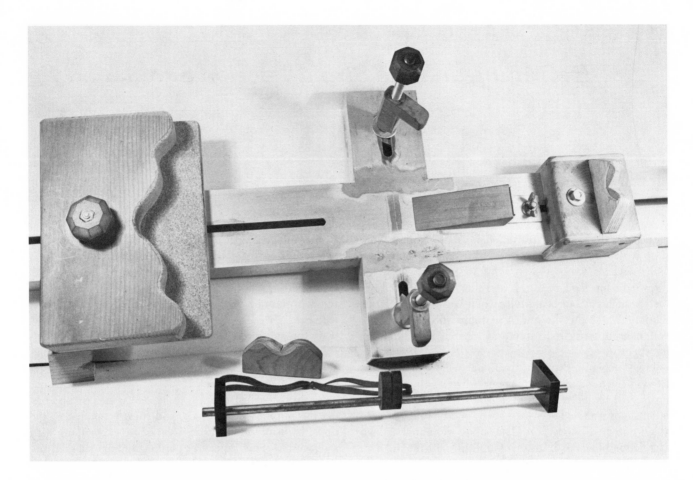

Fig. 101—*The assembled string tension simulation jig and part of its accessories. Missing are the long straightedge and nut–end pointer. Two heavy rubber bands are looped together to provide the proper length for use with the jig.*

On nonadjustable necks—Martins etc.—wood will have to be removed at each end of the fingerboard. In other words, I split the difference so that I don't weaken the neck in one spot by removing too much wood in a given area.

I've had instruments with nonadjustable necks with a .030 to .040″ forward bow, which sounds bad. Actually we need a .010 to .015″ forward bow, so that only leaves .020 to .025″ of wood to plane off, which isn't so drastic.

When the instrument is strung up to pitch with the proper-gauge strings, the tension rod, if so equipped, has tension on it, and the instrument is settled down, we're ready for the next step.

Step 2. On a flattop guitar, when the strings are relaxed or removed, the belly of the guitar settles toward its original unstressed position. This would thoroughly screw up any measurements made with the straightedge if the bridge saddle were to be used as the point for the belly end measurement.

I've removed this factor with the bridge elimination

gauge shown in Figure 102. This gauge consists of two moveable blocks and a guide mounted on a section of ⅜″ drill rod. To use, slide the support blocks toward each end of the rod until they are spaced where they rest on the guitar's face at the very edge of the instrument. Set the gauge where it rests slightly behind the bridge and tape into place. Then take a pair of large rubber bands (available from any good office supply) looped together to hook over one end of the ⅜″ rod, stretch them around the back of the instrument, and then hook the other end around the other end of the rod. If you look closely at Figures 102 to 104, you can see the rubber bands. They ensure a tight fit between the gauge support blocks and the guitar face. This is important, for any sloppiness in the bridge elimination gauge will result in an inaccurate measurement.

Next center the slotted straightedge guide so that the straightedge splits the third and fourth bridge pins, or strings if it's an electric or classical guitar.

Step 3. Fasten the pointer snugly to one end of a 30 to

96

Fig. 102—*The bridge elimination gauge taped into place. The rubber bands are hooked over one end of the shaft, around the back, and over the opposite end of the shaft. This insures a solid contact for an accurate measurement.*

36″ straightedge and set the straightedge into place with the pointer end resting in the center of the fingerboard immediately ahead of the nut. Tape into position. The opposite end should be resting in the slot of the bridge elimination gauge's guide and *contacting* the ⅜″ rod.

Step 4. Make a pair of pencil marks on the instrument fingerboard halfway between the eleventh and twelfth fret. These marks should be separated enough that the depth-

gauge tip of the vernier calipers will sit between them and will be a reference mark to position the calipers properly when setting the stress simulation brackets.

Set the calipers in position on top of the straightedge as in Figure 103 and measure the distance from this point to the instrument's fingerboard between the two pencil marks. Record this measurement.

Step 5. If the fingerboard was planed down using this

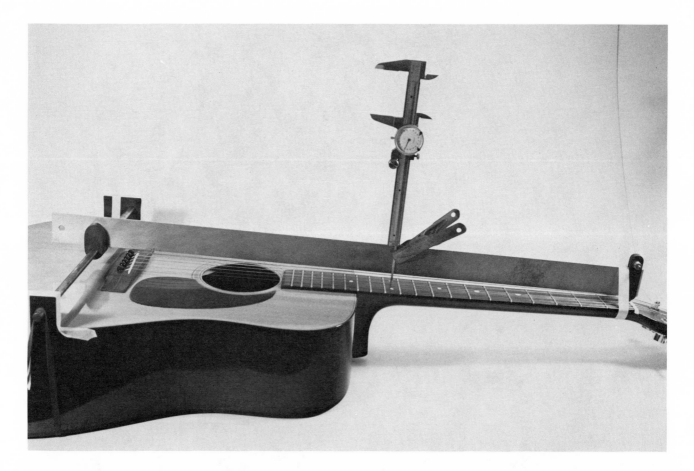

Fig. 103—*The bridge elimination gauge being used with the straightedge. Note the pointer clamped to the nut end of the straightedge. The vernier calipers (held in place with a spring clamp for photographic purposes) are used to measure the distance from the top of the straightedge to the fingerboard.*

measurement, it would be perfectly straight when we finished with it. However, a certain amount of forward bow in the neck is necessary, so we subtract .015″ from the measurement in Step 4. This is the measurement we will be working with. Record it and lock it on the calipers, too. If the calipers should slip or have to be used for something else, the recorded measurement means that you won't have to do it again. Back to the .015″. The neck is not stressed the full amount in the jig that the strings exert on the instrument, and when dressed true at this measurement and refretted, the neck will bow up the fifteen-thousandths over true when it is tuned to pitch. The bow will follow the point of least resistance or from around the center of the neck back toward the nut, since the neck is thinner in this area—the exact spot that we need the bow.

Step 6. Remove the straightedge, leaving the pointer in place on the nut end, and lay it up out of the way. *Do not* remove or shift the pointer on the straightedge or the bridge

elimination gauge or all the measurements are for nought.

Step 7. Plug in your electric soldering iron to heat. Remove the instrument's strings and nut. If the instrument is a Martin equipped with Grover Rotomatic or Schaller machine heads, remove the number-one and number-six machine heads. The long sanding block will make contact with the tops of the machine-head string posts and remove the plating if they are left in place. Machine-head removal is optional on other brands of instruments or Martins with other types of machine heads. Check for interference and proceed accordingly.

Step 8. The soldering iron should be hot enough to use by the time you have finished the disassembly. Use the hot soldering iron and the reworked end nippers (Volume I, pages 42 and 97, Figures 34 and 78) to remove the old frets, and you're ready to set up the instrument in the string tension simulation jig.

Step 9. Blow any previous sanding dust or chips from

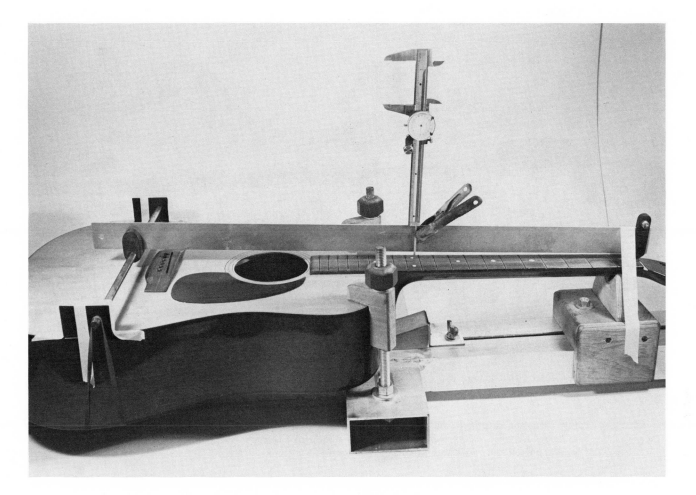

Fig. 104—*The guitar is suspended in the string tension simulation jig and stress is applied with the two center knobs and stress brackets to duplicate the string tension. See text.*

under the butt support and out of the neck *v* block socket. Set the proper *v* block, the tall one for acoustics and the short one for thin- and solid-body electrics, in the socket and loosen the locking nut on top of the sliding neck support. Set the instrument into the jig and slide the upper bouts against the cork-padded stress simulation brackets. The bracket rods should be adjusted to where the brackets contact the instrument's upper bouts at the point where they start curving down (or anywhere you can find a place on the weird cutaway bodies of the electrics) and the rods locked into position. *Do not* apply stress yet.

Step 10. Slip the jig's butt support under and against the butt of the guitar and lock it down. The fit should be snug but not excessively tight. The jig will now be making contact with the butt support and with the leading edges of the stress brackets with the cork-padded *L* of the brackets extending over the top of the instrument.

Step 11. Slide the jig neck support, with the proper *v*

block, up to where the cork-padded V supports the neck in the immediate vicinity of the nut and tighten the support's locknut. The instrument should be closely centered along the jig's main beam. Of course, in the event that you are jigging a cutaway electric, centering may be out of the question—but the jig will still work. That is why the butt support pivots around its locking knob. See Figures 66 and 67 for a look at two different electric guitars in the jig.

Step 12. We are now ready to simulate the stress of the strings, less, of course the .015″ subtracted earlier to allow for the proper neck bow. Slip the straightedge back into the guide on the bridge elimination gauge and tape the pointer on the nut end of the straightedge back in *exactly* the same location used to take the previous measurements.

Step 13. Reset the previously recorded depth measurement on the vernier calipers. Make sure the tapered stabilization wedge is back out of the way and adjust the knobs above the stress brackets equally until they lightly contact

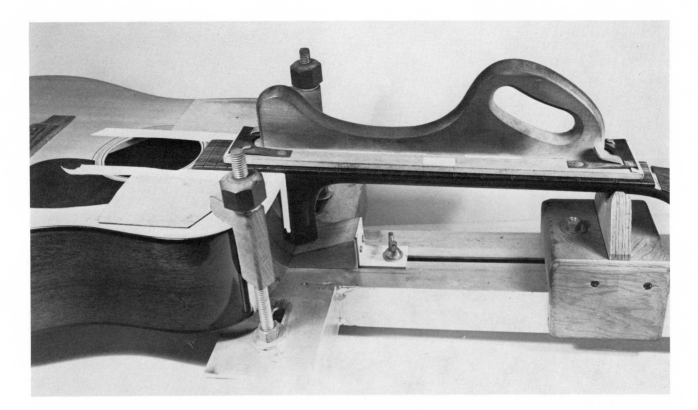

Fig. 105—*The straightedge and bridge elimination gauge have been removed and cardboard is taped to the top to protect the finish from slips. Note the stabilization wedge slipped under the heel of the neck to prevent movement while sanding.*

the instrument's top. You might rock the instrument a bit from side to side to be sure of full contact.

Set the calipers in place on top of the straightedge to where the depth gauge reaches the pencil marks between the eleventh and twelfth frets (See Figure 104). In the photo the calipers are held to the straightedge with a spring clamp for photographic purposes only. Hold the calipers in place with your hand. Adjust each stress block knob in small but *equal* increments until the tip of the calipers moves freely across the surface of the fingerboard with only the slightest drag.

Step 14. Slide the stabilization wedge in place under the heel of the instrument until it is nice and snug and lock the wingnut. Figures 104 and 105 show a good view of the wedge in place. On electric guitars, you might have to lay a ½″ to ¾″ block on top of the wedge to make a contact. The wedge is necessary to prevent any downward movement of the neck or body when you are applying pressure to the plane or sanding block (Figure 105) in dressing down the fingerboard. After going to all this trouble, we sure don't want to mess up now. Check the straightedge-to-fingerboard measurement again and readjust if necessary. We

are now ready to dress out the fingerboard (finally—but the results are worth the extra trouble).

Step 15. Now some cosmetic and caution measures. Place a rag in the sound hole to collect the sanding dust—it's a lot easier to collect it on the rag than trying to clean it out later, and tape cardboard to the instrument's face on each side of the fingerboard as in Figure 105. That is to prevent scratching the face of the instrument if you get a little rambunctious with the sanding block. The straightedge and bridge elimination gauge may be removed before inserting the rag and taping off the top.

Step 16. If there is more than .010″ or .015″ of wood to be removed in the area of an inlay, you might want to remove the inlay rather than risk sanding through it. I use the long sandpaper file with 80-grit paper (Volume I, pages 96 to 98, Figures 77 and 79) to true the fingerboard. Remove only as much wood as absolutely necessary so as not to weaken the neck. On badly warped fingerboards I try to remove wood from both ends of the fingerboard, working the sandpaper file lengthwise and from edge to edge to maintain the original fingerboard's convexity (contour). At times I use a small, razor-sharp block plane with the blade

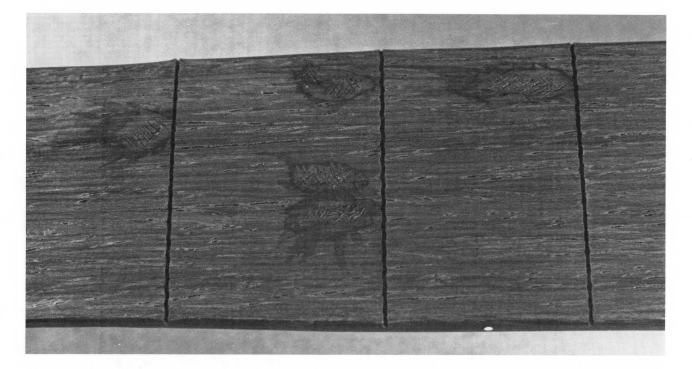

Fig. 106—Wear holes in a dressed fingerboard have been washed clean with acetone and cross-hatched with a sharp–pointed scribe or knife in preparation to filling.

set *very shallow* to spot-plane the high points before sanding. An alternate method is to use 40-grit paper to rough-sand and then switch to 80-grit to finish truing the surface. When the straightedge will lie end to end on the fingerboard (check in several places from edge to edge) with no gaps, you are finished with the jig.

Step 17. However, occasionally you will have deep wear spots or holes in the wood (caused by fingernails digging into the wood between the strings or just plain wear through many years of playing) after the rest of the fingerboard is true. Don't try to cut the wood down any farther; the wear spots can be filled satisfactorily with sanding dust and cyanoacrylate glue.

Wash the wear holes with a solvent such as alcohol or acetone to remove any old body oils and waxes and let dry (don't let this run down on the finished part of the neck as acetone or alcohol will mess up the finish). Repeat a time or two to ensure cleaniness. Scratch a crosshatch pattern in the wood at the bottom of the wear spot (Figure 106). Use a piece of 180-grit sandpaper on the long block and sand dust from the fingerboard into the hole. You might brush a little extra dust from the surrounding area into the hole and pack it down with a small spatula or knife to where it's slightly above the rest of the fingerboard.

Remove the water-thin cyanoacrylate glue from the re-

frigerator and flow it into the packed dust (Figure 107) until saturated. It will penetrate to the solid wood, and there will be some minor swelling. You might also observe some minor "smoking" as the glue sets and cures. Allow to set hard for ten or fifteen minutes minimum—longer if you're not in a hurry—and dress down with a file or the sandpaper block. If there are still some minor pits or air bubbles, repeat the process. This repair (Figure 108) is hardly noticeable on a rosewood fingerboard after waxing and is all but invisible on ebony.

This process can also be used to fill chips lost when you remove the frets. The instrument may now be removed from the string tension simulation jig.

Step 18. Occasionally you will be called on to dress down a maple fingerboard such as those on the "white-necked" Fender models. The "fingerboard" on these is integral with the neck itself, and the surface must be refinished after the dressing procedure.

After the initial truing, and before refretting, I wash the wood surface with alcohol or acetone to remove any body oils that may have penetrated a cracked or worn finish on the original surface. Such penetration is easily spotted; the acids and oils of perspiration will have blackened the white maple.

Next I seal the fingerboard surface by working a couple

101

Fig. 107—Three of the five wear holes have been sealed with "Hot Stuff" cyanoacrylate glue after filling with fine sanding dust. Note the scratch pattern filled with dust on the remaining two wear holes.

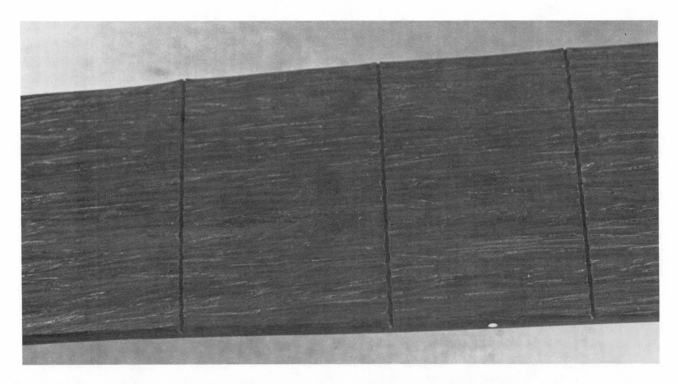

Fig. 108—After dressing down and waxing, the cyanoacrylate–and–dust–filled holes are nearly invisible in a rosewood fingerboard. You will have to hunt for them in ebony. The fingerboard is now ready for refretting.

Fig. 109—*Gibson method of trimming fingerboard binding to cover the ends of the frets. These "nubs" are lost when the fingerboard has to be dressed down unless the binding is removed.*

of coats of cyanoacrylate glue into the wood with the *smooth* side of a piece of Wetordry sandpaper. The glue will not penetrate the sandpaper's backing, so you won't end up with your fingers glued to the sandpaper. The thin cyanoacrylate may be used for this, but I prefer to use one of the thicker, more syrupy cyanoacrylates here.

This treatment may also be used for hardening the surface of deteriorated antique fingerboards or for sealing rosewood fingerboards when a customer wants a slick, finished surface.

Work in a couple of coats of the cyanoacrylate as mentioned earlier, and allow it to dry for an hour. Sand it level with 400-grit Wetordry or 220-grit TRI-M-ITE finishing paper. Give the surface another coat or two, let dry, and resand just enough to level the glue. You should have a smooth, thin, hard seal coat over the wood surface. On porous wood such as rosewood, however, you may have to give it a third treatment. The liquid plastic I use when necessary to finish a fingerboard *will not set up when in contact with bare rosewood, so the seal job has to be perfect.*

I will incorporate the rest of the steps to a finished fingerboard with the rest of my refretting technique as I come to them.

Step 19. Most of the next few steps are explained thoroughly in the refretting chapter of Volume I, and I will mention them only for the sake of continuity except for where I have changed the technique.

Wax the fingerboard with a good *nonsilicone* paste wax. Clear Trewax (brand name) is good for this, as well as most top-grade furniture paste waxes that do not contain silicone. *Do not* use automotive paste waxes. Most of them contain a very high percentage of silicone. *Do not wax* the fingerboard if you plan to apply a finish over a cyanoacrylate-sealed fingerboard.

Step 20. The fret slots are now ready to clean out. There is something else to think about here. Is the fingerboard plain or bound? On most Gibson products and a few others they bind the fingerboard after fretting at the factory and trim the binding down between the frets, leaving a nub of plastic (Figure 109) at each end of the fret.

Martin goes about it with a different method. They bind their fingerboards before fretting, and then during the fretting procedure they notch out the fret tang (Figure 110) and allow the fret crown to extend halfway across the binding. This works fine, but occasionally a fret will work up or the binding will shrink slightly (usually after subjected to extreme heat) so that the trebel "E" string will hook under the end of a fret (Figure 111) after a "roll-off." This is disconcerting to say the least if it happens in the middle of a number.

Fig. 110—The fret tang is notched out on the Martin bound fingerboard with only the crown extending over the binding.

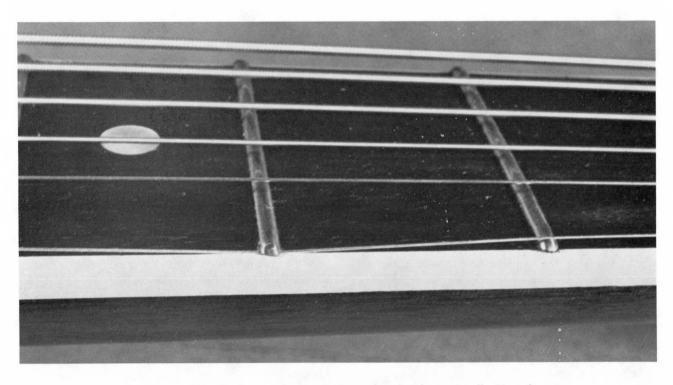

Fig. 111—A problem develops on the bound Martin fingerboards occasionally. Note the string caught under the end of the fret. The fret end may be sealed with cyanoacrylate to remedy this, or it can be cured permanently during my system of refretting. See the next photo.

Fig. 112—I cut the fret groove halfway into the binding when refretting a bound fingerboard, using the Dremel and a dental burr. The fret crown now has a tang below it for support. No more hangups.

My solution is seen in Figure 112. Set up your Dremel Moto Tool with the router base and proper-size dental burr (Volume I, page 99, Figure 80) and go to work. I extend the fret slot halfway into the binding so that the fret crown is supported by the fret's tang when the new fret is installed. That way it's impossible for a string to catch under the end of a fret.

Step 21. Cut your frets to the required length with an X-acto razor saw or jeweler's saw (my preference) as described in Volume I, pages 101 and 102, Figures 82 and 83.

Step 22. Here is one of the changes in technique mentioned earlier (see the last paragraph of page 101 in Volume I). I now *always* shape the frets to the exact contour of the fingerboard. It takes a few minutes longer to do this, but the results are better, and that's what it's all about.

To keep the frets in their proper order, I use a long block with a series of ⁵⁄₃₂″ holes drilled along its length to hold the frets (background of Figure 84, Volume I, page 103) after they are curved or flattened as for a classical guitar. Keeping the frets in order is important, since occasionally you might have to remove a little more wood from one side of a fingerboard to true it up, and the convexity or curvature will vary slightly from side to side. Thus a precurved fret will lie down properly when laid across the fingerboard in one direction only. Reverse it, and the fit is off.

I keep track of which end of the fret goes to which side of the fingerboard by placing the end of the fret away from me in the hole of the drilled board. When you are ready to glue in the fret, the top or exposed end of the fret in the board will be the end facing you when you insert it in the fret slot.

Step 23. For the waxed fingerboards tape off the fret slots as described in Volume I, pages 102 and 103.

Step 24. Sealed fingerboards. The cyanoacrylate-sealed and to-be-finished fingerboards require a different technique. I set the preshaped frets into their respective slots and apply masking tape over the fingerboard, laying the edge of the tape to within a few thousandths of an inch of the edge of the fret's crown. *Do not* apply the tape too close, or the edge of the fret crown will rest on the edge of the tape. This tape *is not to be removed* until after the frets are clamped into place and the glue has cured. Since the sealed board is not waxed because of future finishing, any excess glue will stick to the fingerboard and leave you with a real mess to clean up. Use the tape and save yourself some hard work. After taping, remove the frets and place them back in the drilled block.

Step 25. Lay out all the required clamps, clamping pads, etc., needed for clamping the frets where they are handy before mixing the epoxy glue. After a few jobs (quite

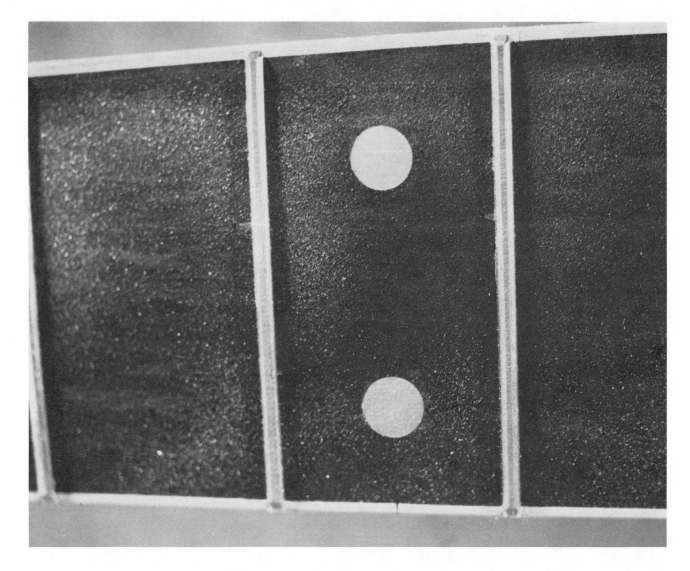

Fig. 113—*The new frets have been dressed lightly with the long sanding block to insure that each fret is level with its neighbor. Note the silver dust on the fingerboard and the small flat area on the crowns.*

a few, actually) the process becomes automatic, and I usually set up and do two fret jobs at the same time, laying out all the clamps and blocks for both.

For gluing in the frets, I use the regular Elmer's brand epoxy (not the five-minute stuff), which is slow-enough drying to enable me to do two fret jobs with one batch of glue. Other brands of epoxy may be used, of course, but the tests that I ran indicate that the Elmer's brand sets up as hard as the wood itself, and I have yet to have a fret work out after using this particular brand. This epoxy, or any epoxy for that matter, should be mixed thoroughly on a piece of *glass* or *plastic* only. A porous surface can absorb some of the chemicals needed to ensure proper setting of the glue.

Fill the fret slots with epoxy, remove the tape (not on the to-be-finished fingerboards), set the frets into their respective slots, and clamp into place as described in Volume I, pages 103 and 104, Figures 84 to 87.

Step 26. Set the instrument back out of the way and allow the epoxy to cure for eight hours. Remove the clamps, and clean off the excess glue, and tape on the to-be-finished fingerboards. The squeeze-out on each side of the frets should come right off on the waxed fingerboard easily with a chisel.

Step 27. Dress off the ends of the frets with the 45-degree file block (Volume I, Figure 88, pages 105 and 106). I use two file blocks now, a left and a right, to simplify the process.

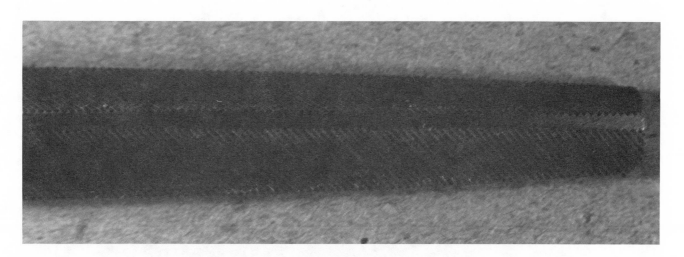

Fig. 114—A neat trick that I picked up at the Martin factory. Grind and hone the corners smooth on a 6" three-cornered file. The smooth edge rides on the wood of a fingerboard while the slanted teeth rounds off the sharp edges of the frets after beveling. It will cut the fret and not the wood.

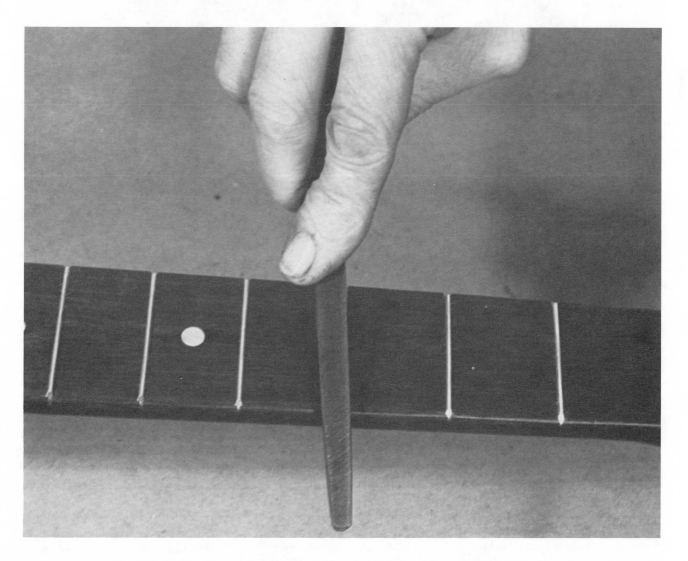

Fig. 115—Position the reworked file at a slight angle with the smooth edge against the fingerboard and push with a rounding motion. The frets to the right (nut end) of the file have been rounded. Note the difference between their ends and the ones on the left.

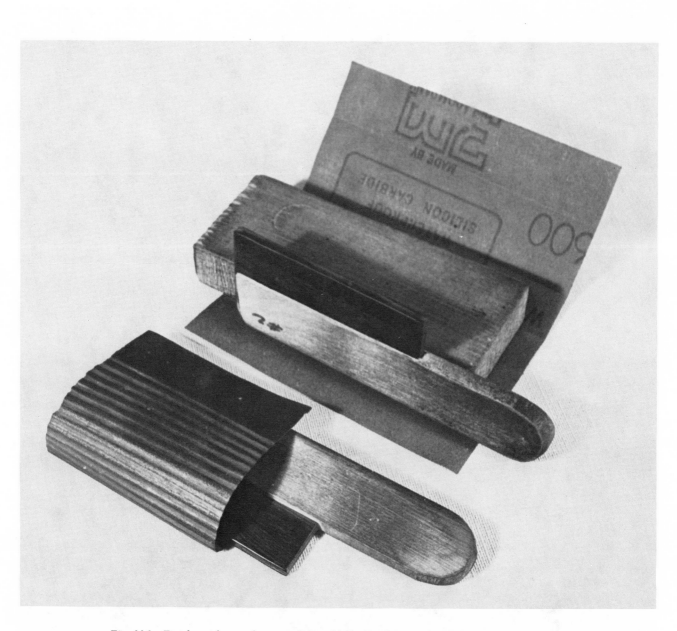

Fig. 116—*Fret burnishers and cross–polishing block. See the special tool chapter on how to make the burnishers.*

Step 28. Finish smoothing off the edge of the frets and fingerboard with a mill bastard file, protecting the top with a piece of metal or cardboard where the fingerboard lies over the face of the instrument.

Step 29. Set the instrument back in the string tension simulation jig and adjust the tension brackets until the fingerboard is true, checking with the straightedge on top of the frets. Actually this step can be omitted if the neck has a uniform backward curve in it. However, if the neck was real squirrely, it's good insurance to use the jig again. Dress the tops of the frets *lightly* (Volume I, pages 106 to 109, Figures 89 and 90) to ensure that all the frets are level with

each other. Sand until you take a trace of silver from all the frets (Figure 113). Some repairmen prefer to use a 12″ fine-mill bastard file or a large hone for this purpose, but I still prefer to use the long sandpaper file with 180-grit finishing paper.

Step 30. Here is where I have made another change in technique. Remove the instrument from the string tension simulation jig. Use a reworked three-cornered file (Figures 114 and 115) to round slightly the sharp end of each fret where the crown contacts the edge of the fingerboard, then smooth the frets with Wetordry sandpaper as in Volume I, page 106 and Figure 91 on page 110.

Fig. 117—A comfortable way (for me) to hold the fret burnisher and sandpaper.

Step 31. Use the proper-size fret burnisher (Figures 17 and 18, Figures 116 and 117 in this volume) with 400-grit Wetordry sandpaper (Figure 118) and go over each individual fret. If you should have a fret that didn't seat down fully and has a wide, flat crown after the initial dressing, use a fret file to recrown it first, then use the burnisher with the 400-grit Wetordry. I suppose you may be wondering by now why I keep mentioning the use of the Wetordry sandpaper. Well, it's tough and long lasting and does a lot better job than finishing paper, which lasts only a short time.

Step 32. Go over the whole fingerboard with 00 steel wool until it is nice and clean and wax it thoroughly, except the to-be-finished fingerboards. *Do not wax these.* After waxing, smooth out the wax with a rag with a couple of drops of lemon oil on it. Then buff vigorously with a soft rag.

Step 33. There will almost invariably be some lengthwise scratches left on the tops of the fret crowns from the initial dressing, so I use a wooden block with 600-grit Wetordry sandpaper (Figure 120) and cross-polish the crowns to remove any such scratches.

Step 34. The final touch is to use the fret burnisher again with a piece of 600-grit Wetordry sandpaper and carefully burnish each fret. They will end up appearing as if they were chrome-plated as in Figure 121. You should hear the customers yell when they first see the job if they're used to seeing a regular fret job. My main complaint is that the frets are too "fast" and that they have to learn to play all over again. That kind of complaint I like to hear.

Step 35. If you are working on a to-be-finished fingerboard, we have a way to go yet. Carefully wash the sealed area with naphtha (cigarette-lighter fluid) to remove any

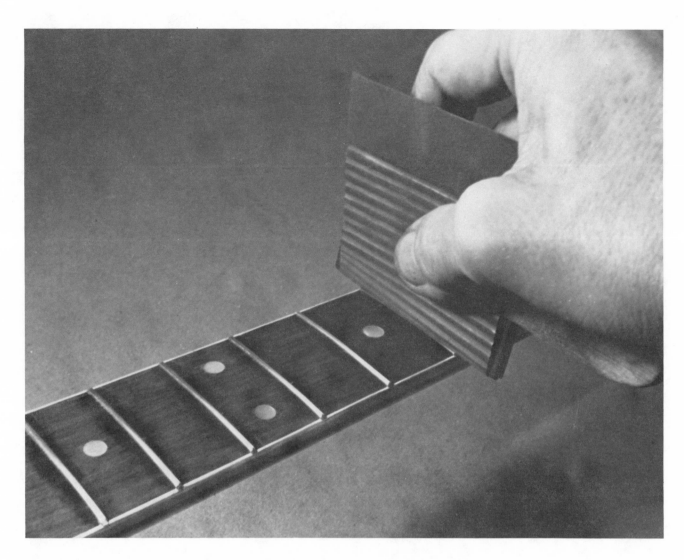

Fig. 118—The fret burnisher is use.

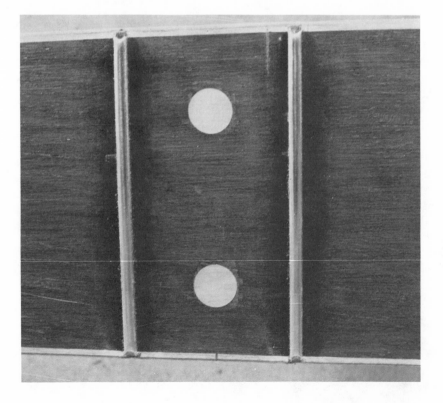

Fig. 119—The frets have been rough burnished with the burnishing tool and 400–grit
Wetordry sandpaper to remove marks left by
the fret files, etc.

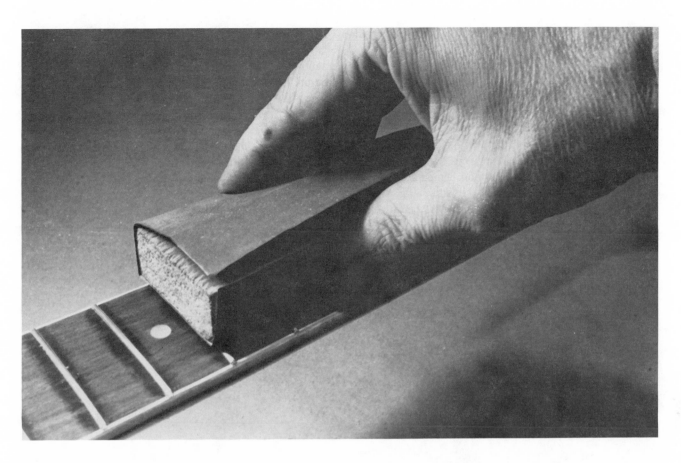

Fig. 120—Cross–polishing with a 5″ block and 600–grit Wetordry sandpaper to remove any fine lengthwise scratches not removed during the rough burnishing. Next to the last step in finishing the refret job.

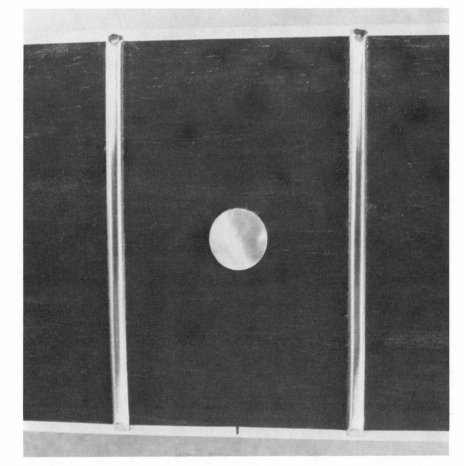

Fig. 121—After the fret crowns are cross–polished with the block, they are finish burnished with the fret burnisher and 600–grit Wetordry sandpaper. I've dulled these frets with wax (unbuffed) to kill the glare for photographic purposes. They shine as if they are chrome–plated.

body oils from where you have handled it, then tape off the areas not to be finished.

Spray the to-be-finished area, frets and all, with a *high-gloss*, clear polyurethane plastic. I usually use the Sears plastic in a spray can and apply a *very fine mist* coat. Allow this mist or tack coat to dry for ten to fifteen minutes, then go over it with a heavier coat. The mist coat will be slightly sticky or have a "tack" to it that will help prevent the second, heavier coat from developing runs.

Allow to dry for four hours at room temperature, longer if the humidity is high, and scuff well with 320-grit Wetor-dry and/or #1 steel wool. There *must not* be any shiny areas left, or the second coat will not bond.

Apply a second double coat (tack and heavy coat) and allow to cure for at least a day, and preferably two days for maximum hardness. Repeat steps 33 and 34.

If you have calculated and used the string tension simulation jig properly, when the instrument is restrung and the action checked and set, you should have a beautifully accurate neck with exactly the proper amount of forward bow—the ultimate in a fret job.

Steps 31 to 34 may also be used after dressing and recrowning worn frets on an instrument. However, I prefer to do a complete refret if the worn frets must be cut down to more than one-third their original height. Otherwise, you may end up with a "fretless wonder."

As mentioned earlier, since I've started using the string tension simulation jig and fret burnishers, my refret load now occupies 50 to 60 percent of my time, and the raves over the improved playability of the instruments are music to my ears, and dollars in my pocket.

9

More on Tension Rod Installations

The theory of operation and many different types of neck reinforcements, adjustable and nonadjustable, are thoroughly covered in Chapter 10 of Volume. I, and I won't go too deep into the material again. Primarily, the intent of this chapter is to demonstrate the use of the counterbore tools shown in the special-tool chapter of this volume. They make installing the hidden and regular tension rods in an assembled instrument much easier and faster.

Redesigning the hidden rod installation is the main subject to be discussed. Installing a hidden rod is not too difficult when the neck is removed (Volume I, page 117, Figure 98), since a nice, neat socket may be cut into the neck itself for the adjustment nut and a mating hole drilled in the neck block for access to the nut. This type setup has been almost impossible to create while the neck is still in the guitar. In Figure 99 of the same page, I diagramed a hidden rod setup that I normally used when the neck was not removed. Frankly, this is not the ideal solution. If the neck should have to be removed at a later date, the rod through the neck block would have to be sawed off at the butt end of the neck. Trouble with a capital *T*. Also, unless a large metal plate is used between the adjusting nut and the neck block, the wood can collapse into the gap between the dovetail at the end of the neck and the neck block.

The ideal setup would be to seat the washer and adjustment nut into the butt of the neck as in Figure 98 in Volume I. The problem is to cut an aligned $\frac{1}{2}''$ hole through the neck block into the neck's butt. It's easy with the long-shanked counterbore tool and guide I've designed. Once the guide hole is drilled and the counterbore tool is inserted, it takes all of thirty seconds to cut a perfectly true $\frac{1}{2}''$ hole through the block and into the neck. The series of photographs and drawings shows the hidden rod being installed in an old D-28 Martin that almost died from heat prostration.

Remove the fingerboard, leaving the frets in place, and pull out the *T*-bar or square steel-tubing reinforcement as is used in the later models. Clean out the old glue, glue in a fitted piece of Honduras mahogany to fill the area, let cure, and trim down flush with the neck surface.

Next I cut the new contoured tension rod slot with the anchor provision at the nut end of the neck as discussed in Volume I, beginning on page 114 (note Figure 101 there).

The $\frac{3}{16}''$ contoured slot should be .500" or $\frac{1}{2}''$ deep at the dovetail end of the slot. This, however, is not deep enough to clear the strut under the face of the instrument with the adjustment wrench. The rod slot must be angled down slightly to provide the necessary clearance. To find out exactly how much deeper the rod must be angled, measure from the face of the instrument to the bottom of the main strut that crosses under the end of the fingerboard, or $\frac{3}{4}''$ on the D-28 Martin used to demonstrate the installation. Subtract $\frac{1}{16}''$ from the $\frac{3}{4}''$ measurement, which leaves $\frac{11}{16}''$. Therefore, the depth of the tension rod slot at the end of the dovetail needs to measure $\frac{11}{16}''$ from the fingerboard contact surface as in Figure 122. Regardless of the job, always subtract $\frac{1}{16}''$ from the top-strut measurement to find the maximum depth at the end of the rod slot.

Make a pencil mark in the bottom of the slot $1\frac{3}{4}''$ from the butt of the neck, including the dovetail portion, and chisel the wood in a slant from the mark until it is $\frac{11}{16}''$ deep at the very butt of the neck. Round the sharp edge where you started at the $1\frac{3}{4}''$ mark so that the tension rod will not have to make an abrupt bend.

Measure $6\frac{1}{4}''$ from the butt end of the neck (be sure to include the dovetail portion of the neck) and set the wooden drill and counterbore guide block (Figure 123) into place and clamp. Run the 14" shanked drill through the guide block hole to the neck block at the bottom of the tension rod slot and drill the guide hole.

Remove the long drill, leaving the guide block clamped in place, and slip the long-shanked counterbore inside the guitar through the sound hole and feed the shank through the guide hole and on through the guide block clamped to the neck. Chuck the end of the shaft in the electric drill. Start the drill and *pull* the counterbore gently up against the neck block (Figures 125 and 126). Maintain a steady pull for a few seconds, push back out of the hole to clear the chips, and continue cutting. The cutter end of the counterbore will come on through the neck block and be

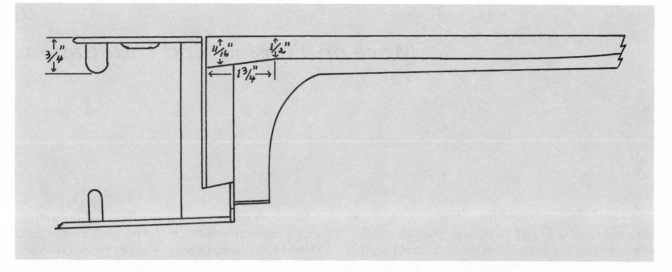

Fig. 122—The hidden rod installation, cutaway view. The maximum depth of the angle cut ($1^{1}/_{16}''$) should be $^{1}/_{16}''$ less than the total thickness of the top/top strut ($^{3}/_{4}''$) measurement. The drawing measurements are from a D–28 Martin and will vary from brand to brand.

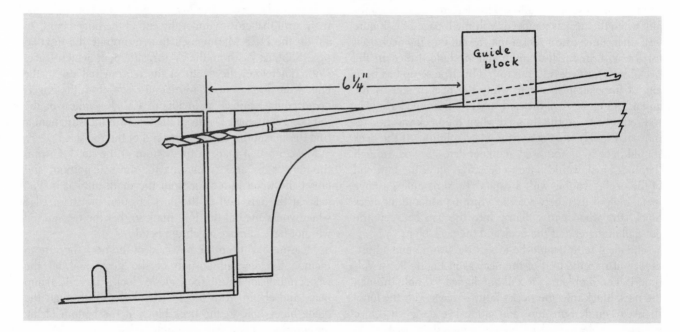

Fig. 123—Hidden rod installation, cutaway view continued. The guide block is clamped to the neck surface 6 $^{1}/_{4}''$ from the butt end of the neck, including the dovetail, and a $^{3}/_{16}''$ hole is drilled on an angle through the neck block.

Fig. 124—Close-up photograph of the special counterbore cutter and spade bit (or drill welded to a long shank) used to drill the guide hole and cut the tension rod seat for the hidden rod setup without disassembling, other than removal of the fingerboard. Both the drill and counterbore have 14″ shanks to be used with the guide block. See Figure 123 and 125.

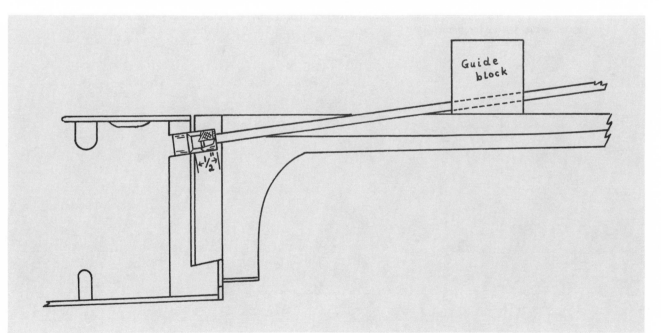

Fig. 125—Hidden rod installation, cutaway view continued. The counterbore tool on the 14″ rod is inserted into the soundhole and the shaft slipped through the guide hole drilled earlier in the neck block. Pull the cutter into the block with an electric drill until you have a ½″ deep socket in the end of the neck. You are now ready to install the tension rod assembly.

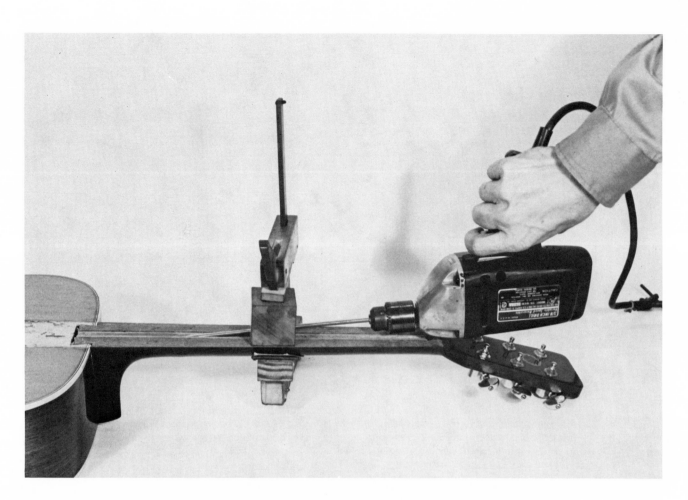

Fig. 126—*Photograph of the special counterbore tool in actual use. See the drawing for the dimensions on setting the guide block.*

Fig. 127—A close–up photo of the counterbore location after cutting the rod seat in the butt of the neck.

guided by the back end of the tool in the neck block hole and the shank guide clamped to the neck surface. Continue cutting until you have a ½″ deep socket (Figure 127) cut into the butt of the neck. Remove the electric drill, slide the counterbore and shaft back into the guitar body, and remove through the sound hole. Unclamp the guide block, and you're ready for the tension rod assembly.

I still make the tension rod as described in Chapter 10 of Volume I, but now I make a template of the bottom contour of the tension rod slot and prebend the tension rod to fit this contour. I also shape the bottom of the wooden fillet used to cover the rod to the same contour to insure a snug fit. The end of the wooden fillet should be notched out so that it clears the ½″ socket for the rod washer and nut.

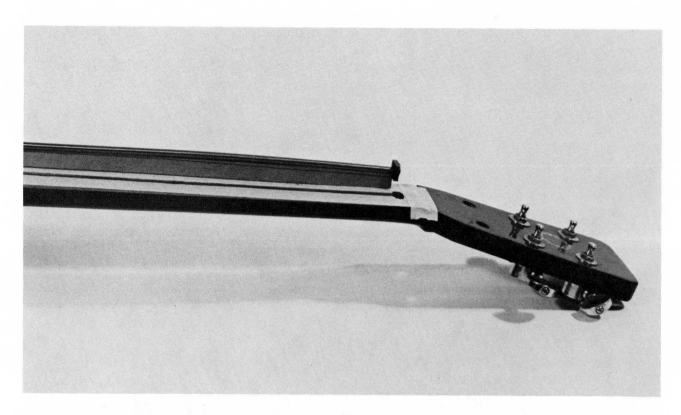

Fig. 128—The tension rod assembly and fillet shaped and ready (upside down) to install in the taped–off slot of a D–28 Martin. The guitar was a victim of "heat prostration" and had close to a ⅛" bow in the neck. Note the pre–bent and contoured rod assembly.

Figure 128 should help make things a little clearer; it shows the contoured rod and wooden fillet, and if you look closely, you can see where the fillet is notched on the adjustment-nut end.

After everything is *prefitted* and double-checked for any interference, wax the tension rod heavily with beeswax, particularly the threads for the adjustment nut. The epoxy should completely surround the rod but not stick to it except for the anchor end. Leave the last ³⁄₁₆″ of the rod and anchor unwaxed.

Apply masking tape along the edges of the rod slot to catch the excess glue squeeze-out, mix up the epoxy (I prefer the Elmer's standard epoxy, not the fast-dry glue), and smear the walls of the rod slot with glue. Push the ½″ washer through the ½″ neck block hole and seat it into the socket in the neck. Slide the threaded end of the shaped and *waxed* rod through the washer and push the rod down to the bottom of the slot, *starting at the threaded end first.* Excess glue wiped from the slot walls will be worked back toward the anchor end and will squeeze out there instead of into the ½″ socket where it's not needed—to put it mildly. However, the anchor end of the rod and the cavity cut for it should be completely filled with epoxy.

Slide the *heavily waxed* ³¹⁄₆₄″ temporary tension rod nut (Figure 53 in the special tool chapter) through the ½″ neck block hole and screw it onto the end of the tension rod, *snugly but not tight.* Apply glue to the wooden fillet, press it into place over the tension rod, and clamp it down as shown in Figure 129, applying the first clamp near the adjustment nut end of the tension rod and working back to the anchor end. Apply the wooden cam clamp *last.*

Let the epoxy set until you can no longer dent it easily with a fingernail. Then remove the temporary nut, using a wrench to break it loose if necessary. If you waxed it well as suggested, it should come right out, leaving a smooth round hole. Set the ⁵⁄₁₆″ *brass* nut into a socket wrench with an extension, and you should be able to slip it through the neck block hole (see Volume I, page 91, Figure 74) and screw in on easily. *Do not apply tension* to the tension rod, however, until you have glued the fingerboard back on.

Remove the clamps after the epoxy has cured, for eight hours or so, and trim the fillet down flush to the neck surface. I find a cabinet scraper handy for the final clean-up of the surface before regluing the fingerboard.

Earlier in this chapter I suggested removing the fingerboard with the frets still in place. That was for a purpose.

Fig. 129—*The tension rod is seated in epoxy with the fillet well-clamped to insure a full contact between the rod and the bottom of the fillet. Actually, the epoxy will fill minor discrepancies, but try for as good a fit as possible for proper operation.*

After regluing the fingerboard and cleaning up, string up the guitar and tune it to pitch. Now you can adjust the tension rod. Allow the instrument to settle down for a day or two and retune it to pitch and readjust the tension rod to see what it is like.

The chances are that you will find the initial adjustment of the rod has resulted in an irregularity or two somewhere along the fingerboard surface. It will have to be planed out and refretted in 80 to 90 percent of the rod installations. Any rod adjustment after the initial one will be perfectly accurate.

After things are settled down and adjusted as well as possible (there should be some tension on the new rod even if you have to pull a small hump in the fingerboard), then set it up in the string tension simulation jig and do a plane and fret as described in the refretting chapter of this volume.

This all sounds terribly complicated, but after you have the proper tools and have installed a few, it's not so bad. Actually I install only three or four a year and then only in really bad cases that cannot be corrected with a plane and fret. The Martin used for the demonstration had been ex-posed to extreme heat, the neck planed out until the nut end of the fingerboard was only about ⅛″ thick (I had to replace the fingerboard), refretted, then exposed to heat again. The only solution was a new neck or a tension rod in the old one, and my customer chose the least expensive route, the tension rod. Besides, it still has the original neck for aesthetic purposes and the adjustable tension rod is ef-fectively concealed from view without the use of a mirror. The owner is now able to make adjustments on the neck whenever necessary to maintain an optimum action when changing string gauges, etc.

Another version of the counterbore (Figure 52 in the spe-cial-tool chapter of this volume) does a good job of cutting adjustment nut sockets at the head end of instruments. It removes less wood than cutting it out by hand, and the difference in time saving is tremendous. I use this one to install rods in old warped–neck *f*-hole guitars, Dobros, and any guitar where I cannot get to the inside to install a hid-den rod, or in renecking electrics.

The slot in this system is cut on through the nut area and out into the face (Figure 130) of the head. I clamp a scrap

119

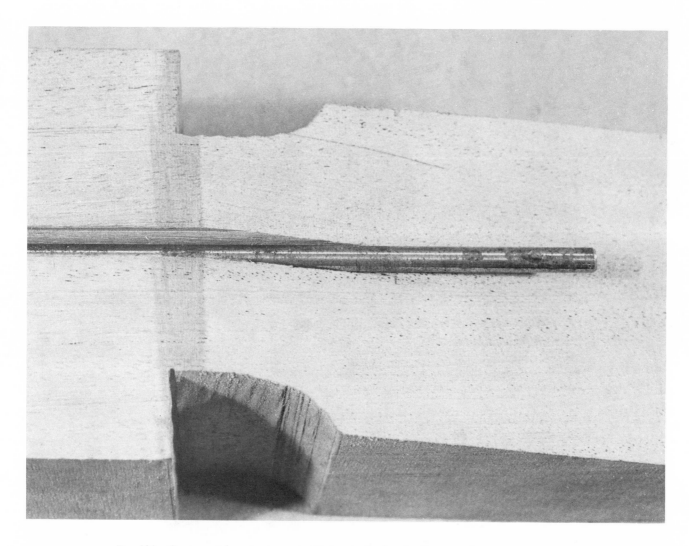

Fig. 130—*Groove cut for a tension rod utilizing the headstock adjustment feature. The ³⁄₁₆″ guide rod for the counterbore is laid into position.*

of ³⁄₁₆″ drill rod (Figures 130 and 131) into the slot, chuck up the long-shanked counterbore, slip it over the end of the rod (Figure 131), and moments later have a nice, neat socket for the tension rod nut and washer (Figure 132).

Occasionally, you will get a guitar where the wood behind the tension rod washer has been crushed back in under the end of the fingerboard by zealous overtightening of the tension rod, or just soft wood.

Remove the adjusting nut, pry out the washer, slip the long-shanked counterbore over the threads (very carefully to prevent ruining them) and cut out the damaged wood. A ½″ plug of hard wood, rosewood, etc., with a ³⁄₁₆″ hole in the center can now be slipped over the *waxed* rod and glued into place with the nut and washer holding it tight until the glue dries. I get three or four of these a year.

I would suggest, in closing this chapter, that you try your first tension rod installation on an "el cheapo" to get the feel of the system. If the instructions in Volume I and II are followed closely with the described special tools, however, the surgery should be an unqualified success.

Fig. 131—A temporary fillet has been clamped over the guide rod and the counterbore tool is in use.

Fig. 132—The results. The ½"
counterbore leaves a nice, neat
cutaway for the tension rod adjustment nut and washer with a
minimum of wood removed. The
demonstration is on a scrap block
of wood. For a real headstock, the
veneer should be glued in place before the cutout is made.

10

An Update on Intonation and Bridging

Intonation: The act of modulating the voice to a certain predetermined frequency, or in an instrument, modulating a string to a certain pitch by depressing the string to a fingerboard or a fret set into the fingerboard at a certain specified interval.

In the guitar the accuracy of the intonation is determined by two primary factors (assuming that the strings, action height, etc., are correct): accuracy of the fret spacings and the accuracy of the bridge location. Fret spacing accuracy can usually be ignored, for even the most inexpensive instruments nowadays are fretted within reasonably accurate tolerances, but bridging? That's another story.

A real problem seems to have developed in this area, especially in the past few years. During the guitar craze of the sixties the ready supply of naturally aged tonewood was pretty thoroughly depleted through production demands. All the major instrument manufacturers, and most of the smaller outfits too, have been forced by this acute shortage into substituting kiln-dried woods.

Some companies are drying their own wood under carefully controlled conditions to ensure the proper moisture content and shrinkage of the raw materials.

The C. F. Martin Organization has taken this one step farther and actually set up its own sawmill on the factory premises. They import huge logs of Indian rosewood, ebony, mahogany, spruce, etc., in the green state, rough-saw it, and kiln-dry it to their own specifications in their own kiln.

However, wood, even naturally aged wood, continues to shrink to a certain degree down through the years, and we repairmen are receiving instruments for repair that would appear to have been bridged short at the factories. Usually when discussing the problem with the customer, I learn that this discrepancy was not apparent when they purchased the instrument new but developed progressively through several years of playing.

Why? Well, I may get a few arguments on this wood-shrinkage theory, but it's the only logical answer that I can conjure up. Look at some of the really old-time instruments. Check the frets at the edge of the fingerboards and

around the sides where the tops and backs are glued. Metal does not shrink and you will find the ends of the frets protruding slightly, more so on ones that have been stored in hot, dry attics etc. Or perhaps you will find a certain amount of distortion or shrinkage around the bodies. Now most of the old-timers had naturally aged wood to work with, and it took quite a few years for this shrinkage to occur, but it did happen.

"But we can kiln-dry a piece of wood to any degree of moisture content that you specify," the kiln operators argue. Granted, but suppose that we take a piece of kiln-dried wood that is identical to that of a piece of ten-year-old natural-dried wood? There are still a certain percentage of volatiles and resins in the kiln-dried wood that have had a chance to dissipate or oxidize in the natural-aged wood. The collagens, or natural glues that bind the wood fibers together, have broken down to a certain degree, and this process has continued through the years.

Another "fer-instance": One of the manufacturers discovered in brand-new instruments a problem with intonation discrepancies before they cleared inspection. They had been using the same bridging standards for years with no particular problems. Upon inspection, they found that the well-cured wooden standards had actually shrunk. Now they use metal standards. Make sense? It does to me.

There are several other factors to be considered. We have the string tension for one. The tremendous pull of steel strings exerts a collapsing effect on the grain of the neck, actually shortening the neck a few thousandths of an inch in time. And this same stress will shorten the soundbox of an instrument another few thousandths in combination with the vibrations of playing. Then we add climatic conditions. Modern musicians are a well-traveled group, from the high humidity of the coasts to the low humidity of the deserts and high country, from extremes of heat to extremes of cold. Hot and cold plus high and low humidity. An instrument tends to shrink when subjected to low humidity as it looses moisture. The opposite occurs in a moist climate. You might say that the wood is "breathing."

"So what?" you ask. "What" is that we have encountered

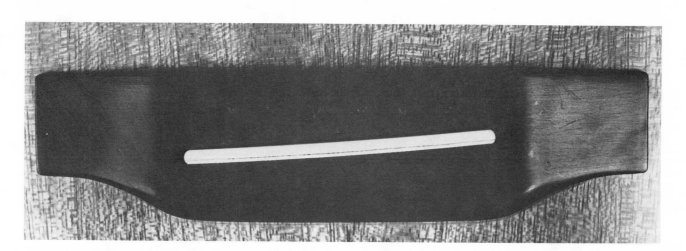

Fig. 133—*The bridge on this circa mid–1960s LGO Gibson looks like it is made of a nice piece of ebony. Or is it?*

Fig. 134—*Surprise, surprise! It's made of carefully wire–brushed, injection–molded nylon and is held on by four sheet metal screws with washers. These are found on certain models of mid–60s Gibsons and Epiphones in both adjustable and nonadjustable versions. I still get them in my shop occasionally for a glued–on wooden bridge replacement.*

Fig. 135—Rosewood replacement of the nylon bridge matches the rosewood fingerboard. A glued–on wooden bridge is much stronger and the improvement in sound is quite noticeable.

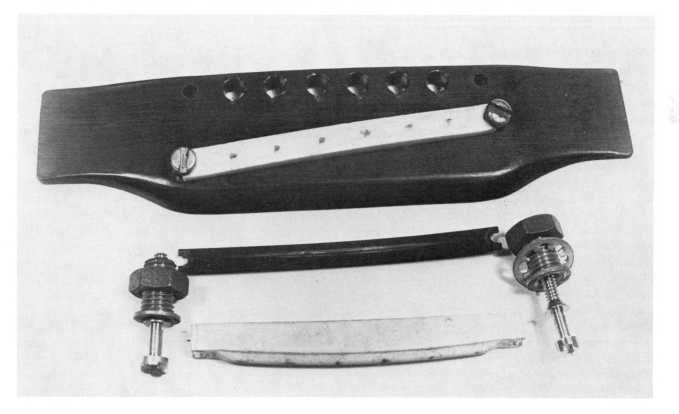

Fig. 136—An adjustable variation of the injection–molded nylon Gibson bridge. The ceramic saddle ate strings like popcorn and is hard enough to make an excellent grinding wheel dresser. Although discontinued, they still crop up occasionally. The brass and steel adjustment pieces are good mutes for the higher frequencies.

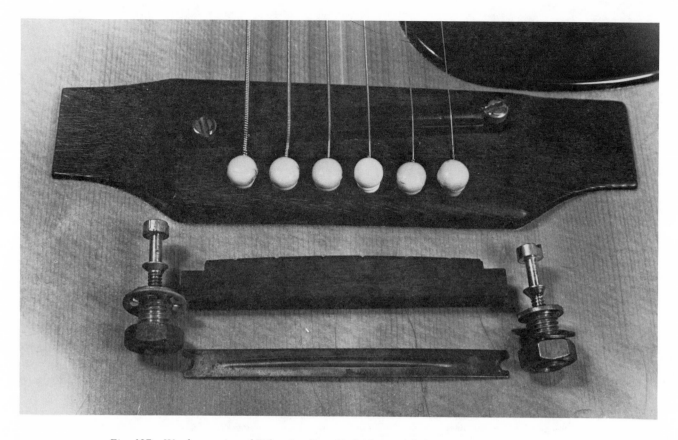

Fig. 137—Wooden version of Gibson's adjustable bridge used before and several years after the injection–molded job. Replacement with a solid wood, bone–saddled bridge brings a definite improvement in sound.

another reason for wood shrinkage. The wood contracts and expands with these climatic changes, but the contraction rate is usually a tiny fraction of an inch more than the expansion rate because of the climatic factors, string tension, etc. Therefore, we have to add a few more thousandths of an inch to the minus side of the ledger. Our instrument is literally growing smaller through the years. An accumulation of sixty-thousandths of an inch in three or four years is not uncommon in the new instruments constructed of kiln-dried wood. That, my friends, is close to a sixteenth of an inch. Enough to throw the intonation off approximately 5 percent at the twelfth fret, a noticeable amount when playing double-string lead work down the neck, and I quite often run into discrepancies of $\frac{3}{32}$ to $\frac{1}{8}''$, which is bad news. Luckily, however, this shrinkage seems to stabilize after two or three years of playing, and further shrinkage is minuscule.

If it sounds as though I'm trying to make excuses for the modern instrument makers, you can bet your sharp "B" string I am. It's a problem that we have to live with and contend with, like it or not. In most instances the compa-

nies are doing their dead-level best with the materials at hand, and most of them are turning out excellent merchandise.

You keep hearing such comments as, "They don't make guitars like they used to way back when." Very true. In many ways the new instruments are better: better glues, better finishes (sometimes), better bracing designs, etc. Some manufacturers—The C. F. Martin Organisation for one—have invested many thousands of dollars in expensive acoustic test equipment and hired experienced acoustical engineers to man the labs. They are constantly conducting tests and experiments in an effort to better their products. I only wish that I had the knowhow and access to some of the fancy equipment that I've seen while visiting the Martin sound laboratory. Special frequency generators, sonic drivers, a huge twelve-dial Stroboconn, computer. . . .

Back to the intonation problem. This "short-scale" phenomenon is apparently industry-wide; I have had the problem occur in a wide range of instruments from the "el cheapos" made of plywood (workmanship could be a large part of the problem with these) to the most expensive instru-

126

ments in nearly every brand. The only logical solution is to redesign the existing bridge, or barring that, because of the original design, to completely replace the bridge with a redesigned one.

But first we have to determine the degree of discrepancy of a given instrument. If you have studied the bridging and intonation chapter in Volume I, you will know that the twelfth fret is only theoretically the central point of the scale when it comes to figuring the bridging mathematically. To achieve the correct intonation acoustically at the twelfth or octave fret, the distance from the twelfth fret to the bridge *must necessarily be longer* than from the twelfth fret to the inside or take-off point of the nut. Why? Because the strings are stretched when we press the strings to the frets while playing the instrument.

The lower-tuned strings are wound with a heavier metal, usually brass or bronze on an acoustic instrument, to add weight to the string to increase its performance at the lower resonant frequencies where they operate. The string vibrates slower and, with the extra weight, swings farther than the higher-pitched treble strings, and must be set higher from the frets to prevent string interference or rattling on the frets. This necessitates setting the wound strings higher than the treble strings, which in turn causes them to sharp more than the treble strings when fretted. Also each individual string delivers its own particular rate of sharpness because of its metalurgical composition, diameter, whether it is wound or unwound, its particular tuned frequency (tension), plus reasons that I will probably never fully understand.

This is why you will find the bridge saddle slanted on properly bridged steel-stringed instruments, and you will find the longer part of the slant favoring the bass or wound strings. At best, however, this slanted saddle is only a compromise, usually with only four of the six strings anywhere close to being perfectly true at the twelfth or octave fret.

But then we have the nylon-strung classical guitar. The wound strings on these have a multifilament core rather than a solid core and sharp out at a rate nearly equal to that of the solid nylon treble strings. These instruments usually have little or no slant to the bridge saddle, although there is some minor inaccuracy at the twelfth fret on the "B" and "G" string—unless, of course, you are using a wound "G" such as that found in certain Savarez or Iberia string sets. Then the "G" will be right on to slightly flat.

Confusing, isn't it? Wait until you try a twelve-string on for size. You will usually find only five strings close to accurate pitch down the neck on a properly bridged, slanted saddle job. Again we are confronted with compromise and must carefully "temper" the tuning, tuning some strings slightly sharp and others slightly flat to come up with a sound that is pleasant to the ear.

On a twelve-string guitar in particular, this is difficult to do if you are attempting to do lead work down the neck rather than rhythm work. Bronze-wound string sets are really rough to tune to achieve this compromise or tempered tuning on a twelve string while the silk-and-steel sets will usually temper out closer because of a difference in core diameter. They use a smaller core and have a layer of silk between the core and outer windings to bring them up to the proper outside diameters.

I find that the only way really to satisfy a critical ear on a twelve-string guitar is to set it up with a fully compensated bridge saddle, shaping the configuration of the saddle top to be compatible with the particular type and brand of string the guitarist plans to use. For instance, the configuration for silk-and-steel strings will invariably be different than that for bronze-wound strings. The bronze-wound strings use larger cores and sharp out more. The unwound strings of both the bronze and silk-and-steel sets, however, will usually be close in a comparable gauge. What a mess!

I know that I'm doing a certain amount of repetition from Volume I, but I am trying to clarify things. When I design a compensated bridge, I design it for the particular brand and gauge of string my customer prefers. I use a brand-new set and warn my customer that if he switches brands and gauges I may have to design a new saddle with a different configuration to achieve optimum intonation accuracy with the different set, at his expense. In fact, the string manufacturer might change to a different metalurgical formula in manufacturing his strings and a set that was once perfect in intonation might be off again. I have had this happen once on my personal instrument. After three years I started running into all kinds of tuning difficulties and had to redesign the compensated saddle for my six-string guitar.

When am I going to get down to the method of determining the degree of discrepancy for a given string? In just a moment. First on the agenda is to determine if the problem might be elsewhere. Check the string height at the nut, at the neck to ensure that the amount of forward bow is not excessive (see the string action and tension rod adjustment chapters in Volume I and this volume), and that the strings are set at the proper height over the twelfth fret. The action *must* be right to suit the individual customer's playing style. Also this checking should be done with a reasonably new, preferably brand-new, set of strings. Old strings are a major cause of intonation troubles.

Is your customer using a "cheater" or capo? The intonation can be within reason without one of these beasties and go all screwy when the clamp (capo) is applied. Why? Well, all six—or twelve—strings are sharped when the capo is set in place, invariably more than with one's grip. Then you lay a chord on the guitar. Some of the strings are being double-sharped, and when using a bar chord ahead of the capo, some are being triple-sharped. You will have to do a certain amount of tempering or retuning to correct the intonation when using a capo.

There is a solution to the capo problem. A new design of capo (patented) is on the market that provides little or no discrepancy when applied as it presses the strings directly to the top of the fret rather than to the fingerboard behind the fret. Ask your supplier or music store for the Sabine capo manufactured by the Sabine Musical Manufacturing Company of Gainesville, Florida.

All other factors being correct, the action, new strings, etc., the final factor to check for is worn frets. If the frets have deep wear notches, you are forced to press the strings farther to fret them, thus increasing the sharpness owing to the extra distance. Quite often you will find some of the frets filed flat while the rest have nice, rounded crowns. The fretted string will make contact with the back edge of the flat fret and near the center of the crowned fret. Either replace or recrown the flat-filed frets. See the refretting chapter for more on this.

As mentioned before, you can usually eliminate the fret spacing themselves as even the cheapies nowadays are figured to a reasonable degree of accuracy unless someone has replaced the fingerboard with one of the wrong scale. If you prefer to confirm this, however, you may use the formula for calculating a given scale (Volume I, page 152) as a double-check.

Now we get down to the brass tacks. With all the previous factors eliminated, if the intonation is still off, it must be the bridge-saddle location. But how much is it off? One method is to use a Strobotuner, if you have access to one, and try to figure out the amount of discrepancy with percentages by using the calibrate dial. Calibrate the strobe to a gnat's whisker and zero the calibrate dial pointer. Tune a given string until the strobe dial "freezes" and then fret the string at the twelfth fret. Move the calibrate knob until the strobe freezes with the string still fretted at the twelfth fret and check the amount of percentage the string is off. Multiply half the scale of the individual instrument times the percentage of discrepancy shown on the strobe and divide the answer by two. This will give you roughly the amount the string take-off point at the bridge must be moved to correct the intonation on that string. This can vary a plus-or-minus 20- or 30-thousandths of an inch, depending on your ability to calibrate and read the strobe accurately.

I used to tear my hair out using this method and decided that there had to be a simpler, quicker, and easier method to come up with the *exact* measurement, one that didn't necessarily require the use of a strobe, since not everyone can afford one. I found it, too. In fact, it was so simple that I've been mentally kicking myself for not figuring it out years ago.

Since we are primarily concerned at the present with getting the octave true, the only fret that we are concerned with is the twelfth, or octave, fret. All the others are irrelevant, so we ignore them. When the octave is right, assuming that the frets are accurately spaced, the rest of the frets will be accurate within reason. When a given string is sharp at the twelfth fret (the overwhelming problem with most acoustic guitars with intonation problems), this means that the distance from the center of the twelfth fret to the string take-off point of the bridge saddle on that particular string is too short—or that the *distance from the center of the twelfth fret to the take-off point of the nut is too long.* Does a glimmer of light begin to glow in the distance?

The tools required are a good ear, or strobe, an accurate steel rule marked in sixty-fourths of an inch, or preferably, a good pair of vernier calipers, and, the most sophisticated tools of all, a half-dozen *round* toothpicks. Read on for the disgustingly simple solution.

As stated previously, when the string is sharp at the octave fret, the distance from the twelfth fret to the take-off point of the nut is too long. If we were to effectively *shorten* this distance down near the nut until the octave is right on, we could calculate exactly how much that particular string is off. Right, the round toothpicks. Slip the end of a toothpick in between the fingerboard and the string being checked, as in Figure 138, (clip off a short section of toothpick for the in-between strings) until the toothpick makes positive contact with the string. Don't force it. It needs to be only snug enough to make contact, to change the pitch of the string, not to raise it appreciably, or you will defeat your purpose.

Check the octave. If you are using a strobe, the dial should "freeze" both when fretted at the twelfth and when played open. If you are doing it by ear, the string should be the tiniest bit sharper when fretted than the harmonic or "bell tone" immediately over the twelfth fret. Move the toothpick in small increments toward or away from the nut until you achieve this result. Measure the distance from the *center* of the toothpick to the inside edge or take-off point of the nut and record this measurement.

Do this on all six (or twelve) strings if you are planning to make a fully compensated bridge saddle. If you want to relocate only the standard slanted saddle, use this method on the treble "E" and the fifth or "A" strings and record the measurements as before.

Wait now; don't get ahead of me. These measurements *are not* the amount the bridge is off. We have determined the amount the intonation is off in both directions from the octave fret, and we need only *half* that amount since we are correcting the scale from the twelfth fret to the bridge, or *half the scale.* Divide all your measurements by *two.* Say, for the sake of argument, that the distance from the center of the toothpick to the inside of the nut on a given string is .125" or an eighth of an inch. Half of that or $\frac{1}{16}$" is the *exact* amount that has to be added to the string length at the bridge to bring the intonation of that particular string

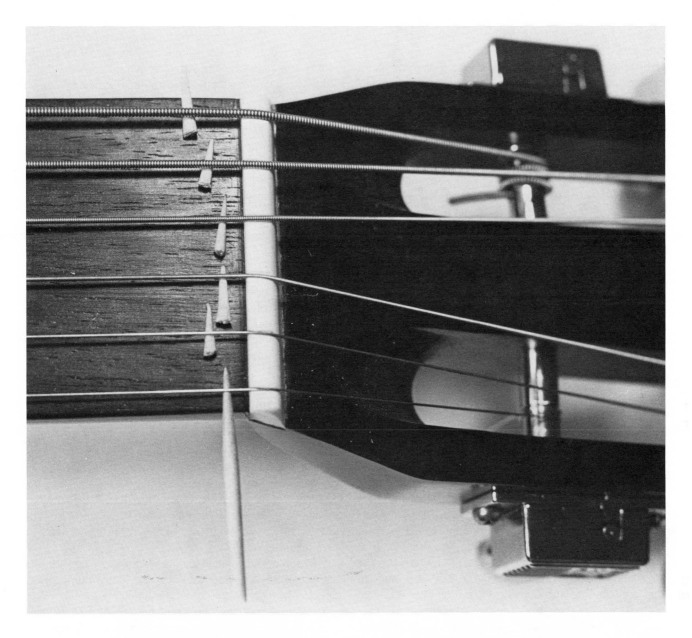

Fig. 138—Pieces of round toothpicks in place to determine the amount of discrepancy on each string for a fully compensated bridge. The bridge is not as far off as it would appear. The actual discrepancy is one–half the distance from the inside of the nut to the center of the toothpicks. I should have thought of this beautiful idea ten years ago.

into line. Now wasn't that hard? See why I've been kicking myself? Sometimes I can be so ingenious, and then again I can be so slow.

Another point to stress here: Check the bridge saddle closely to locate the exact take-off point of the string being corrected. When adding to the discrepancy, add it at that point and figure the new saddle location to where the new take-off point will be near the *center* of the saddle.

What if a particular string is flat at the twelfth fret after correcting all the factors and the string action? Slip a piece of ivory, bone, hardwood, or what-have-you between the string and the wooden part of the bridge immediately in front of the bridge saddle, again with only enough force to ensure a good contact. Move it to and from the saddle until the octave is right and measure the distance between the contact point of the piece of scrap and the string take-off point of the bridge saddle. This is the *exact* amount that the particular string has to be shortened to bring the intonation into line. Since we are working at the end of the scale where the discrepancy lies, we *do not* halve the measurement as when working at the nut end of the scale. Again, if you are simply relocating a standard slanted saddle, figure the new saddle location where the *first* and *fifth* string take-off points will be near the center of the new bridge saddle.

When the first or treble "E" string and the fifth or "A" string are correct on a steel stringer, the second or "B" string and the sixth or "E" string will be sharp. The other four strings will be nearly perfect, and all six will be well within temperable limits.

I've found that, on the average steel-string instrument such as the Martin dreadnought with the 25.4″ scale set to a moderate action, the treble "E" string must be set ³⁄₃₂″ over scale, and the "A" string ⁷⁄₃₂″ over scale to achieve a workable compromise. It will vary with different scale lengths and higher, or lower, string actions.

The next step is to apply our findings to the bridge itself. If you should happen to get lucky, it might be possible to recontour the existing bridge saddle slightly to change the string take-off point enough to correct the intonation. You should be so lucky. Of the jobs 99.9 percent will entail relocating the bridge saddle slot or going so far as replacing the existing bridge with a new, redesigned one.

Some brands of instruments have the bridge pin holes far enough behind the bridge saddle—some ridiculously so—that the solution is relatively simple. It's not even necessary to remove the bridge for the job.

Remove the strings and bridge saddle. Cut a piece of hardwood (rosewood for a rosewood bridge, etc.) and trim and fit it into the saddle slot for a snug fit. Try to match the color and grain pattern of the scrap as near as possible to that of the bridge, and allow the top of the wooden fillet to protrude slightly above the highest point of the bridge. This will be trimmed down to the contour of the bridge top after gluing.

Our new friend, the water-thin cyanoacrylate glue, comes into use here. You may, of course, use Titebond or epoxy and apply the glue before inserting the fitted fillet, but you will have to wait for the glue to cure. With the cyanoacrylate you insert the fillet, flow a few drops of glue around the edges of the fillet until it no longer sinks from sight, and wait ten or fifteen minutes for it to cure (it takes longer than a few seconds to cure in an application such as this). Trim off the excess wood and glue and sand it smooth. If there should be a small gap left because of a poor fit of the fillet, sand wood dust into it and apply a few more drops of cyanoacrylate. It should now sand out smooth after it cures for a few seconds.

We're now ready to lay out the new saddle-slot location.

I think that I had better digress for a moment here to discuss the easiest way for measuring for the new saddle location. I use a long straightedge and apply half-inch masking tape to each edge, covering the area of the bridge saddle as seen in Figure 139. Before removing the old saddle, lay the straightedge on the fingerboard with one end butted against the nut and the taped area over the bridge. Mark the string take-off point of the first and fifth (or sixth for a compensated bridge) on the tape on their respective side of the straightedge as in Figure 139 and add the respective discrepancies to the tape with new marks. Transfer the new location to the bridge and rout out the new slot. The Dremel Moto Tool jig (Volume I, page 39, Figure 31 and the improvement on it found in Figures 38 and 39 of the special tool chapter in this volume) was designed for this job.

Set up the jig, rout out the new saddle slot, set in the saddle, and restring the instrument. If the intonation was off considerably, you will find a definite increase in volume (in every instance if you decided to opt for the fully compensated saddle route). You will no longer have the "beats" or slightly off-pitch notes and harmonics canceling each other out. The improvement in an acoustic instrument's projection with a fully compensated bridge must be experienced to be fully appreciated.

I used to work the coffeehouses quite a lot and used both a voice and instrument mike, until I installed a fully compensated bridge. I was forced to discontinue the use of the instrument mike because I was no longer able to sing over the newfound projection of my guitar.

In recording work I highly recommend a fully compensated bridge, especially when a twelve-string guitar is used. It's the only way to set up one of these instruments where it will record clean.

On some bridges such as the Martin and Martin types, there is little or no room to move the saddle slot rearward because of its proximity to the bridge pin holes. Don't get me wrong: I'm not knocking the closeness of the pin holes to the bridge. This is the way it should be to insure the proper tension of the strings over the bridge saddle. The best quality and volume of sound seems to be achieved when the strings leave the pin holes and meet the bridge saddle at an angle of 30 to 40 degrees. At a lesser angle the sound is a little mushy; steeper, and the sound seems to be too crisp, and there can be a problem with string breakage.

The problem with this close proximity when the intonation is too sharp, however, is that the bridge will have to be removed and a new one designed which has the pin holes located farther back. This way the saddle slot can be relocated and still maintain the proper angle of attack of the strings to the saddle.

Make the necessary measurements to determine the amount of discrepancy and remove the strings and then the bridge. Set the bridge back in place with locating pins in

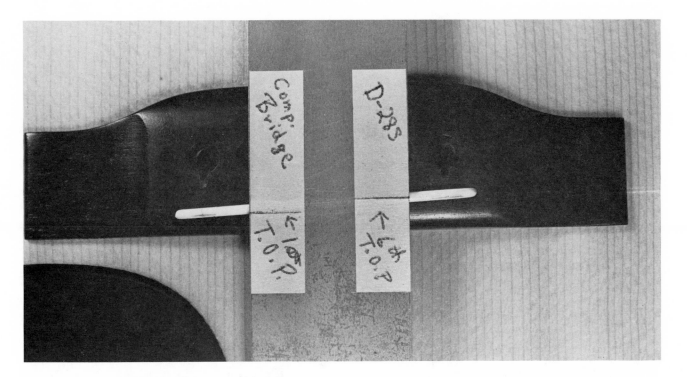

Fig. 139—The T. O. P. (take–off point) of the first and sixth are marked on masking tape applied to a long straightedge placed with the opposite end against the nut. The above is for setting up a fully compensated bridge saddle. When figuring for a relocated standard slanted saddle, mark the T. O. P. of the first and fifth strings. See the text.

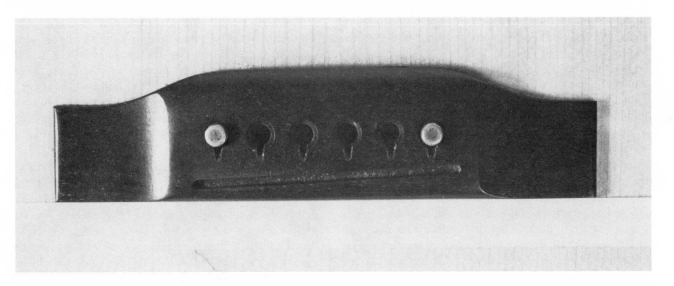

Fig. 140—Masking tape is applied to the top at the leading edge of the old bridge prior to plugging the old pin holes and will serve as a guide for positioning the new bridge blank with the relocated pin holes.

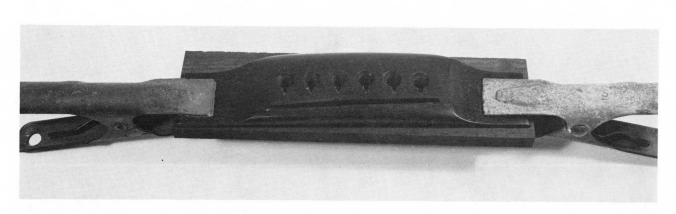

Fig. 141—The old bridge is clamped to the new blank as a drilling pattern. See the text for an explanation on the slanted positioning of the old bridge.

the first and sixth string holes and apply masking tape to the instrument face along the leading edge of the bridge, as in Figure 140. The tape should actually touch the leading edge of the bridge since it will be used to position the new bridge blank when you are drilling the new pin holes through the instrument top later. Do not apply positioning tape at each end of the bridge yet. That also comes later.

Remove the bridge again and measure the over-all height of the old bridge and saddle. This should be the total height required for the new bridge and saddle since you should already have the action set to the proper height when calculating the intonation discrepancy. The new saddle should ideally protrude .125″ or ⅛″ from the surface of the bridge, so subtract ⅛″ from this total height. The remainder will be the thickness to cut the new bridge blank. A "fer-in-stance": Suppose the total height of a given bridge is .425″. Subtract .125″. The thickness of the new bridge blank should be .300″, or slightly under ⁵⁄₁₆″.

Now, how far off was the original bridge? I'm talking about the maximum discrepancy—usually the fifth or "A" string measurement for a slanted saddle. Suppose that, for the sake of argument, the saddle needs to be moved back ⅛″. This might seem to be a rather large discrepancy, but it is not as uncommon as one would think. Measure the original bridge from front to rear. Say that it measures out at 1.400″. Add the amount of maximum discrepancy. The front-to-rear measurement required for the new bridge blank would be 1.525″, or slightly over an 1½″. Add one-half the discrepancy, or ⅛″, to each end of the old bridge measurement for the total length of the new blank and saw it out.

Do not saw the contour on the back of the new bridge yet. It's easier to make your measurements, drill the new pin holes, and cut the saddle slot when the blank is in the "square." Why add length to each end of the new bridge? We are adding new wood to the back of the new bridge and

the small amount of wood added to each end adds congruency to the shape of the new bridge. In other words, if the extra length is not added, the new bridge will appear to be "fat."

Now to locate the new pin holes. Suppose that the discrepancy at the first string was only ¹⁄₁₆″ while that of the fifth string (standard slanted saddle) was ⅛″? Position the old bridge on top of the new blank and clamp with small spring clamps as in Figure 141. Measuring from the leading edge of the new blank, slip the old bridge back ¹⁄₁₆″ at the first string location and ⅛″ at the fifth string location. The old bridge will, of course, be setting at a slant (see Figure 141 again). Why? To maintain the proper string-to-saddle angle discussed earlier. The new pin holes will be slightly slanted, but with the bridge saddle slanted also, the optical illusion created will negate the appearance of the slant. It will have to be measured to be noticed once the instrument is strung up. Drill out the new holes in the blank using a ¹³⁄₆₄″ drill bit and the pin holes in the old bridge as a pattern, and remove the spring clamps.

Place the drilled bridge blank on the face of the instrument and locate it with guide pins—only one pin if you have drilled the holes on a slant. The leading edge of the new bridge blank will rest on top of the masking tape that marked the leading edge of the original bridge. Square up the new blank to the tape and apply masking tape down the guitar's face at each end of the blank. The tape in front and at each end will give us an exact location for the new bridge when drilling the new pin holes in the face.

Remove the new blank and plug the original pin holes in the top with carefully fitted hardwood dowels, as shown in Figure 142, and glue in place. The dowels should be a snug press fit with the fingers (I machine the plugs on my lathe) and should be perfectly level with the instrument's face on the underside of the top. If you cut the plugs slightly long, make sure they are flush to the bridge plate underneath and

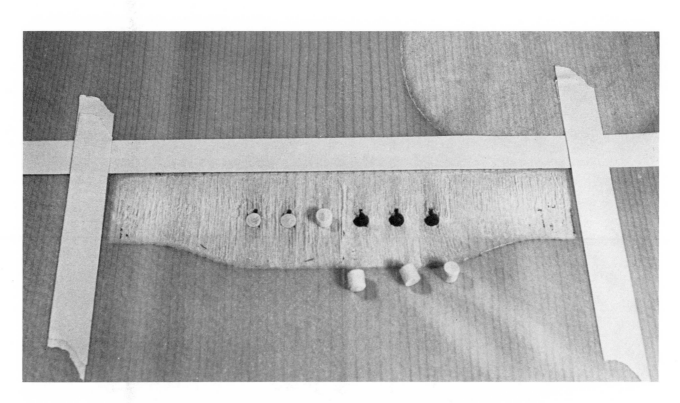

Fig. 142—*Alignment tape in position to locate the new corrected bridge. The original pin holes are plugged with hardwood dowels of the proper size and length. See text.*

Fig. 143—*The original string T. O. Ps. are indicated by the first line while the new corrected take–off points for each string are indicated by scribe prick marks. Scribed rectangle around the prick marks is the area to be cut out for the new compensated bridge saddle.*

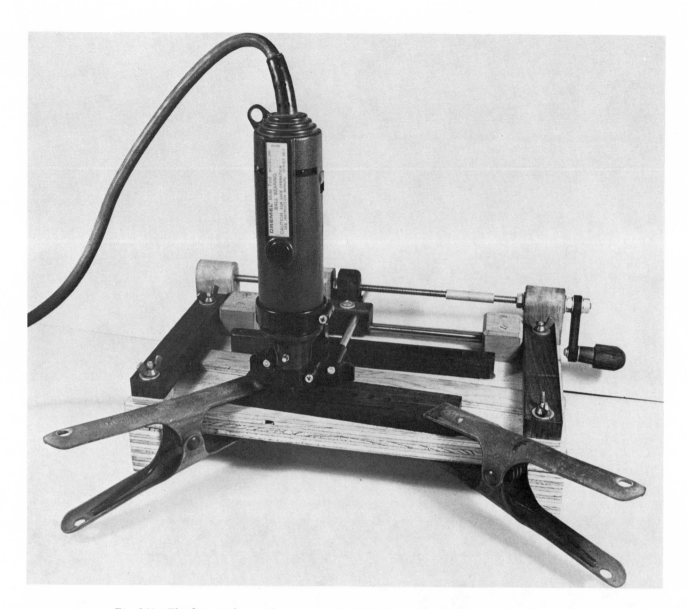

Fig. 144—*The first cut for a wide compensated saddle slot completed. Reset the slotting jig and make the back cut to the width of the saddle you plan to use, cut out the slot, then reset the jig to clean out any remaining wood. I use a .200″ slot for six strings and a .300″ wide one for a twelve string.*

trim them flush on the outside surface. I use Titebond to glue them and allow to cure thoroughly.

Clean off any excess glue inside and out and carefully position the new drilled bridge blank inside the boundaries of the masking-tape guides and clamp it down with a cam clamp. Run the 13/64″ drill bit through the first and sixth string holes (I drill out the rest of the holes when the new bridge is completed and glued down) for the guide pins and remove the camp clamp and tape. The new bridge blank can now be properly positioned with the two guide pins.

Lay out the location of new saddle slot from the calculations marked on the tape on the straightedge. I lay out the

location of the original saddle take-off points and add a pin-prick behind it for the new location. Figure 143 shows a bridge laid out for a compensated saddle; for a standard slanted saddle, use only the first and fifth string locations and scribe a line through them for the new saddle location. Remove the bridge blank and cut out the new saddle slot, remembering that the line scribed is for the take-off point of the new saddle. It should be located in the center of the saddle slot. The new bridge can now be completed and glued on as in the instructions in Volume I, pages 125 to 133.

I have, however, designed a new jig (Figure 144) which

I now prefer to use in cutting saddle slots with the Dremel Moto Tool and a router bit which you may wish to make and use in place of the miniature saw (Volume I, page 128, Figure 109). See the special-tool chapter in this volume for instructions and plans to make and use this jig. I prefer to use this jig because I can cut the saddle slot deeper than I can with the saw. The saw is limited to ⅛″, and I like to cut the slot at least .140″, or %4″, deep for more support when the wooden top of the bridge blank is contoured.

Now, more on fully compensated bridges. I will begin with the classical guitar. As mentioned before, there are usually few problems with the intonation on these except for the plain (unwound) "B" and "G" strings. These are usually within temperable tolerances, but if you wish to get picky, a simple way to compensate them is to use the toothpick method to determine the discrepancy, then cut a notch behind the regular saddle for a short length of bone or ivory. Glue this short length to the original saddle (off the guitar) with cyanoacrylate glue, lay out the new take-off point, and bevel the saddle with small files to the layout marks. The front bevel should be steep to the mark and the rear slant slightly rounded to prevent chipping as might occur with a knife edge.

A simple method of laying out a fully compensated bridge saddle for a pin-type bridge for the six- or twelve-string guitar is as follows: With the new bridge blank pinned to the top with guide pins, mark the original take-off points of the first and fifth strings and lay out a pencil or scribe line through these two marks (back to Figure 143). Remove the bridge for working ease and lay out the amount of discrepancy (figured with the toothpick method) for each string as shown in Figure 143. I use a simple prick from a scribe point for this. You will notice that a single-thickness saddle will not cover all the scribe marks. I use a pair of bone saddles carefully lapped for a perfect contact—three for a twelve-string saddle—and laminate them with cyanoacrylate glue as shown in Figure 145. While these are drying, measure the exact distance from the front edge of the bridge to the center of each scribe mark and record these measurements for future use.

Cut out the new saddle slot to match the thicker blank saddle (Figure 146). Cut a piece of ebony scrap to fit the new saddle slot and contour the top so that the total thickness of the new bridge and temporary saddle is the *same height as the original bridge and saddle less .018″*. Mark the string take-off points in pencil, measuring from the front of the bridge with the previously recorded measurements on the wide ebony temporary saddle. Remove the temporary saddle, complete the new bridge, and glue it on the guitar.

Clean up the excess glue, drill and chamfer the pin holes, cut and radius the string s slots (Volume I, page 134, Figure 115), set in the ebony temporary saddle, and string it up.

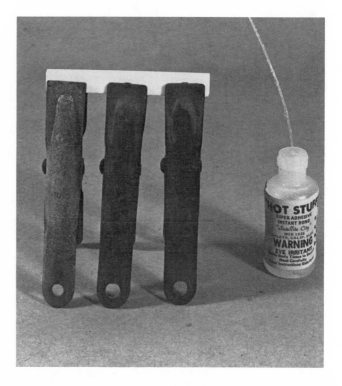

Fig. 145—Two bone saddles lapped and laminated together with cyanoacrylate glue to form a thick one for a compensated bridge. Most twelve stringers will require a third lamination.

Cut six (Figure 147) or twelve (Figure 148) short pieces of .018″ "B" string and position a piece under each string at the pencil marks on the temporary saddle, tune to pitch, and let the instrument settle down for a few hours—a full day if you have the time. Check the string action again. If you have measured things accurately, it should be correct. If not, correct it now. That is why I use the temporary saddle. Ebony is much cheaper than bone or ivory if you've blown it.

If the action is correct, check the intonation. It should be nearly perfect, but if not, move the pieces of "B" string back if too sharp, toward the soundhole if flat at the octave. Should you have to move the pieces, remeasure the distance from the front of the bridge to the center of the pieces of string and record the distances. These are the final measurements used to lay out the bone saddle.

Use the temporary ebony saddle to lay out the proper height on the bone saddle, remembering to add the height of the pieces of string. Sand down the top of the bone saddle to the proper contour, set it into place, and mark with a pencil each string take-off point as in Figure 149. Remove the saddle, contour the top to the lines with small files, reinstall the saddle, and string it up.

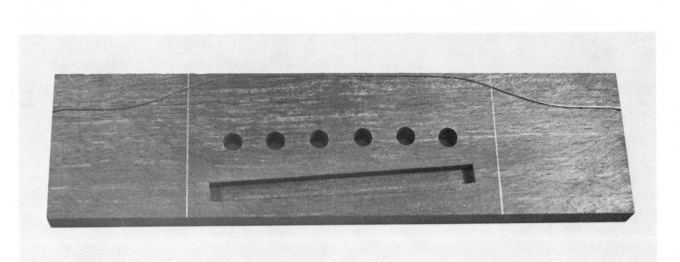

Fig. 146—The compensated saddle slot is cleaned out and the blank is laid out for the final shaping as per Figures 110 to 114 in Volume I. Glue to the guitar after waxing the top surface and contours of the bridge.

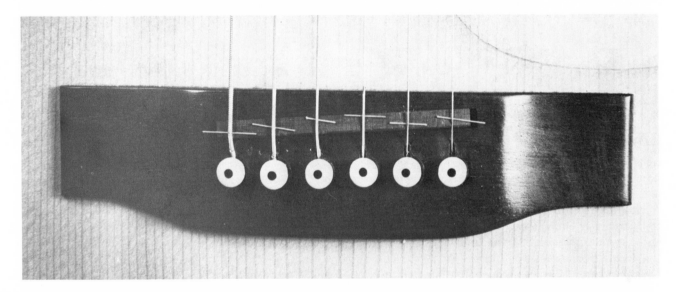

Fig. 147—The bridge has been glued on, the pin holes chamfered, and the string slots cut. The instrument is tuned to pitch with pieces of "B" string in place to double–check the intonation. After the locations are finalized, the locations are transfered to the new bone saddle for shaping.

Fig. 148—Final positions for a twelve-string guitar being finalized for silk–and–steel strings and "D" tuning. The positions will vary somewhat with different tunings and type of strings.

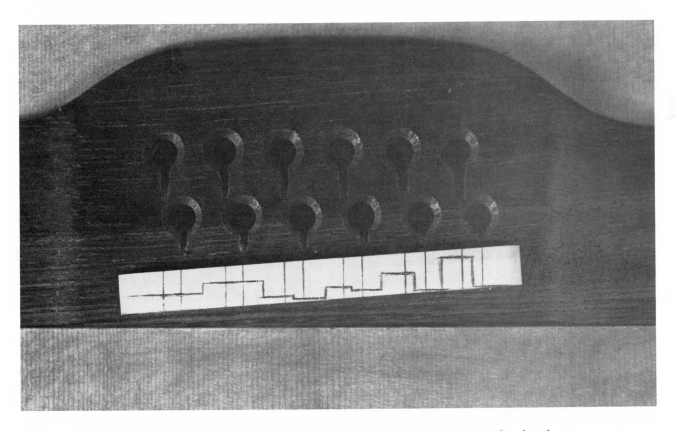

Fig. 149—Laminated bone saddle laid out with the final measurements in pencil and ready to complete.

Fig. 150—Adding a 1/16" plate to the bottom of the bridge plate to compensate for the wood thickness removed from the top of the bridge to correct an action. This prevents the ball-end string winding from coming through the bridge pin holes far enough to chip the saddle. Note the brass pins used for alignment until the clamp is in place.

Between the two volumes, I've pretty well covered bridging and bridge making. I mention using the ball ends cut from old strings (Volume I, page 134) to pull the string windings down away from the bridge saddles on those bridges that have been planed down thin. An alternate method, which is less hassle in the long run for your customer, is to glue a 1/8" thick strip of hardwood to the underside of the bridge plate as in Figure 150 and drill the pin holes on through this. Actually this trick adds a certain amount of strength that is lost when a bridge is thinned down and does not affect the sound to any noticeable degree.

Another item not discussed in Volume I is a method to achieve a near-perfect fit between the base of a movable bridge and the top of an f-hole acoustic guitar. Replacement bridges for these can usually be ordered from a supply house or the original manufacturer or purchased from the local music store. There are many styles and shapes that can be adapted to almost any job. Or, as a last resort, you can make one from scratch using the old base for a pattern.

The fit of the bridge base to the top is important for good sound conduction. Most of the older f-holes have, through shrinkage, warpage, stress, misuse, etc., developed their own particular configuration in the bridge contact area through the years, and the base of a new bridge has to be fitted accordingly.

A rough fit can be achieved by pressing a contour gauge such as the Copy-Cat brand to the bridge area, using a piece of masking tape to prevent marring the finish, and transferring this contour to the base of the new bridge. Sand or saw along this new contour line very carefully.

Now the finishing touch. Tape a sheet of fairly coarse (100-grit) sandpaper to the instrument top in the bridge area. Make a mark lengthwise with a pencil on each side of the sandpaper to mark the outer reaches of the bridge's feet. Keep the bridge within these marks and square with the guitar's top and work the bridge base sideways but lengthwise to the guitar top as demonstrated by the dust pattern shown in Figure 151. You will notice streaks in the dust. These are high spots. Work until you get a uniform dust pattern with no streaks, and you have a full contact. If you are unsure whether or not you have a good fit, mark up the base's contact area with a soft-lead pencil and sand until all the pencil marks are removed. Remove the sandpaper and check the fit against the top. If done properly, it should be a perfect fit.

Fig. 151—Fitting the base of an f–hole bridge to the arched top by using a sheet of sandpaper taped to the top. The bridge is worked lengthwise with the top. Note the sanding dust pattern. When the pattern is solid with no discernable streaks, the base is properly fitted to the top.

Another problem that I've occasionally encountered with f-holes is string alignment—where the strings have shifted closer to one edge of the fingerboard than the other owing to carelessness in aligning the tailpiece during construction or when the neck has been removed and reset slightly crooked or perhaps when the guitar's body has shifted or shrunk more on one side than the other. This last occurs primarily on the "cutaway" models. You shift the bridge over to realign the strings, but after playing the instrument for a while, the vibration causes it to shift back and misalign the strings again. The proper cure is to remove the tailpiece, plug the screw holes, and redrill the holes in a proper alignment.

If the customer is in a hurry and the misalignment is minor, or the customer doesn't want the tailpiece shifted, there is a Q&D cure for a shifted bridge. Move the bridge to where the strings are properly aligned and the intonation is correct. Apply masking tape to the face of the instrument around the bridge base. This tape is for alignment purposes. Relax the strings and remove the bridge. Glue a piece of 400-grit Wetordry sandpaper to the contact area of the bridge base with the sandpaper grit *facing down*. Set the bridge back in place, aligning it between the tape markers, and tune the instrument up to pitch. Remove the tape, and the Q&D job is complete. The fine grit of the Wetordry sandpaper will "bite" into the finish slightly, and the bridge will not slip. Personally, I prefer to shift the tailpiece.

There are other problems that develop occasionally with

Fig. 152—A ¾" plywood clamping pad with carbon paper (carbon side against the plywood) taped to it to determine the strut patterning of a classical guitar top in preparation for clamping a warped bridge and top. The pad should be cut longer and wider than the bridge to provide full support.

the *f*-hole bridge. Unlike the glued-on, pin-type or tie-type bridges which use the pin holes or string-tie holes to space the strings, the *f*-hole bridge utilizes notches exactly like those in the nut to space the strings. Sometimes these wear enough for the strings to jump out, or you have funny, citarlike buzzes emanating from the bridge saddle.

Sand down the top of the saddle to new wood, being especially careful to maintain the original curvature, and recut the notches to where the strings fit *snugly*. There should be no sideways play, and the notches should *slant down* slightly from the string take-off point toward the tailpiece. If the notch is left flat from the leading edge to the rear, you may end up with that citarlike whang when the strings are plucked.

One final point on notched bridge saddles. You *should never notch* a pin-type steel string or tie-type classical bridge saddle. This will cause problems of rapid string wear and breakage at the point of contact. The saddles (especially the plastic ones) will become notched somewhat through normal playing, and they should be sanded down clean occasionally when they get bad. The soft plastic one should be replaced with bone or ivory when encountered for the betterment of the sound if nothing else.

After you clean up a saddle two or three times, the action may be a little low. If so, replace with a new saddle of the proper height.

There is one final problem that I've encountered quite a few times in the past several years that concerns regluing classical guitar bridges. When one of these starts pulling loose, whether from normal stress or exposure to heat, a certain amount of distortion will often show up in the top. It usually takes the form of dips between the fan struts or braces, leaving a high spot on the face at the location of each strut.

I've had no end of trouble getting these to clamp flat since you cannot use enough cam clamps through the small sound holes to clamp all of them flat. Some classical guitars, such as the Jose Ramirez, use a small bridge plate and trim the fan struts to fit over them. I've had no problems with the ones that use the small bridge plate, but the average fan-strutted instrument has only the thickness of the top wood between the fans, and that is where the distortion problem lies.

Most luthiers use seven fans on a classic and five on a flamenco model, and there are usually three to five struts running under the bridge. It would require a clamp be-

140

Fig. 153—The pad is taped into position under the face of the guitar and clamps are applied. The pressure of the struts transfer their location to the pad via the carbon paper.

tween each strut to ensure a full contact, and there is just not enough room to set that many clamps in place.

The solution? A clamping pad, notched to fit over each fan brace with the notches cut deep enough to clear the braces when the major part of the pad contacts the underside of the top.

Yes, I know that there are dozens of variations in fan-brace patterns, but it's not as difficult to make a clamping pad for a particular instrument as it might seem. I keep some scrap ¾" plywood on hand for this job. A piece cut to around 2" by 8½" or 9" will usually be large enough to handle the job.

Tape a piece of carbon paper, carbon side against the wooden pad, as shown in Figure 152, stick a couple of long pieces of masking tape to the underside of the pad, and insert it into the sound hole. Position the pad against the struts and press the tape against the underside of the face. Check with a mirror to see if it's located properly. To assist in aligning the clamping pad, I use two pieces of ⅟16″ hay-wire inserted in the alignment holes drilled through the

saddle slot and top of the guitar (see Volume I, page 132) before removing the bridge. I slide the pad up against these, push the pins up out of the way, then slide the block another ¼" toward the sound hole to cover the full bridge area before sticking the tape to hold the clamping pad in place.

Another method of double-checking the alignment of this clamping pad is to use a bright light (useless if the guitar has a plywood top) over the belly of the instrument. Good spruce will transmit light and shadows. Move your fingers around the bridge area, and if the whole glue area is covered underneath, you will see no shadows. Shift and retape the clamping pad until it is properly located.

Now insert a cam clamp and clamp the pad tight against the struts. I use two clamps as in Figure 153 and take turns shifting and locking them tight over each strut that the pad covers. Remove the clamps and pad and the carbon paper, and you should have a mark on the clamping pad (Figure 154) wherever the pad made contact with a strut. Make a pencil mark parallel with the carbon paper mark about ⅟16″

Fig. 154—Remove the pad and carbon paper. The center mark of each trio are pencil–darkened carbon marks. The area between the outer marks of each trio is to be cut out to the proper depth to clear the fan struts.

Fig. 155—The strut cutouts are made with a band or backsaw and chiseled clean. It may now be taped back under the face and used to clamp the bridge perfectly flat.

to each side and saw out the notches with a bandsaw or dovetail saw to about ¼″ or ⁵⁄₁₆″ deep. Figure 155 shows the cut-out pad.

Once in a while one or two of the fan struts will be lower than the others, and you may have to repeat the carbon paper trick to deal with these, or you may have to do some minor trimming on the clamping pad before it straddles the struts properly and fits flush to the top. Tape it into place, and you are ready to glue down the bridge for a perfect fit.

To further ensure a perfect fit, I use redwood clamping pads with concave bottoms to fit the lengths of the ends of the bridge (Figure 156) and another nearly the length of the bridge's center secton. Of course, I use masking tape to protect the top and catch glue squeeze-out and the metal align-

142

Fig. 156—Topside clamping blocks used to insure full contact of the glue area on a classical guitar. The notched pad is in place under the top. Note the taped–off area and guide pins between the clamping blocks. The pins may be removed when the clamps are locked into place.

ment pins in the saddle slot to keep the bridge from shifting until the clamps are in place and locked down. You can see the metal pins in between the clamps in Figure 156. I've used this method for the last three or four years and have been able to pull the worst of the warped tops into place for a good join in every instance.

11

More Miscellaneous Repairs, Shortcuts, and Tricks to Make Life Easier

STRINGS AND THEIR PROPER INSTALLATION

One criticism that I've received concerning Volume I is that I didn't show the proper way or method of installing strings and that I should remedy the omission in this volume. Other questions concerning strings are what particular gauge and type of string should be used; when the strings should be changed; should all the strings be removed before installing a new set; what about mixing new strings with old ones; what about mixing gauges; should the excess string ends be clipped before or after installation, on and on. All right, you asked for it, and I'll try to field as many of the questions as possible here.

Perhaps one of the most common questions asked is what gauge strings should be used and why. That is a rather difficult question to answer. There are so many factors to be considered in determining the gauge and type of string to use. What type of music do you play? What kind of playing style? Are you using thumb and fingerpicks, playing barefingered, or using a flat pick? Are you using an electric pickup mounted across the sound hole or one of the many transducer pickups? Is your instrument one of the smaller guitars or a large "dreadnought"? Is the instrument a six or a twelve-string?

Sounds complicated, doesn't it? It can be. I'll start with the playing style and the type of music played. I recommend something light if you are playing just for your own enjoyment or just learning to play. Not one of the Super Slinky sets, however, if you're playing an acoustic instrument. These should be used only on the electric guitar; they just don't have the strength (tension) and weight to move the top on a flattop guitar—and the unwound "G" or third string is hard enough to set for an electric guitar with the adjustable bridge pieces. It's an abomination on a flattop guitar and will give all kinds of tuning troubles on a standard bridge. There's no way it will be right.

Silk-and-steel strings are about the lightest-gauge string that will work satisfactorily on a flattop. They have light tension cores and a layer of silk is wound over the core before the plated brass outer windings are added. These strings have a soft, easy action, but there are a couple of drawbacks. They won't stand up to heavy playing, and they don't have the weight to move a large top such as the dreadnought instrument. In other words, they provide less volume than a heavier string, but if you're playing for your enjoyment, they're fine.

On antique instruments I wouldn't recommend anything heavier than a silk-and-steel set because most of the pre-1900 instruments were designed for gut strings. Most of the Martins were designed for gut up to the mid-1920s, and if you *must* use a steel string on the older ones, *do not* use anything heavier than the silk-and-steel sets. Keep a close eye on the top, and if it starts bellying behind the bridge or caving in between the bridge and sound hole, either tune down to "D" or, preferably, go to nylon strings.

I also recommend silk-and-steel strings for twelve-string guitars. My personal preference is a medium-gauge silk-and-steel set such as the La Bella 710-12M tuned down to "D". They are easy on the guitar, easier to fret, and are not as "tinny" sounding as the light-gauge silk-and-steel sets tuned up to concert pitch.

Bronze-wound sets are available in several gauges and usually give the best tonal response and volume for the average flattop guitar. If you play folk style with the thumb and finger picks or use a light flat pick for quieter-style ballads, etc., a light-gauge bronze set is ideal. The longevity is not quite that of the medium gauge, however, but they are easy on the guitar and fingers, and they have enough weight to move a dreadnought top satisfactorily.

Then we get into the heavy-handed country-and-western and bluegrass styles. A stiff flat pick is usually used, and you can destroy a set of light-gauge strings in nothing flat. I recommend medium bronze for any up-tempo requirements. What about heavy gauge? I don't like them—period. They've caused too many bowed necks and bellied tops, and my personal preference is to stay with medium gauges and replace them more often. I prefer to use the lightest-gauge string possible to give the desired sound, and unless the guitar is built like a tank, I would definitely shy away from the heavy ones. I consider them bad news.

What about using the bronze sets for twelve strings? Well, be sure to read your warranty papers thoroughly to see if the manufacturer recommends anything along that line. Some of the manufacturers are very specific about the maximum gauges, and I for one would not exceed their recommendations. Even the light-gauge bronze sets exert a lot of stress on the neck. If you *must* use a bronze set, I would highly recommend tuning down a full step ("D" tuning).

What about the proper string to use with the many various types of pickups available for use on the accoustic guitar? Can you use any kind of string? Yes and no. This depends entirely on the type of pickup used. The ones designed to be installed under the strings and across the sound holes operate on a magnetic principle. They consist of many windings of copper wire around a permanent magnet. The magnet is surrounded by a magnetic field, and the strings pass through this field. The string, when plucked, vibrates rapidly, causing minute variations in the magnetic field, which in turn are sensed and picked up by the windings around the magnet. These variations are then fed into an amplifier for boosting into an audible sound.

A bronze-wound string can be used with the magnetic pickup but will usually be weak in bass response. Bronze is a nonferrous metal. In other words, it is unaffected by magnetism. When it is used with a magnetic pickup, only the steel core of the string will "tickle" the magnet. A string wound with a high nickel content wrapping will give the best results with a magnetic pickup.

Transducers? Go ahead and use any kind of string your heart desires. The many various transducer and contact-type pickups amplify the vibrations of the tops themselves, and you can use any string that will give you the best sound.

Nylon-string selection for the classical guitar is more a matter of taste rather than gauge per se. There are different gauges, of course, which are usually referred to as low, medium, or high tension. The wound strings consist of many fine strands of nylon filament covered with silver-plated brass to give them weight. Some of the more expensive sets use silver altogether for the bass windings, which gives considerably more volume. These can be used to balance out a guitar that is more responsive to the treble strings but on an already balanced instrument can overbalance it.

The first three strings are usually plain nylon, some black in color, and others plain or translucent. A few special sets have wound "G" or third strings. Savaraz offers a plastic-wrapped, filament-cored "G", while Iberia (National) offers a metal-wrapped "G". Most classical guitarists shy away from the wrapped "G" because they "squeak" when they make a rapid slide without lifting the finger, but the intonation is usually more accurate with the wrapped than with the plain string.

On the imported, plywood-topped classical guitars, I recommend the highest-tension nylon string you can buy to improve the deplorable lack of sound, although the high-tension strings are usually harsher in tonal qualities. For the better classical instruments play around with the various tensions and brands until you find the sound that pleases you. I wish I could be more specific here, but a classical guitar can be a cranky creature. A particular string that does wonders for one instrument will do nothing for the next. Experimentation is the way to go.

How can you tell when to change the strings? On a classical guitar the deterioration is slow and gradual, and the average person doesn't realize that the strings are dead until one breaks or he starts having tuning problems. You break down and replace the whole set and wonder what happened when the instrument comes alive in your hands.

I guess that perhaps the best way on a classical guitar is to change the strings on a regular basis, depending on how much you play. If you practice or play every day, change every two or three weeks, more often if you are performing professionally.

If you play only occasionally, another system of checking on the condition of a set of strings is to check for wear spots in the windings on the wound strings where they contact the frets. If you find definite notches, change the whole set. Also keep an eye on the plating of the string windings. When the plating shows a brassy or copper color, the strings are overdue for a change.

Don't bother to change only one string out of a set unless the set is nearly new. Mixing a new string with old ones will invariably cause tuning problems. The molecular structure of a string changes immediately when tension is applied and continues changing throughout the life of the string until it gives up completely and breaks. Look at it this way. If you were as skinny as a string and were treated in the same manner, you'd get tired, too. A new string will not balance properly with the old ones. Install a new set. This holds true with both nylon and steel strings.

The breakdown of steel strings is more rapid and dramatic than that of nylon. Instead of a nice, clean, resonant ring, you will have a dull-sounding thud with little or no sustain. Again, the frequency of change depends on how much you play and on the type of music you play. A heavy-handed bluegrass guitarist can kill a brand-new set of strings in a couple of hours, while another guitarist, playing soft, easy ballads might get two or three weeks or more out of his set.

Probably the best indicator of when to change a set of steel strings is the fifth and sixth strings. When they lose their brilliance, change the whole set. Severe tuning problems are another indication. If the guitar tunes easily when a new set is installed, it's time to change when the tuning becomes difficult. If the strings won't tune when they are new, see the bridging and intonation chapter.

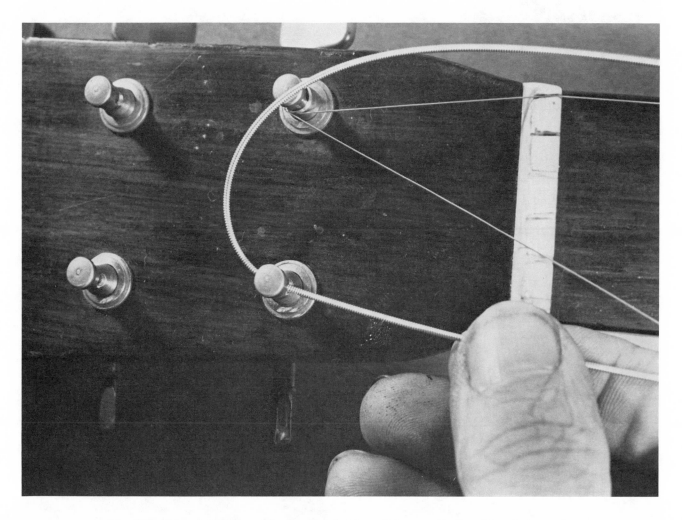

Fig. 157—*Proper installation of heavier wound strings. String post is adjusted lengthwise to the headstock. Run the end of the string down toward the name on the head and loop it back through the string post hole. Leave enough slack for three windings minimum.*

Now, changing the strings. Unless you need to work on the instrument or the fingerboard needs cleaning, change only one string at a time. This is not as critical with steel strings as with the nylon ones. If you remove all the strings on a classical guitar, it often takes a day or even longer for the stress to set up again. I've worked over classical guitars that I've had the strings off for a while, and I've also noticed this phenomenon on the handful of classical guitars that I've made through the years. String it up, and the sound is maybe so-so but nothing to write home about, but wait until the next day. The guitar seems to have suddenly doubled in volume and became alive. It has to do with stress alignment in the wood, I believe.

The one main problem many people have in installing new strings seems to be the proper way to connect the string to the machine head string post. People come to me with chronic string breakage problems, and not only amateurs

either. The string slips or breaks at the string post, and they blame it on the string quality, the machine heads, or anything but themselves. It's really weird how so many people who have been playing for years don't know how to install a string so that it won't slip or break.

String breakage at the string post is almost invariably caused by the string cutting itself. In nearly every case I find from one-half to one turn of the string around the machine-head post. There should be at least three turns with the wound strings and four or five with the unwound strings—and the unwound strings must be locked properly to prevent slippage.

I believe that the series of photographs and captions will better explain how to install and lock the strings than trying to spell it out, so please refer to Figures 157 to 163. Follow these guidelines, and your string breakage and slippage at the machine heads should be cured.

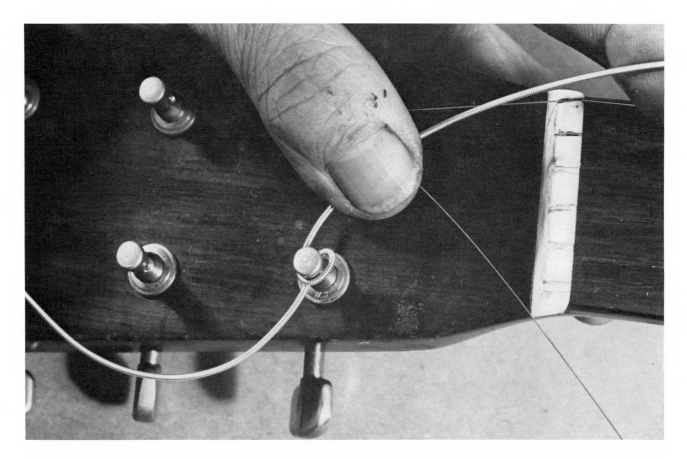

Fig. 158—Bass string installation continued. Make your first winding around the string post over the top of the string's "tail".

Fig. 159—Bass string installation continued. Wind the rest of the string slack under the tail. There should be at least three turns around the string post when the string is tuned up to pitch. The "A" string (center post in foreground) gives the best detail on this.

Fig. 160—Treble and smaller wound string locking technique. Run the string down and back as in the first step on the bass string installation. Remember to leave some slack. You should have a "U" shape in the string.

Fig. 161—*Treble string locking technique continued. Bring the tail on around the opposite side of the post from the main part of the string in an "S" shape, continue on around toward the head, under the top of the "S" and up. It should now resemble a handwritten "O". Pull the tail on up tight, hold, and apply tension to the working part of the string while winding the slack under the tail end.*

150

Fig. 162—*Treble string locking technique continued. The strings are now locked and tuned up to pitch. Note the windings underneath the tail which is locked solid and will not slip.*

Fig. 163—The strings should be bent as in the photo before clipping to prevent the windings from slipping from the shock. Also, another good look at both methods of locking the strings.

Left-hand Conversions on Right-Hand Guitars—or Vice Versa

Left-handed guitars are available from most of the major instrument makers on special order. But what of the left-hander who stumbles onto a real buy in a right-handed guitar, one that he or she cannot afford to pass up? Or perhaps someone has been given a right-handed instrument.

Well, they have two choices: learn to play right-handed or have the instrument converted. Most of my left-handed customers choose the first alternative—learning to play right-handed. A left-handed guitarist playing a right-handed instrument can do some unreal things on a fingerboard with the dominant hand, and it's about as easy for him to learn to pick with the right hand as it is for the right-handed person to learn to finger a neck with his left hand. However, if you've been playing left-handed for some time, this can prove to be nearly impossible. I know from experience. I play right-handed, and when I cut a half-inch off the long finger on my left hand, I tried to learn how to fret with my right hand. No way. I invented a rubber-tipped plastic boot for the cut-off finger and learned to cope with it.

Most of the better-quality steel-string instruments and many of the cheapies use the Martin style of x-bracing under the face. The two tone bars are butted against the x-brace on the treble side and angle across the belly (see Figure 164) to the lower bout on the bass side. The idea is to stiffen the treble side somewhat so that it responds better to the higher frequencies of the treble strings. The bass side, being more flexible, responds better to the lower frequencies of the bass strings.

Ideally, the tone bars should be removed and slanted in the opposite direction as in Figure 164, but this entails removing the back or top of the instrument to do the job—an expensive proposition.

Classical guitars are usually braced more symmetrically, except in instruments like the Ramirez with its so-called Ramirez strap and some of the other expensive models. On handmade classics I use a tight-grained wood for the treble side fans and a coarse-grained wood for the bass side to help with the balance.

There are also, of course, external changes required, and most of the left-handed conversions I have done were strictly external conversions. There is some tonal loss to be expected, obviously, but to tell the truth, they were not at all that noticeable, and I have yet to receive any complaints. Don't get me wrong: the best way to go is to go the whole route, both external and internal, but if the owner doesn't have the money. . . .

Now to the external conversion. Since the bridge will have to be replaced or reworked, the first thing I do is to check the intonation and lay out the proper positioning of

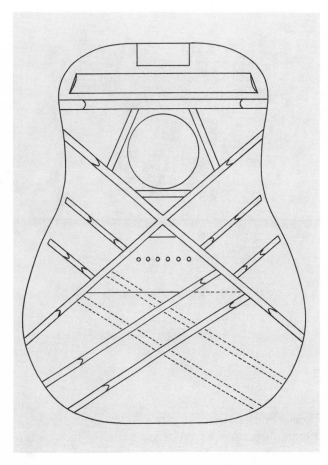

Fig. 164—Martin style (D–28) left–hand top strutting. Imagine that you have removed the top and turned it upside down. It's reversed on the guitar. The dotted lines represent the original right–hand strutting and bridge plate location. Only the tone bars and bridge plate are changed interiorwise to make a lefty.

the new saddle location on my straightedge as described in the bridging chapter in this volume.

Remove the strings and nut and rough out a new nut designed for the reversed strings. The string spacing can wait until you are ready to reassemble the instrument and, of course, the nut action is set after reassembly.

I prefer to make a new bridge, since the old one is usually cut thinner on the treble side, but if the intonation wasn't off and you have enough "meat" on the bridge to work with, the original bridge can be left in place. If so, cut a scrap of wood that matches the bridge wood and trim it for a snug fit in the original saddle slot. Press into place and flow in some of the water-thin cyanoacrylate glue and let cure. Trim the scrap flush with the top of the bridge, lay out the new string take-off points, and recut the saddle slot with the slant in the *opposite direction*. One time I had a new bridge completed and was ready to glue it on when I

*Fig. 165—Deluxe machine heads, three–to–a–plate and individual, which are found as original equipment with a half–dozen different knob shapes on many American guitars. These are available from most musical supply houses with the pictured style knobs. They are "self–tighteners" (note bradded end on t*he *gear end of the string post) and may be lubricated through the hole in the cover.*

realized that I had blown it. I make so many new right-handed bridges that I had automatically cut the slot right-handed rather than for a left-hand model. With the exception of being backward, completing the bridge is the same as for a right-hand model, so refer to the bridging chapter.

On a classical guitar the saddle is usually not slanted, and all that needs to be done is to reverse the saddle so that the lower side is opposite the original position. If the saddle is slanted, however, as on a few models that I've encountered, make a new bridge.

The original nut on a classical guitar can often be used as is with the exception of setting the nut string action. It might have to be shimmed slightly under the bass side for a little extra clearance.

Pickguards on the steel string jobs can be a problem. The spruce under a pickguard is almost invariably lighter than the rest of the top because it has been protected from the light. Sometimes this can be shaded to match and the top refinished, but the simplest method is to leave the old guard in place and make a matching left-hand guard for the opposite side. If you don't have any matching material, make a matching pair from material you have on hand and glue them on.

Machine Heads and Their Problems

This section will be somewhat of a rehash of the machine-head section of Volume I with some added information. The main, overwhelming problem encountered with machine heads is that of neglect. More machine heads

have been ruined by the lack of lubrication than all other reasons combined. A simple drop of 3-In-One oil at the bearing ends of the worm gear and one where the worm gear meets the string post gear every few string changes would cut our repair shop's machine head replacements by a good half. Of course, replacing machine heads helps to boost our income, but it's an unnecessary added expense to the owner, and a needless waste.

Friction adjustment, or rather the improper adjustment, accounts for another large percentage of replacements. The owner has tuning problems, such as a sudden jump above or below pitch while tuning, accompanied by a grating or screeching sound, and he or she automatically assumes that the problem is in the machine heads. These sudden jumps in pitch while tuning are caused by the string catching in the nut notches, but the owner tightens down on the friction adjustment of the machine head. It still jumps, and out comes the screwdriver again. The first thing you know, the string shaft is almost locked and the worm and gear gall from this treatment. The job of the guitar repairman is to free up the string slots in the nut and replace the ruined machine heads.

There are tuning problems, however, that do concern the machine heads. Several popular and not-so-popular machine heads are what is known as self-tighteners. These, excluding some of the aged machine heads, are all covered machines. The gears are protected from dust with covers riveted and bradded in several different manners (Figures 165 and 166) and have the shaft gears bradded to the string shafts. To remove the housings for adjustment is futile;

154

Fig. 166—Another variety of the "self-tighteners". The hollow rivets may be drilled out and the cover removed for lubrication, but if they are loose and sloppy, replace them.

Fig. 167—A pretty decent Japanese made machine head, many times found with a cover as shown separately. The cover is held in place by the machine head retaining screws and may be removed for adjustment and lubrication.

there is no provision for this when they become loose. They have to be replaced with new ones.

Not all machine heads with dust covers are self-tighteners, though. On these (Figure 167) the covers are usually held in place with the same screws that hold the heads to the instrument, and they can be pried off the plate after removing the heads from the guitar. They usually have a Phillips head screw to hold the shaft gear in place (as on Japanese models) and may be adjusted normally. A snug fit with a small amount of drag is sufficient. If the knob is stiff and hard to turn, back off on the screw slightly until only a slight drag is felt.

Oil can be used to lubricate these covered machines, but since they are covered where they won't collect dust and get the mess all over your hands and clothes, I prefer to pack the worm gear and shaft gear teeth with Lubriplate or a lithium grease. These lubricants last longer than oil.

Grover Rotomatics and Schallers are supposed to be permanently lubricated at the factory, but under constant use they too sometimes need cleaning and lubricating. The friction adjustment is a machine screw located in the end of the knob instead of on the shaft gear as on most machine heads. If you find one that is rough and feels like metal-to-metal when the knob is turned, this machine screw may be removed, and the knob will slip off the worm-gear shaft. You will find two or three washers, one a spring washer,

between the knob and housing. Lay them out in the order you removed them so that they can be replaced in the proper order (Figure 169) and slide the worm gear out of the opposite end of the cast housing.

Check the worm and housing for metal "filings." If they have galled, you'll find these filings in the old grease. Wipe the pieces clean. If metal flakes or filings are present, dunk the housing and gear in naphtha or lacquer thinner and let them soak for a while. Swish the parts around and blow them out good with an air hose. Repeat if necessary until the shaft gear and inside of the housing are clean.

I don't know what kind of grease the factories pack them with, it looks like petroleum jelly, but I prefer to use a lithium grease or Lubriplate. It's a white, long-lasting, high-temperature grease that can be purchased in a tube with a long snout. Run the snout inside the housing and rotate the shaft gear until the teeth are packed solid with grease. Fill the threads on the worm gear and slip the shaft back in place. Then reinstall the washers and knob. Wipe off any excess grease, adjust the friction screw, and install the machine heads on the guitar. The lube job should be good for several years. When you find one dry one, it's a good idea to go ahead and lube the rest of the machine heads, too, so that they will all have the same "feel."

If this fails to solve the problem, send it back to the factory (Grovers). They are warrantied for life, unless, of

Fig. 168—A common (too common) problem caused by a lack of lubrication. Note the two full worm gear threads nearest the adjusting knob. One has started to gall and the second is worn to half its original width. Throw it away and install new machine heads.

Fig. 169—Even "permanently" lubricated machines such as the Grover Rotomatic (pictured) and Schallers have been known to need lubricating under constant usage. Be sure to reassemble them in exactly the same order as disassembled. See the text for lubrication instructions.

Fig. 170—A problem encountered quite often on classical machine heads, loose rollers on the string shafts. Use a v–block and drill press to drill and pin the rollers. See the text.

course, the machines have been damaged. Various parts, screws, washers, etc., are available from the factory to replace missing parts.

Other problems involving machine heads are broken plastic knobs and bent worm shafts from impact damage. Sometimes the bent shafts can be straightened—at the customer's risk. About 50 percent of them break if the original impact was enough to bend them badly, and I usually make my customer watch while I try to straighten the shaft. That way he can't argue with you if you have to install a new machine head.

Loose, press-on plastic knobs can usually be repaired with five-minute epoxy or cyanoacrylate glue. If a knob is broken or missing, I check my junk box—I'm a pack rat—and try to remove a matching knob from a junk machine head. I might even have a usable machine head in the box to replace the one with the broken knob. Barring that, sell the customer some new machine heads, or tell him to use a pair of pliers.

A problem that occurs frequently with classical guitar machine heads is loose plastic rollers on the string shafts. Many of the inexpensive sets have metal shafts that extend for only a short distance into the plastic roller instead of the full length. They can loosen up, causing the string to lock in the shaft hole.

Remove the strings and take the machine head plates off the guitar. Use a sharp-pointed scribe or icepick and realign the string hole in the plastic roller with the metal core. Drill a $1/16''$ hole through the roller and shaft, as in Figure 170, where it will be concealed by the wood when the machine head is replaced and pin it. You can use a piece of soft iron haywire (my choice, me being a farm boy) or a piece of brass welding rod. Trim the pin flush with the roller and apply a drop of cyanoacrylate glue to lock the pin in place.

Go ahead and pin all six rollers. Chances are that if one of the six is loose the others will eventually work loose too, so you may as well do a bit of preventive maintenance while you're at it.

In Volume I, page 19, Figure 14, I show a drilling jig for fitting Grover Slimline machine heads to twelve-string guitars. It worked beautifully too, but Grover has changed the dimensions on their later twelve-string sets, and I had to make a new drilling jig. The large holes are now $11/32''$ in diameter instead of $21/64''$, and the center-to-center measurements are .920″ instead of .930″. You'll have to make a new jig to drill for these, but the procedure is the same as outlined in Volume I. The .010″ difference in center-to-center spacing doesn't sound like much, I know, but multiply that by five, and you have a .050″ difference from end to end, and that's almost ¹⁄₁₆″. Make a new jig.

"Voicing" of Guitar Struts

Perhaps one of the most sought-after acoustic guitars, with the exception of the old D-45 Martins, is the prewar D-28 herringbone Martin. These instruments, and other pre-1946 Martins, had the top bracing "voiced," or scalloped, and with light- or medium-gauge strings, they by far outperform most of the later instruments. With the advent of heavy-gauge strings, however, Martin and other manufacturers were forced to go to heavier top bracing.

Martin has recently revived the herringbone as the HD-28, and it has the old-style scalloped braces, but there are limitations on the types of strings that can be used on these to keep from voiding the warranty. I have had several in my shop for minor string action adjustments, and I have only one thing to say so far . . . great. Even new, the ones I've worked on have had the sound and tonal quality of the standard-braced Martins ten or fifteen years older. After aging and a lot of playing, they should be fantastic. Many kudos to Martin for reintroducing the herringbone.

Now to the problems with voicing. Many owners of the heavier-braced instruments are asking me to scallop the braces of their instruments to the old-time configuration. Some are going so far as attempting the jobs themselves, working through the sound holes with pocket knives, scrapers, coarse sandpaper, and even broken glass. This can be bad news in more ways than one.

The one overwhelming reason not to attempt to do this is that any attempt at altering the configuration of the original bracing will void your warranty and is done at your own risk. Even warranty repair stations such as mine *are not* authorized to do this job without voiding your warranty.

However, if the job is to be done regardless of warranty considerations, I advise caution in trying to do the job through the sound hole. Don't get me wrong: it can be done—by someone with smaller hands and forearms than mine. But I wouldn't attempt the job with any kind of a sharp-bladed tool. A scraper—maybe, but coarse sandpaper and caution would be a surer bet.

Reason? You're working blind. Say you have a razor-sharp knife and are whittling away when the edge catches in a grain and splits out half the strut. Norton Abrasives makes a cloth-backed "utility roll" in various grits which would be ideal for the job. I have a 1″ by 60-grit roll that I use for rough sanding when shaping necks, struts, etc., that I would recommend if you must go this route.

Another reason I would advise against working through the sound hole is the difficulty in attaining the right configuration and measuring the same. I suppose you could make some cardboard templates and work with those, but I just don't like working blind. Must be the machinist in me.

Now if the back or top were removed, that would be a different matter. You can see what you're doing and measuring for the exact dimensions are simplified.

The two photographs, Figures 171 and 172, of scrap Martin tops will give you an eyeball reference of the standard late Martin x-bracing and two methods of "voicing," the Martin scalloping and the early Guild (altered to my own specifications) style of taper trimming. A word of caution here. Do not mix the two styles of voicing. Use either one or the other. The mix on the top is for demonstration purposes only. I've used both methods but have settled on the taper-trimmed braces on the handful of steel-string guitars that I've made. No specific reason for the choice, except perhaps the technique for building speakers comes to mind. The central area of the belly is stiffer and "floats" freer around the edges. On my handmade instruments I even went so far as thinning the tops .015 to .020″ thinner at the edge of the belly area, starting at around three inches from the edge of the tops. Results, excellent. Results with the scalloped bracing? Also excellent, but with slightly more bellying of the top.

If you're interested in knowing how I can take an exact amount off the edge of a top, I'll tell you. I use a Dremel Moto Tool with a router attachment. Chuck in a small dental burr or router bit and set it to the depth desired for the amount to be removed. Start the Dremel and set it in place about ¼″ from the purfling. Lift it and move it down a few inches and set it down again. Keep doing this until you have a line of holes an inch or so apart all around the area where you plan to do the thinning. I start where the waist begins to flair out at the lower bout. When you do the sanding, sand until the marks just barely disappear and you're in business.

The drawings in Figures 173 and 174 give you the dimensions of the standard Martin x-braces and tone bars, those I took from a 1938 D-28 herringbone, and those of my last two steel-stringed instruments. Since the Martin braces are individually hand-trimmed at the factory, there will be some variations in other scalloped Martin braces, but the variation is minor.

Whichever method you use, work only on the legs of the "x" that extend under the bridge and belly area. The ends of the "x" in the sound hole area should be left untouched to counter the rotational stress of the strings on the bridge.

Both tone bars are also scalloped or taper-trimmed. If you like, the tone bar nearest the butt of the instrument can be trimmed slightly lower, perhaps ¹⁄₁₆″, but unless you

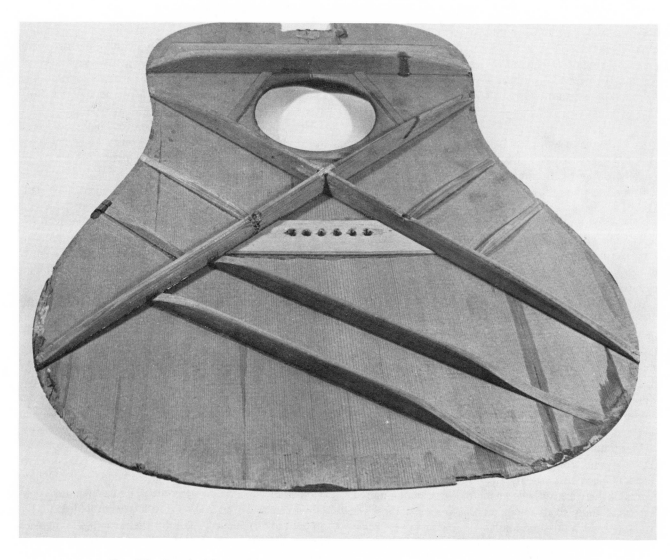

Fig. 171—Standard late model Martin dreadnought top strutting (on scrap top) before "voicing".

plan on using only light-gauge strings, I wouldn't lighten it any more than that.

The flat tops left on the struts after scalloping or taper trimming should be rounded nicely and sanded smooth. While you're sanding, go ahead and sand the underside of the top and the rest of the braces with fine finishing paper. A certain amount of sanding is done at the factory, but, being a production-line operation, it can be improved on.

You will sometimes find a small amount of glue squeeze-out (a lot of it on some brands), and now is a good time to remove it. The variable-speed Dremel with a small wire brush can make short work of old glue messes.

After clean-up and fine sanding, a wad of 0000 steel wool will put a silk-smooth, almost polished finish on the spruce. Why? Rough wood collects dust, and dust collects dampness, all of which can affect sound, and a smooth surface ensures a freer flow of air. A guitar is an air pump, and anything that will increase the flow of air will increase the sound.

Replacing Completely Loose Struts

Many more times than I care to remember, customers have brought in instruments with one or more struts rattling around loose inside. Loose struts are bad enough when they're still partly attached, but completely loose ones can be real woolly-boogers.

Take an *f*-hole instrument for instance. These have, in most cases, two longitudinal braces running the length of the top, carved to fit the contours of the carved or lami-

160

Fig. 172—Two methods of "voicing". The bass side x–brace and first tone bar have been scalloped a la Martin (scrap top for demonstration purposes. Do not mix the two methods) and the treble side x–brace and second tone bar have been taper–trimmed similar to the early Guild. See the drawings for the exact dimensions and the text for a warning on warranty considerations.

nated top. When one of these comes loose, usually from an impact to the top, you have to remove the top or back to reposition and glue them properly.

I've evolved a technique, however, that works in most cases on flattop guitars. If you can reach the area through the sound hole, you're in business. If not, remove the back.

Now the procedure. In perhaps 90 percent of the cases the completely loose brace will be a cross brace, usually from the back but occasionally a top brace from a ladder or lute-braced top. The ends of these braces almost invariably extend into notches cut in the linings between the top or back. One end of the brace will often be broken off at the point where it extends into the lining, but the opposite end will be intact. The intact end gives us a starting point.

Scrape or sand away the old glue from both the strut and the contact area on the top or back. Insert the good end of the strut into its respective notch in the lining and see if it

will stay in place long enough to apply a piece of masking tape over the brace to hold it to the top.

Slip a strut jack into position near the end of the strut where it fits the notch (Volume I, Page 139, Figure 118) and tighten it just enough for a snug fit. Inspect the positioning with a machinist's mirror. If it's out of position—you should be able to see exactly where it came from with the mirror—slip the strut around until it's located properly. Next tighten the jack down a little more. Position a second jack in the middle of the strut and tighten it snugly, then place a third one at the opposite end. Apply the outside cam clamps and reinspect the strut for positioning. If you have located it properly, there should be no gaps between the strut, back or top. If there is, try again and again until it clamps into position properly.

Now we're ready to glue. Remove the outside cam clamp from one end only and slack off of the strut jack below it

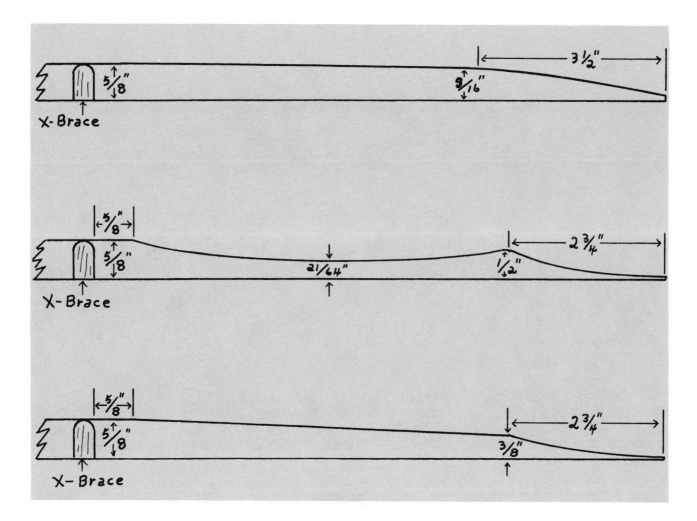

Fig. 173—"Voicing" dimensions. The measurements on the top x–brace were taken from a 1954 D–28 Martin, the scalloped brace in the center from a 1938 D–28 herringbone, and the bottom drawing is a taper–trimmed style similar to the very early (F–40) Guild.

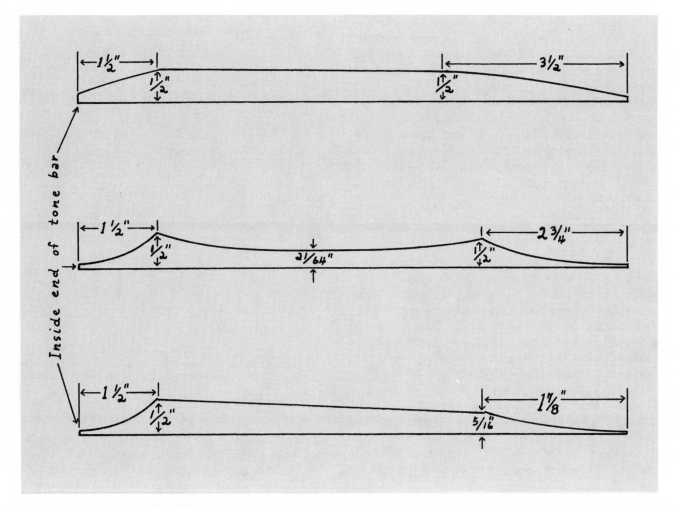

Fig. 174—"Voicing" dimensions continued. Tone bar measurements. The top drawing is from the 1954 D–28, the middle from the 1938 herringbone, and the bottom similar to the early Guild.

until you can insert a sleeved hypodermic needle and syringe (Volume I, page 138, Figure 117) between the strut and back or top. Inject Titebond along a two- or three-inch section, tighten up the strut jack again, and reapply the outside cam clamp. Set the instrument back out of the way for two or three hours. If you feel brave, go ahead and relax the other two strut jacks and cam clamps, one at a time, and inject glue under the rest of the strut. It's chancy, however, and if the strut should slip, you're in trouble. Once one section of glue is cured, though, you can release the other clamps for gluing without fear of slippage. I prefer the more cautious approach myself.

If both tip ends of the strut are broken off and there's no notch in the linings to use for the preliminary fitting, what do you do? A good question; but it's still possible to position the loose strut properly with masking tape. It just takes a little longer—but not as long as removing a back.

Trim off any splinters on the ends of the strut, but no more than is absolutely necessary. Lay a piece of masking tape over the strut, position it by guestimation, and press the tape against the top or back. Tear off a second piece of tape and stick it across the strut in a second location.

Check the positioning with the mirror. The odds are overwhelmingly against getting it right the first try—or the second or third—but keep after it. You will also have to keep applying new tape as the original tape loses its sticking power. Once you have one end in position, you can insert a strut jack to help simplify things. From there on the procedure is the same as before—gluing one section, then the rest of the mess.

After the complete strut is glued and cured, I like to cut and glue a small gusset (Figure 175) in place for added reinforcement at each end of the strut. If one end was intact and still fits into the original notch in the linings, the extra reinforcement is unnecessary on that end. Sometimes a piece of the lining will come down with the strut. In this case a new piece of notched lining can be fitted into place for the support. Since it is impossible to clamp these gussets, I use five-minute epoxy and hold the gusset in place with a finger until the epoxy gels.

Repairing Loose Bindings

I have a much faster and just as satisfactory method for repairing loose bindings than that described in Volume I. The secret? Our new friend, the cyanoacrylate glue again. It will stick loose bindings and purflings in seconds.

The only precaution is that same one mentioned several times in this volume. Tape off the finished areas *very carefully* and make doubly sure that the tape is pressed down firmly to eliminate the wrinkles. After taping, flow a drop or two of Hot Stuff or other water-thin cyanoacrylate *de-*

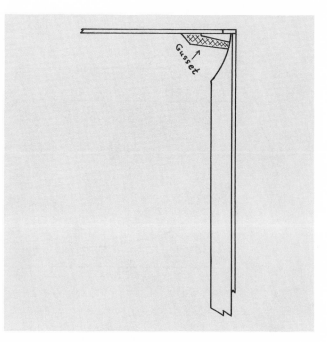

Fig. 175—Gusset to reinforce loose brace that has been reglued. Use a smaller gusset under the top struts in the belly area of a top.

signed for use with woods into an inch or so of the gap at a time and press the loose binding tightly into position with a waxed stick or X-acto knife handle for thirty seconds. More on over and repeat the operation on the next section. Use only a small amount of the glue, and don't try to do more than an inch or two at a time.

When the loose area is solid, pull the tape, scrape or sand off the excess glue, and touch up. Simple—and fast.

Transducer Installation in the Acoustic Guitar

I won't get into the merits of one type or brand of transducer over another because each customer usually has his or her reasons for choosing one brand or the other, and for me to do so would only start an argument. Also, I will leave it up to the individual whether or not to use a preamplifier with the installation. The preamp will, however, boost the signal on an installation that is weak. I will stick with the installation procedure.

There are many arguments about where and how a transducer should be placed. Most companies include a mastix or sticky putty with their kit, so you may stick it where you want it. I lean toward a more solid type of installation without the dampening effect of the soft putty. I glue the transducer to a thin piece of spruce 1/16″ to 3/32″ thick and glue the spruce to the underside of the guitar's top with five-min-

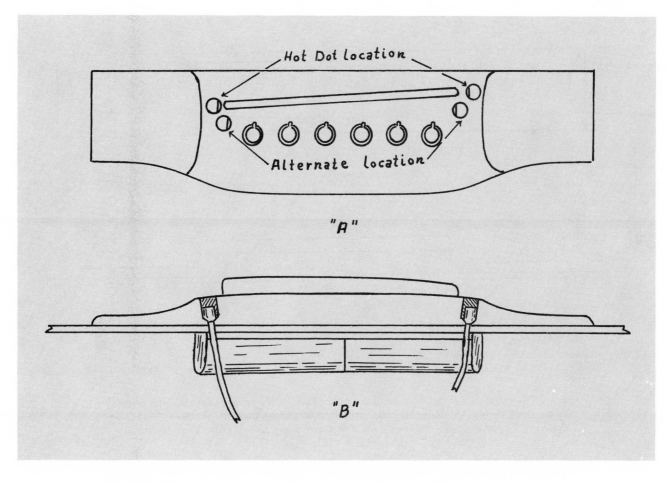

Fig. 176—"Hot Dot" transducer installation in a steel string guitar. Part "A" shows two locations to mount double dot system. Note the flat sides of the transducer is to the inside. Color of the dots (see text) is important. Part "B" shows a cutaway picture of the double dot installation in an x–braced (Martin) bridge. Note that the holes are drilled on a slant to miss the struts and that the flat sides of the Hot Dots are facing to the center. Shaded area is epoxy filler.

ute epoxy. It may be removed without damage to the transducer when necessary by simply splitting the spruce scrap with something sharp. This type of installation, of course, applies only to the log-type transducer.

The Barcus Berry Hot Dot requires a different type of installation. The first decision is whether to use one or two dots. A single Hot Dot should be placed on the treble side of the bridge, close to the end of the bridge saddle (Figure 176) or immediately behind it. Two Hot Dots are a better choice and will give a better balance in sound. The second dot is mounted on the bass side of the bridge in the same location as on the treble side. Be sure that you have *two different colors of* Hot Dots for the double dot installation, *one black*, and *one brown*. Two of the same color are not designed to work with each other to the best of efficiency.

One particular thing to watch for in the Hot Dot instal-

lation is in drilling the holes. Both legs of the x-braces on an x-braced top run under the outer edges of the bridge, and I have had several do-it-yourself installations in my shop with the lead wire holes drilled through the x-braces. Drill a small, 1/16″ or less, hole through the area where you decide to place the Hot Dots and check beneath the top. If the drill went through a brace, plug the hole, and then redrill at an angle to clear the braces.

Use a .203″ (13/64″) drill for the body of the Hot Dot. Drill into the wood of the bridge until the tip of the drill just touches the spruce top. Be careful here and check several times while drilling. The bridge wood is hard, and if you apply too much pressure, when you hit the softer spruce, you can easily go all the way through the top before you can catch yourself. Look for a trace of white wood at the bottom of the hole when it's drilled to the proper depth.

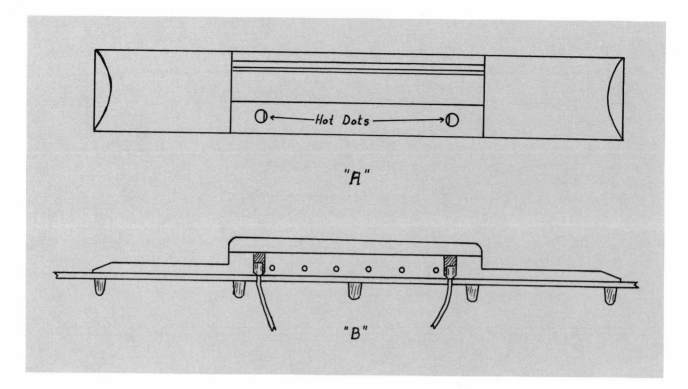

"A"

"B"

Fig. 177—About the only practical location for "Hot Dots" in the average classical guitar bridge is in the string tie part "A" at the back. Be sure that you miss the fan struts shown in the cutaway drawing "B", and again, the flat sides of the transducers should face the center of the bridge.

The hole for the lead wire is drilled on through using a 3/32″ bit. Epoxy is recommended for cementing in the transducers. There are two ways of doing this. I own a precision metal lathe and machine fitted wooden plugs of scrap wood to match the bridge's wood, but you may use dyed epoxy or pearl dots in the top of the holes. I like the wooden plugs because the installation is all but invisible when finished.

Study the Hot Dots closely. You will find a small flat spot on one side of each dot. On a single-dot installation, this flat spot should face toward the center of the bridge. The same applies for the double-dot installation. In other words, the flat spots should face each other.

Run the wires through the small holes and check to make sure that the dots will bottom out in the larger hole, then push them back up above the surface of the bridge while you mix the five-minute epoxy. Regular epoxy will work, but you will have to wait for it to cure.

Apply a small amount of epoxy to the bottom of the Hot Dot—not all over the wire—and push it down into the hole until it bottoms. Fill the rest of the hole with dyed epoxy, a pearl dot, or a fitted wooden plug and let cure thoroughly. (See Figure 176)

Figure 177 shows the installation in a classical-guitar bridge.

The one objection I have to the Hot Dot installation is having to remove and reglue the bridge should it ever come loose. It's very easy to pull out or cut the lead wires during the removal process. The epoxy squeezes down through the lead wire hole and cements it solid to the top. I've started waxing the lead wire heavily with beeswax, which helps some. I've removed several bridges with Hot Dot installations so far and have managed to salvage all but one Hot Dot, but I make no guarantees. It's cheaper to make a new bridge than to purchase new transducers so I just destroy the bridge in the removal process and make a new bridge.

A Dremel Moto Tool with a small router bit, and no base is the answer. I start cutting out a circle of wood around the hole where the transducer is mounted until I reach the spruce top. The bridge may then be lifted while leaving the transducer in place.

Cut or unsolder the lead wire at the butt peg, and start chipping away the plug of epoxy very carefully with a sharp knife or chisel until only the transducer itself is left. Try to wiggle it free, but don't force things. If it's stubborn, use a small dental burr in the Dremel and cut away the spruce

166

around the lead-in wire until it's free. Drill out the lead-wire hole with a large enough drill bit to cover all the damage, drilling only three-quarters of the way through the spruce top. Plug the hole with a scrap of spruce or a dowel, then trim flush. After the new bridge is made and glued on, drill and reinstall the transducers as previously instructed. That should about cover the Hot Dots.

Now for the other types of transducers. Many companies recommend mounting them on the bridge. I find that in most instances this results in an unbalanced sound between the bass and treble. Of course, this varies, depending on the individual instrument and the sound and tonal quality required by the customer. Some like more bass, others more treble, etc. I insist on my customer telling me where to place the transducer, located by his or her personal taste.

Start by mounting the pickup on the treble side of the bridge with the supplied mastix and try it out on your own amplification equipment. Don't be satisfied with the first location. Move it around on the top. Try several spots behind the bridge, maybe even halfway to the butt of the instrument. You will probably end up with it on the treble side of the top's centerline and anywhere from the bridge to three or four inches behind the bridge. Don't be afraid to move it a dozen times until you find the sound you want. The actual volume of the transducer can depend on the location and might be increased enough to eliminate the need for a preamplifier in some instances. The mess left by the putty is easily cleaned up with a rag moistened with cigarette lighter fluid (naphtha).

Some people prefer to use the mastix and leave the transducer stuck to the outside of the instrument (I've seen some screwed to the tops), but a neater way is to mount it inside. Stick a dime to the top of the guitar in the desired location—a small piece of masking tape will work, too—and glue the aforementioned scrap of spruce to the contact side of the transducer with five-minute epoxy. Remove the strings while the epoxy is drying and aim a bright light at the dime or tape while checking inside with a mirror. On a natural spruce top, you should see a shadow cast by the dime. You may have to shift the location a fraction of an inch to clear a top strut, but try to locate the transducer as close as possible to the predetermined spot.

This may be easier said than done if the top is plywood and doesn't transmit light or if the desired location falls on the bridge plate. A measurement from the bridge pin holes can be useful to find the bridge plate location. On a non-translucent top? Place the fingertips of one hand gently on the predetermined spot externally and tap the underside of the top with a fingernail of the other hand. You should be able to find the spot with relative ease. Check the feel of the struts in the immediate locale so that you can find the spot again when you insert the transducer.

Clean off any excess epoxy from gluing the spruce scrap

to the transducer and trim the spruce to the dimensions of the pickup. Dress the contact surface of the spruce scrap perfectly level on a piece of sandpaper placed on a flat surface, mix up a few more drops of five-minute epoxy, press it in place under the top, and hold it tight until the epoxy jells. An easy way to tell when it's time to turn loose is to mix slightly more epoxy than needed and keep it within reach of your free hand. When it sets, turn loose. *Do not* try to wiggle the transducer to tell if it's set as this may result in a bad glue join with the resultant loss of sound. Use the same method to glue in a transducer in the classical guitar.

The plug-in is next. I prefer to install the Barcus Berry–type butt peg with the miniature jack hole in the peg itself rather than drilling a hole in the side of the instrument for a ¼″ phono plug, but that's up to the customer. If a ¼″ phono jack must be installed, glue a piece of nylon or thin fiberglass cloth to the area inside the guitar to help prevent the splitting out the side in the event of an impact on the plug, etc. The cloth should surround the hole for at least an inch.

Some people object to the small butt-jack system because the cord keeps falling out. No problem. Tie the cord to the guitar strap with a small amoung of slack. The jack can then be plugged into the butt peg, and any sudden jerk on the cord will be taken up by the neck strap instead of the jack pulling out. Simple. The installation of the Barcus Berry butt peg is not so simple. The portion of the peg that fits into the butt-peg hole has two different diameters—both larger than the standard plastic butt pegs. Some shops just drill out the larger diameter for the full depth. It works, but why do a halfway job when it's not that much harder to do it right (see Figure 178 for the dimensions)?

I use a .406″ (13⁄32″) drill for the first step and drill it 13⁄32″ deep, measuring from the butt of the guitar. A piece of masking tape wrapped around the drill at the proper depth is the easiest way to measure the depth. The larger diameter of the butt peg—depending on how thick it is plated—is .408″ in diameter, or .002″ larger than the hole. You might have to wallow the drill very slightly to keep the fit from being too tight, but go easy on this until you drill out the second smaller hole.

The second hole is drilled with a ⅜″ bit and is ½″ deep (the total depth of the 13⁄32- and ⅜″-diameter holes), measuring again from the butt of the guitar. The second diameter of the butt peg mikes out at .375 (⅜″) but has a small knurled portion which is .002″ larger. This one might have to be wallowed slightly too, if the fit is too tight. It should be a tight press fit with the thumb. If a light tap from a plastic hammer doesn't seat it, wallow it out a trace more until it does fit. Got it too loose? A drop of Titebond on the knurled portion will hold it in place. If it should have to be removed after gluing, unscrew the center part and heat the pressed-in sleeve with a soldering iron. It will come right out.

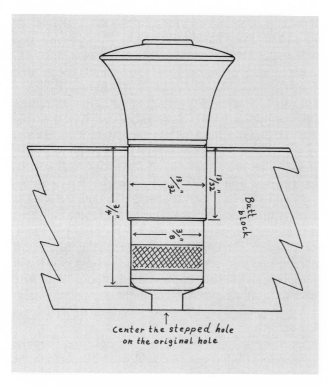

Fig. 178—A cutaway drawing showing the installation of the Barcus Berry butt peg. The ¹³/₃₂" hole may be drilled a full ¾" deep, but it's much neater to step–drill the hole for a fit.

Another thing to watch for—a peculiarity that I've run into on some models of Guild guitars—is a thin butt block. If you drill only the larger-diameter hold for the full depth, you'll go through the butt block. You might have to glue a small ¼" plate on the inside of the block in the vicinity of the butt-peg hole to gain some extra thickness.

Unscrew the center section of the butt peg, and you're ready to solder the wiring. On a double-dot installation strip the plastic coating from the braided shielding and un-braid a short section of each wire. Trim the plastic from the center core of both cables. Twist the center cores—the signal carriers—together, then the ground shielding. They will then be soldered to the butt peg as though a single-wire job. Check out the continuity of the solder job on an amplifier or Strobotuner and you're in business. You don't have to string up the guitar for this check. Use a 440 tuning fork on the body of the guitar and the amplifier or strobe will pick this up. It'll save some labor removing the strings again if you've blown it.

ANOTHER WAY TO AMPLIFY AN ACOUSTIC GUITAR

One of my customers, Bob Farrell, was not satisfied with the sound quality produced by a transducer pickup and wanted a more natural acoustic sound such as that pro-

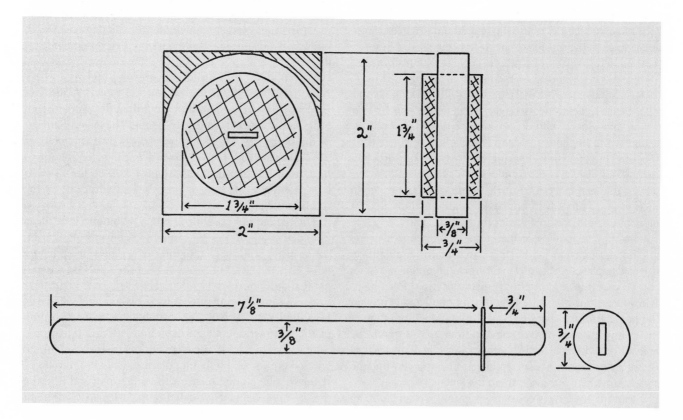

Fig. 179—Vibration–dampened mount (two needed) for a lapel microphone. The two wooden pieces needed should be cut from a soft wood such as redwood, cedar, etc. I used redwood. Use a very soft foam plastic or rubber (crosshatch-shaded area in drawing) for the shock or vibration absorbing material in the center hole. The line–shaded area is wood to be removed. The disk mounted on one end of the ³/₃₂" x ³/₈" x 7 ½" mike-mount stick may be cardboard or plastic and is tacked in place with a drop of Titebond.

duced by a microphone. He didn't want to be tied to one spot on the stage by using a microphone on a stand, however. His answer? A lapel mike mounted across the sound hole in such a manner that it wouldn't pick up any appreciable vibrations from the top itself, thus promoting feedback. My job was to design a dampened mount to eliminate the vibrations.

I used scrap redwood and a 1¾" holesaw for the job. I cut the holes first in a single piece of ¾" by 2" redwood, then split it into two pieces approximately ⅜ in thickness. I rounded off all but one side and glued nylon tape to the edges for reinforcement. The dimensions are in Figure 179.

Cut two pieces of ¾"-thick soft plastic or rubber foam into 1¾" circles and set into the 1¾" holes, tacking it to the wood in a couple of places with Titebond. Cut a ⅜" slit in the center of the plastic foam running parallel with the flat base of the blocks and glue the blocks under the face of the guitar (Figure 180) where the mike mount will cross the center of the sound hole.

The mike mount is simply a piece of hardwood ³⁄₃₂" thick by ⅜" wide and 7½" long to fit through the slits in the foam. A small circle of cardboard can be glued (see Figure 179) to the mike mount on the treble side to keep it from sliding on through the slit from the weight of the mike, or if you like, it can be tacked into place with a drop of Titebond.

Clip the mike cord and solder it to a Barcus Berry–type butt peg for a neat installation. It would be a good idea, however, to experiment with different top-quality lapel mikes before making the installation permanent. I have yet to hear the results, but Bob says it works well and wants me to do an installation on another of his instruments. I'll leave it up to you if you wish to experiment with this system.

"RED EYE" BRIDGE PINS AND SIDE MARKER DOTS

Someone is always asking me if I know where I can find some of the old Red Eye bridge pins such as those used in old Martins or where they can get position-marker dots for the edges of fingerboards.

I've used two different methods for making the dots, the first one very simple, and the results are not too bad. Punch the head of a plain bridge pin or the edge of the fingerboard with a sharp scribe or an awl to mark a center for the drill and drill out the mark with a ¹⁄₁₆" drill bit. You will have to scare up a long-shanked aircraft drill to drill the holes in the edge of the fingerboard over the top area. Brookstone stocks them.

Mix up some epoxy with the desired color and fill the drilled holes. After it sets, clean off the excess and touch up

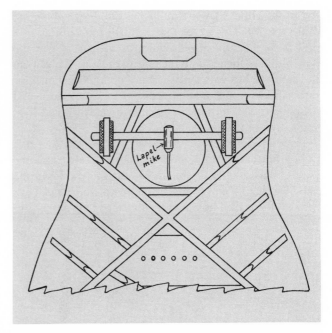

Fig. 180—Lapel mike isolation mount installed in a D–series Martin guitar. The microphone cord may be clipped and soldered into a Barcus Berry butt peg if desired.

with lacquer (fingerboard) or buff the heads of the bridge pins with jeweler's rouge to slick them up.

The second method is to punch the dots from scrap binding, old imitation-tortoise pickguards, colored plastic, etc. You will need access to a drill press and a drill-press vise for this job. The only other tools needed are a square nut, either ⅜" or ½", it doesn't really matter, and a ¹⁄₁₆" drill bit.

Set the nut in the drill-press vise so that you can rake out the punched dots and lock it tight. Clamp or bolt the drill-press vise to the drill-press table with the spindle centered over a flat side and hole in the square nut.

Grind off the shank end of the ¹⁄₁₆" drill bit or a 2" piece of ¹⁄₁₆" drill rod perfectly square. Squareness can be ensured by mounting the flute end of the drill bit in the drill-press chuck and running it at high speed against the edge of a hone laid across the drill-press table. It's important for the quality of the dots that the shank end of the drill bit or drill rod be perfectly square.

Set the shank of the bit into the chuck and drill a hole through the side of the nut into the threaded interior using a fairly slow speed. Before drilling, double-check the drill-press vise to make sure it's bolted or clamped solid to the table. Otherwise you may have an alignment problem.

Once the hole is drilled, remove the ¹⁄₁₆" drill and reverse it—or use the ¹⁄₁₆" drill rod—clamping the flutes or drill rod in the chuck's jaws. Unplug the drill-press motor; the drill press will now be used as a punch press instead of a drill press. Pull the handle down to make sure that the punch-drill is aligned with the hole in the nut. You can tap the punch lightly with a plastic hammer if the alignment is minor. When you can pull the drill-press handle down and the punch enters the hole in the nut smoothly with no drag, you're in business.

Place a piece of plastic, imitation tortoise, etc., over the drilled hole in the nut, pull the handle down until the punch makes contact with the plastic and then give the handle a sharp jerk. A perfectly formed plastic dot will fall through the drilled hole into the threaded hole of the nut.

I usually punch out several dozen dots of imitation tortoise and white and black plastic while I have the punch working to have for stock. It takes only moments to make enough to last for a year or two.

A $1/16''$-thick plastic stock seems to give the best quality dots on the $1/16''$ dots. Thicker stock will sometimes give you deformed pieces.

This drill-press–punch setup works well for $3/32$ or $1/8''$ dots, too, but you can try larger sizes at your own risk. For anything larger than $1/8''$, I generally use mother-of-pearl "ready-cut" dots.

A drop of glue in your drilled holes in fingerboards or bridge pins, and you can tap the dot in place for a snug fit.

12

Salvaging the Plywood Guitar

To salvage or not to salvage? A good question. At the prices some of the imported plywood guitars are selling for these days, many are worth salvaging. Unquestionably some of them have good to excellent sound and tonal qualities, and if the customer is happy with the over-all sound and tonal qualities, and if the repairs don't run over half the purchase price of a new one, repairing should be considered.

Then there are those received as gifts. I've put as much as seventy or eighty dollars' worth of work into an instrument that originally sold for little more than that because of the sentimental value involved. Don't get me wrong. I'm not crazy about working on some of these beasties, but the plywood guitar has become a dominant factor in guitar sales nowadays, and the inevitable repairs have to be dealt with.

Some of the imports in the more expensive price ranges have plywood only on the backs and sides and are topped with single-thickness spruce or cedar (quarter-sawed redwood). This is not too bad, if the top wood has been properly cured. The backs and sides have little or no "give" to them, being plywood, and if the top wood decides to shrink, something has to give, and it's the top that will give in the form of cracks. However, in the imports of the past few years the manufacturers seem to have a handle on this problem, and unlike some of the early instruments of this type construction, they're standing up well with proper care.

How does one tell if an instrument is plywood? Look for a foreign label to start with. Then study the grain pattern closely in a given spot on the outside of the guitar. Find an unusual sworl pattern, a knot, etc., and check the same spot inside the instrument. There should be a corresponding pattern. If not, you can safely assume that it's a veneered job.

Check the edges of the wood on the top where the sound hole has been cut out. Many companies are carefully rounding the edges of the sound holes to conceal the plies, but if you will study the edge of the sound hole immediately under the end of the fingerboard, you can usually spot three different plies. A machinist's mirror will show up a plywood top in a hurry. The grain on the outside of the top is usually a nice, tight, choice piece of spruce, but the underside of the top will usually reveal a different, coarser grain. Some of the "el cheapos" are using only two plies of wood in the tops, back, and sides. You can spot these by the grain running at a ninety-degree angle to the wood on the exterior. Forget about repairing these. They're not worth the trouble.

Also a natural-spruce top will usually transmit a certain amount of light. Aim a high-intensity light source at the top from an inch or two away and you should see a light area underneath with the mirror. A finger between the light and the top will give you a nice shadow.

Then there are exceptions. Some of the thicker, natural-spruce tops will not transmit light—and some of the plywood tops will. I'm talking about the Japanese-made Yamahas. They apparently use a spruce center core and a transparent glue to laminate the plies. You will, however, see a faint cross-grained pattern in your mirror on these. The later Yamahas are made in Taiwan and apparently use a Philippine mahogany or white luan for a center core since they do not transmit light.

There is one definite advantage to plywood among the many disadvantages: there are no body cracks from drying out to contend with. Cracks are mostly limited to the necks, fingerboards, bridges, and finishes.

Bridges are one of the major problem areas in imported instruments. So many of the imports are finished with a polyester finish (catalyzed resin similar to the gel coats on fiberglass boats) that is applied to a ridiculous thickness. I've peeled chips of finish off these that miked out to .030″ or better, about three times as much finish as necessary, and, to compound the problem, many of the factories are gluing the bridges directly to this finish instead of cleaning it off and gluing them to the wood properly (see Figures 181 and 182). I realize that this saves quite a lot of time (and money) when you're working in large volume, but it sure lays a burden on repairmen.

This finish is very brittle, almost as brittle as glass, and has a tendency to crystallize from the string vibrations.

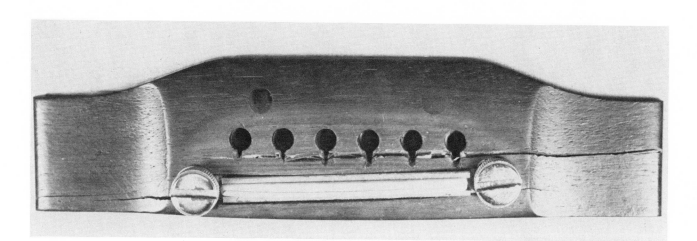

Fig. 181—What caused this bridge to crack and shift in such a manner? See the next photograph for the answer.

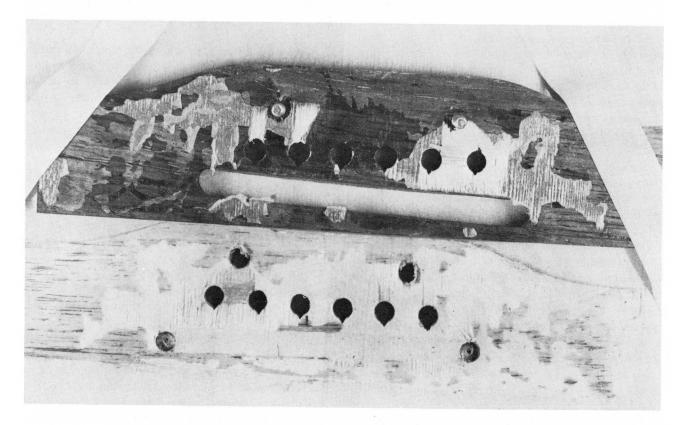

Fig. 182—Because it was glued to the finish (very thick polyester) instead of to the wood. The finish crystalized from the string vibration and turned loose. The large cutout area for the metal saddle didn't help matters, or the sound, and the replacement bridge will have a non–adjustable bone saddle in a solid wood bridge.

172

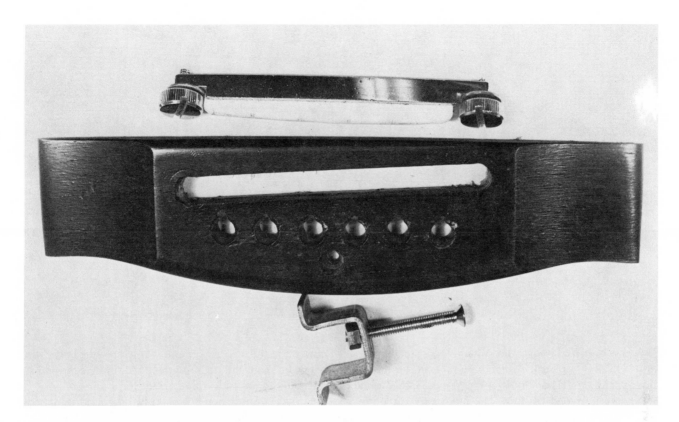

Fig. 183—A favorite with the Japanese. Notice the large cutout, metal and soft plastic saddle, and bolt with bracket. Found on many "El Cheapos". A solid, non–adjustable bridge with a bone saddle invariably improves structural strength, looks, and the sound.

Also, a sharp blow or bump in the highly stressed bridge area can crystalize the finish, and the bridge pops off. Sometimes it will take part of the finish with it or perhaps even part of the top ply of wood (see the mess in Figure 182).

Some of the cheaper models are evidently assembled with an inferior-quality glue, and poor bonding techniques are used in laminating their tops. Most of these will have a single flat-head stove bolt installed to help keep the bridge down with perhaps a fancy bracket on the underside (Figure 183) for supposed added strength.

When these turn loose, they may take more than one ply of wood with them. It is usually impossible to glue the splinters back satisfactorily, and the only alternative is to clean out the area and graft in a piece of spruce to replace the missing wood. In these cases I generally make a new, redesigned bridge, designed ⅛" larger all the way around, and use two flat-head stove bolts with washers to hold it down. I seldom if ever guarantee my work on these jobs.

Heat really wreaks havoc with these cheapies, too. Most of the interior glue work is done with an inexpensive white glue that turns loose almost instantly upon exposure to heat. The struts pull loose, the ridiculous soft-plywood bridge plate shifts, the bridge splits and pulls loose or shifts (Figure 184), and the whole top bellies up, perhaps even pulling the retaining bolt or bolts through the bridge plate and the top. I have nightmares about some of these beasties.

Can they be repaired? Yes—if the customer insists and is willing to pay for it. I remove the strings and bridge and use my bridge-plate heater (see the disassembly and reassembly chapter of this volume) to remove the Mickey Mouse bridge plates. Next I use a small, thin spatula (Volume I, page 140, Figure 119) to locate any loose struts. You will almost inevitably find the main x braces (copied from Martin by most Japanese manufacturers) loose in the area of the bridge and the first tone bar loose where it meets the x-brace—possibly a half-dozen others, too.

Any loose braces should have glue injected under them and then be clamped back in place. Many times these can be reached with the cam clamps via the sound hole, but if not, use the strut jacks and outside cam clamps to pull these into place. Regluing the loose struts should take care of most of the top bellying.

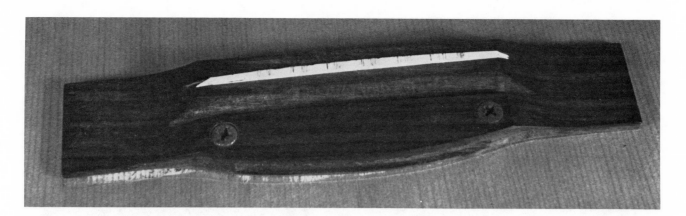

Fig. 184—A "heat treated" Japanese guitar. Even with the two retaining bolts, this bridge has shifted nearly 3/16" on the bass side. Note how the strings have embedded into the plastic saddle. The customer was lucky that the top laminations (plywood top) didn't separate.

A new oversized bridge plate should take care of the rest of it. Do not—I repeat, *do not*—use plywood for the new bridge plate. Use a good quarter-sawed piece of hardwood, preferably rosewood for this. The process for installing a new bridge plate is thoroughly described in the text and pictorial layouts of Volume I, starting on page 141, and I will not repeat it here. However, if you tore up the plywood in removing the old bridge plate, I would seriously consider epoxying in the new bridge plate.

Now that we have the top reasonably flat, the next step is the contact area where the bridge is glued to the instrument face. Have you lost some wood? Are the plies loose? Has the area been finished over?

If the wood is all there but some of the plies are loose, inject glue under them with a hypodermic syringe, cover with a piece of thin plastic or waxed paper, and apply a clamping pad that will cover the complete loose area. Use two or three clamps and pull them down tight until the glue cures.

Should some wood be missing, say more than 10 percent, clean out the missing area and graft in a scrap of spruce to give a level glue surface for the bridge. Any finish under the bridge's glue area *should be cleaned down to the bare wood*.

Now for the bridge itself. What condition is the old bridge in? Does it have a large cutout for an adjustable saddle? Is it cracked or badly warped?

A cracked bridge should be used only as a drilling pattern for the pin holes and then thrown away. I have yet to glue a cracked bridge satisfactorily. Because stress warped the wood, it will almost invariably crack again. The best thing to do is make a new one, particularly if the top was in really bad shape. It's best to make the new one a solid, nonadjustable one with a bone saddle and add an eighth of an inch

of wood to the original contour—at least to the butt of the bridge for more glue area. A solid bottom where the adjustment cutout was adds considerable glue area too.

For added insurance I position two flat-head stove bolts behind the pin holes, lined up between the first and second and the fifth and sixth pins. You should use a thin, flat washer under each nut and a drop of Loctite on the threads before installing. This will ensure that the nuts do not vibrate loose. Cover the heads of the stove bolts with pearl dots or matching wooden plugs.

Nearly all the bridge saddles on the imports nowadays are soft plastic, on both the adjustable and the nonadjustable saddles, and a bone saddle will give a definite improvement to the sound.

A compensated saddle makes a whale of a difference, too. I rebridged a Madeira (Guild's import line) with a fully compensated bridge, and the customer nearly dropped the instrument the first time he played it. It was destined for a knockabout instrument, but he changed his mind and is using it now for recording sessions. It really livened up the old plywood top!

Another major problem area on the imports is the neck. Shoddy fret work (some real nasty), tension rods that don't work properly (though they're getting better), cheap machine heads, hollow plastic nuts (Figure 185), and the next topic for discussion, the neck-to-body joint.

Several brands—the Epiphone pictured in the photos and drawings for one—have a massive neck block with a rectangular cutout where the butt end of the neck is held in place with four huge wood screws. This setup has its advantages and disadvantages. Tapered shims may be used to raise and lower the angle of the neck-to-body relationship or to correct any string-action problems easily. The screws must be checked periodically to ensure tightness, however. I've

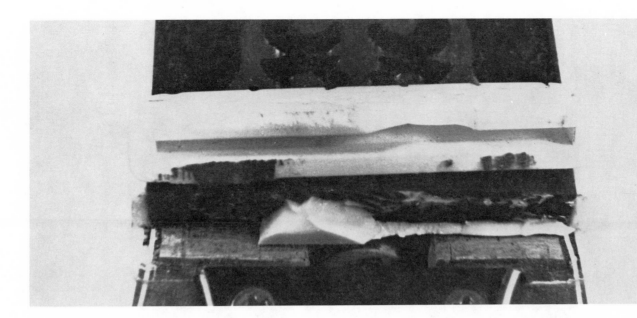

Fig. 185—A hollow plastic nut found on many imports. These have a bad habit of collapsing completely if the instrument is exposed to heat. Replace with bone or ivory.

had quite a few, actually too many, strip out the screw holes.

Stripped threads in the wood are not too difficult to repair. Drill the hole out larger and dowel, then redrill the proper size for the *center core* of the screw. Use your calipers and mike the diameter of the core between the screw's threads. Never drill a screw hole smaller than the core diameter unless you are working with very soft wood.

A Q&D way to repair stripped screw holes is to wax the screw carefully with beeswax, mix up some epoxy, and stuff the hole full of epoxy and steel wool. Screw in the screw, with the neck off of the body, and leave until the epoxy *starts* to set up. Remove the screw *before* it sets hard, or it may be almost impossible to remove. If you do forget to remove the screw until the glue has set and it wasn't waxed well enough to remove easily, heat up your soldering iron and apply heat to the screw where it enters the wood until it will back out. I prefer to plug and drill rather than use the epoxy–steel-wool method, but I've used it a time or two on some real cheapies.

One major problem with the screw-on neck is that, after the neck cutout is made in the neck block, there is only a quarter-inch or less of the block on each side of the cutout left glued to the top and usually less at the end near the sound hole. Of course, the sides of the instrument meet at the outer end of the block, and the back is glued to the bottom of the block—supposedly. I say supposedly because in nearly every one that I have repaired there is a gap between the bottom of the block and the back. Instead of ta-

pering the block to fit the slope of the back, they apparently just cut it off square and only about a quarter- to a half-inch of the bottom of the block is glued to the back. To make matters worse, a back strut runs across the back so close to the block that it is impossible to fill this gap with a wooden wedge or even work it full of epoxy glue.

The neck block breaks loose from the top, and the block pivots down against the back, resulting in an action height high enough to stick a broom handle between the fingerboard and the strings at the body. Bad news.

It can, however, be repaired if the owner has the presence of mind to detune the instrument immediately. Perhaps you have seen an old Fender flattop guitar. They use this style of neck block (glued properly to the back, though) and evidently had the problem of the block breaking loose even with the properly glued block. For added reinforcement they ran a length of composition tubing between the neck block and butt block. This "monkey bar" is adjustable down inside the body (at the butt) with the proper wrench.

I've repaired a few of these by using a length of aluminum tubing slipped over a piece of threaded Ready Rod as an adjustment feature and leaving it in place. Then I tried it on a Japanese-made twelve-string Ephiphone. Six months later it was back in my shop with the neck block shifted again—plus a shifted butt block. There had to be another way. Although I don't guarantee structural work on plywood instruments, I still hate to see one that I have worked on come back in with the same problem.

A partial solution would be more glue area where the top

Fig. 186—A major problem with Japanese bolt–on necks. The neck block has broken loose from the top on this Japanese Epiphone (common occurrence) allowing it to shift and causing the top to buckle. The plywood has started to separate (see arrows).

Fig. 187—The top has separated from the neck block (shown by arrows) and the block has shifted toward the soundhole. The customer was lucky. I've had to deal with shifts measuring as much as 3/16" or more.

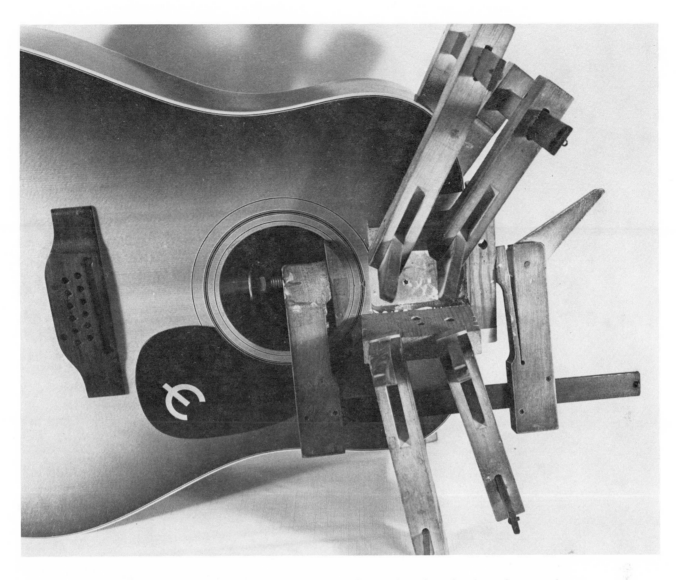

Fig. 188—A complicated setup. The aluminum tubing and Ready Rod jack (inside guitar) has pushed the neck block back into position and the two pairs of cam clamps and blocks have pulled the top back down against the neck block on each side. The fifth cam clamp is used with a contoured redwood caul to pull the crushed area of the top back in place.

was glued to the neck block. First, however, the neck block has to be pulled, or pushed, back into its original position and reglued.

Remove the strings, the plastic plate covering the screw holes on the back of the guitar (Epiphone), then the screws holding the neck itself. The closeup photo (Figure 187) will show you what to expect when the neck is removed. The "monkey bar" or jack (Figures 188 and 189) is slipped inside the guitar, and the nut is screwed against the tubing until the block is pushed back in place where it can be glued. See Figure 188 for the clamping setup.

After gluing, the jack is removed, and two pieces of ¾″

quarter-round (get it from your local lumberyard or make your own) are cut and glued into place as shown in the drawings in Figure 190. These two quarter-round gussets will give you approximately 3.75 square inches more contact area against the top and the same against the sides of the neck block. Try to get as near perfect a fit as possible. You will have to scrape out the old glue squeeze-out to fit the blocks poperly. Use a mirror to check the fit before gluing. A piece of masking tape or a curved rod will hold the corner blocks in place while you are checking the fit. Use epoxy to glue them in, and turn the instrument upside down while gluing them in place. They will stay in place

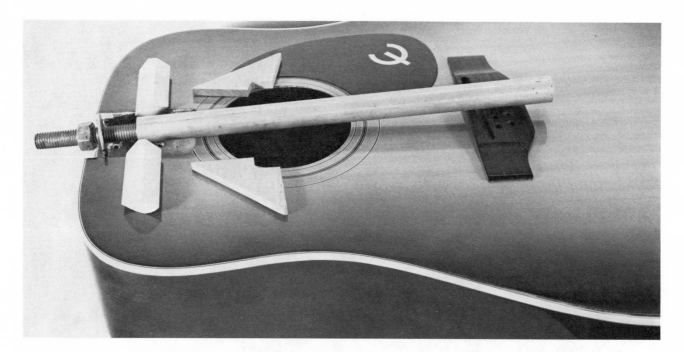

Fig. 189—*The neck block jack (pictured) and clamps have been removed and reinforcing corner blocks and knee braces have been cut, fitted, and are ready to glue in place. When the reinforcements are glued in, as in the next series of drawings, the instrument is ready for reassembly.*

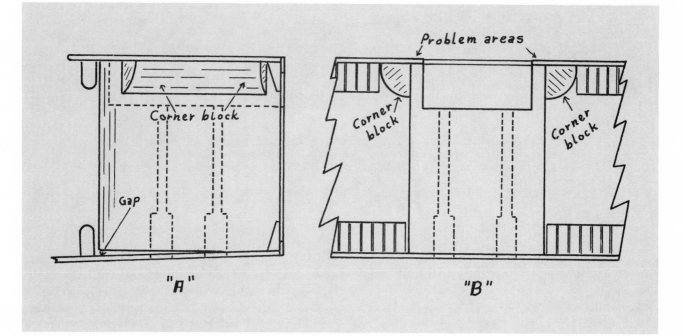

Fig. 190—*"A" shows the cutaway side view of a Japanese bolt–on neck setup (Epiphone layout here). I glue in a length of ¾" quarter–round on each side of the neck block to reinforce this area. The gap between the bottom of the neck block and the back is the problem area. See the next two figures for cures. "B" pictures the cutaway end view showing the location of the pieces of quarter–round.*

178

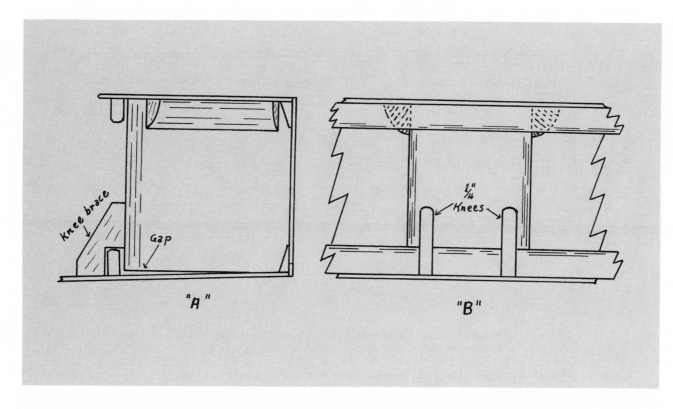

Fig. 191—One way to reinforce the back–to–neck block (gap) problem. Side view in "A" and inside end view is shown in "B". The knees are cut from hardwood such as Honduras mahogany.

then without clamping; it's almost impossible to clamp them satisfactorily in such an awkward location.

For added reinforcement (overkill, perhaps, but I have yet to have a job returned with this technique) I add a pair of ¼" knees (Figure 191) between the inside end of the neck block and the back. This is better explained by the drawings than with words, so I'll just mention that a portion of the paper label (on the Epiphone) should be cut away so that the bottom of the knee will make contact with the back wood rather than the paper when epoxied into place. The main problem in fitting the knees is that the angle between the back and the block is not square (the original problem). A piece of cardboard can be trimmed until it fits the angle and used as a template to make the knees. Be sure you get as near perfect a fit as possible and glue them in.

An alternate method to fill the gap between the neck block and back, particularly if it's a bad one, would be to plug the four holes in the back, along the edges of the neck block, and the gap between the back strut and the edge of the block with children's modeling clay (Figure 192).

Mix up a couple of ounces of casting plastic (available at most hobby shops) and pour it into the gap between the back strut and the neck block. Pour it full, clear up to the top of the strut, let the plastic set, and clean out the mod-

eling clay. Although this is one method that I haven't tried yet, when used in combination with the quarter-round gussets, I see no reason why it shouldn't work as well as or better than the knees.

This technique, the gussets and knees, seems to handle even the stress of twelve strings, although I do recommend silk-and-steel strings with "D" tuning, to be on the safe side.

Another problem that can be a holy terror to handle on plywood instruments is impact damage. Of course, an impact that would crack a single-thickness box might do little more than "star" the finish on a plywood job, but when it is hit hard enough to go through the plywood, that's bad news.

In most cases it's impossible to push an impacted area back in place on plywood as is usually possible with single-thickness impacted areas. The center, cross-grained ply is usually shattered into matchwood or torn in such a way that it is impossible to realign the splinters where the inside and outside plies will flatten out normally.

There are two approaches to this problem. If the outside ply can be trimmed away with a scalpel or razor blade reasonably intact, the center and inside plies may sometimes be realigned and the splinters glued flat enough to where the outside veneer can be grafted back into place. This out-

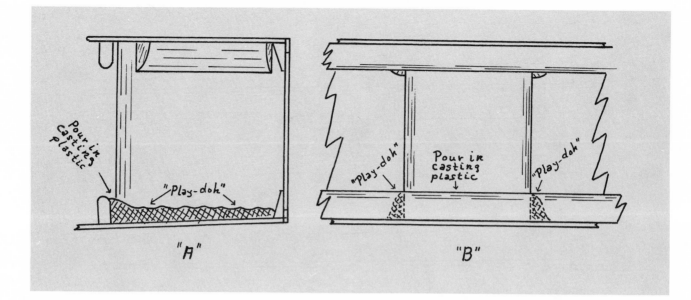

"A"   "B"

Fig. 192—An alternate method of repairing the gap problem. Plug the four neck retaining screw holes, the gaps at the bottom side edges of the neck block, and the small area between the neck block and strut at each side of the block with "Play-doh" or modeler's clay and pour in catalyzed casting plastic to fill the gap under the neck block and between the neck block and back strut.

side ply is usually pretty thin, however, and the odds are against this method. Most of the time you will end up doing a graft.

If you chose to graft in new wood, the first order of business is clearing away the shattered area. An impact will separate the plies to a certain extent away from the immediate impacted area and these will have to be reglued. One method is to slip the tip of a hypodermic needle in between the plies and inject them full of Titebond. Another method that I now use more frequently is the water-thin cyanoacrylate Hot Stuff. It will penetrate into the finest hairline separations when applied to the edges of the trimmed-out hole. Tiny modeler's clamps padded with polyethylene plastic to prevent gluing the clamps to the wood can be used through the hole to clamp the plies. The first application—possibly even the second or third—will sink into the plies from capillary action. Clamp quickly and allow a half-hour or so to cure.

When the area is solid, the hole can be backed for added strength (Volume I, page 149, Figure 129), and a piece of hardwood matched as near as possible to the grain and coloration of the exterior ply is fitted and grafted into place.

Badly bowed necks are a common problem with many of the imports, particularly the "el cheapo" models without tension rods. Most of the instruments have an adjustable rod of some sort, however. It's probably better in the long run not to mess with badly bowed necks on the cheapies

because it will usually cost more than they are worth to try to repair them. One of the full-length, commercially available fingerboard heaters could be tried, but if it didn't work satisfactorily, you could always hang the instrument on the wall with a plastic posy in the sound hole as a conversation piece.

If the guitar has an adjustable tension rod, adjust as much of the bow out as possible, then if it still isn't right, forget it or use the string tension simulation jig and do a plane and fret.

Nuts are a big problem on the imports. They are almost invariably a cheap, soft plastic, although I've run into some hard plastic ones that weren't too bad. The hard ones are prone to chipping, though. The soft ones wear rapidly and many are actually hollow (Figure 185). Any exposure to heat, and they promptly collapse. These are generally found in combination with a fret nut or "zero fret" and used only as a string spacer. The fret nut is a satisfactory (inexpensive) way of setting the nut action, but if the strings have to be raised or lowered, the only way is to file the zero fret down, or if a higher nut action is needed, replace it with a higher fret. In other words, I consider the zero fret a copout.

One potential problem to watch for here is the string-to-zero-fret angle. I have in some instances cut the spacing slots in the plastic nuts below the wood and grooved the wood slightly to obtain a steep-enough angle to the zero fret to stop an open-string buzz on the zero fret. This problem occurs primarily on nylon-strung instruments, however, and is seldom encountered with steel strings. The zero fret will have to be watched for string grooving on the steel stringers and replaced periodically when worn.

In a great majority of the jobs, whether a zero-fret setup or the traditional nut setup, I go ahead and replace the plastic nut with a bone one. The harder material does not have the dampening effect of the softer plastic with the traditional-type nut, and the bone nut—saddle, too—will give you better sound conduction.

There's another problem that is encountered occasionally, one unique to the plywood instruments—buzzes that crop up with no apparent reason. I hunted for the cause on one off and on for a week before I finally pinned it down to a loose ply in the belly area. The makers evidently missed gluing a spot approximately four inches square when they laminated the top. I ended up slipping a sharp-pointed scalpel through the top ply and injecting it full of Titebond with a hypodermic needle, then touching up the finish.

The water-thin cyanoacrylate glue should work very well for something like this, too, with its fantastic capillary action, and the next one I run into will get this treatment.

Major string-action adjustments are too common and are covered in respective chapters of both volumes. Problems with machine heads, also too common are covered in the miscellaneous chapter, and that's all I have to say on these beasties.

13

More on Pearl Inlay

I don't have a lot of material to add to this chapter; most of my pearl-inlay technique remains the same as that outlined in Volume I. I do have a quick alternative to using dyed epoxy for seating pearl-inlay pieces that works just as well—perhaps better, since it's faster. It takes minutes instead of the hours necessary for the epoxy to cure thoroughly.

After cutting out the fingerboard for the inlay and fitting it to make sure it seats properly, remove the inlay, flow a couple of drops of cyanoacrylate glue onto the bottom of the cutout, replace the pearl quickly, and press it down for a minute or two. It should be bonded in place. File the pearl down level to the surrounding wood and blow out all of the pearl dust.

Take a scrap of wood—ebony for an ebony fingerboard, etc.—and sand off some fine dust with 320-grit Wetordry sandpaper. Pack the fine sanding dust around the inlay, filling any descrepancy left from fitting the inlay. Flow the water-thin cyanoacrylate into this fine dust (in a ventilated work area) and let it set up. There may be some minor "smoking" as the cyanoacrylate cures, which will take five to ten minutes. Cut it down with a fine-mill bastard file and take a look. Duplicate the treatment on any pinholes that might be left. File level, sand smoother with the wood grain, and wax, or finish over on a peg-head inlay. The filled area will be practically invisible in ebony, slightly more visible in rosewood.

The cyanoacrylate trick is invaluable when working with an antique instrument where the pearl may be loose or badly cracked up, such as on the border pearl on the old 40-series Martins. Through the years the original glue used to seal the pearl in place deteriorates to a certain degree, and if you should have to strip the finish from one of these for refinishing, you may end up with all kinds of missing pearl chips.

My technique for these is to carefully scrape the finish off the border pearl, or use a small-mill bastard file, then flow the water-thin cyanoacrylate glue over all the border pearl and the purfling on either side of the pearl. The first application will sink out of sight as it flows into all the nooks and crannies and will require a second or third application before you get a surface build. File or sand it level, and the pearl and purfling will be as solid as the day it was originally glued into place, safe to sand without worry over losing any abalone or pearl ships.

This works for sealing down fingerboard inlays in these oldies, too, particularly if the instrument is old enough to have had the pearl bedded in hide glue. You can fill in any missing filler with sanding dust and seal the whole mess down with Hot Stuff or other water-thin cyanoacrylate glue.

Another major problem that you may encounter on some of the oldies—some of the original Washburns, for instance—is the engraving in the mother-of-pearl inlays. I wish I had one of these to work on at the present for photographic purposes, but the sketches I've made from one (Figure 193) will show you what I'm talking about. A certain shape of inlay will look rather plain, but with a few simple engraving lines the simplest patterns take on a new character, and engraving is not all that hard to do in pearl.

I use three types of small gravers, as shown in Figures 194 and 195. The "knife"-shaped graver I use for wide (.030″) lines, such as engraving a name plate. The multiple (twelve lines) line graver is useful for "crosshatch" and fill-in work, but perhaps the most useful one is the square or "diamond-shaped" graver. It is used for most single-line work and comes in several sizes. The one that I purchased is a #3, the smallest (.100″) the supplier had in stock. I made a smaller (.080″ square) one from a square needle file by breaking the pointed tip off, leaving it about 4″ long, and honed (Figure 196) to a graver configuration that is my favorite.

If you like, you can check your local library for a book on the fine points of engraving; I will be discussing only the rudiments here. Check your telephone book for a jeweler's supply or talk to your local jeweler about a source for the gravers and special handles. Better yet, if you talk nicely and explain that you're not going into competition with him, the jeweler might be inclined to demonstrate some

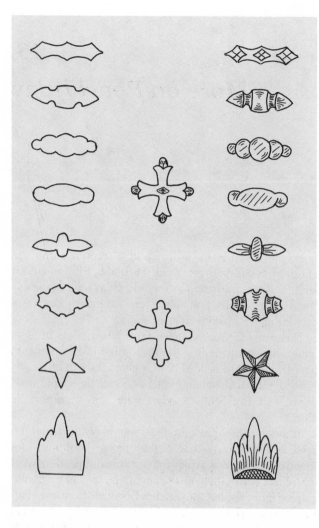

basic techniques, which is all you need for engraving in pearl. It's much easier to learn by watching or doing than by reading.

Sharpening the graver properly is one of the major secrets in engraving. Jewelers use special-degreed holding tools to hone the proper angles on the gravers, but for occasional work they are an added expense that you can skip. I "eyeball"-sharpen mine, and they work well. It may not be exactly professional, but. . . .

The beveled ends of the gravers are ground to around a 45- to 50-degree angle as shown in Figure 197, section "B". The bottom edge of all but the multiple lining graver (it would destroy the lines) is honed to a 5-degree angle for a short distance, as shown in "C" of Figure 197. This is to prevent too much "bite" when the tool is held at an angle to the workpiece and also to allow you to "rock" the handle down to control the depth of the cut and to end the cut.

After the bottoms of the tools are honed to the correct angles, subsequent sharpenings are limited to the honing of the 45- to 50-degree angle only. You can usually tell a person who engraves for a living by the mutilated thumbnail (Figure 198) caused by testing the graver's sharpness. When it digs into the thumbnail from its own weight instead of skidding over it, it's sharp enough to use.

Now we are down to the actual engraving. In normal engraving of jewelry and other small pieces, the workpiece is held in a special vise mounted on a heavy metal ball

Fig. 193—Relatively simple patterns of mother–of–pearl appear to take on a new exotic dimension with a few simple engraving lines. Take this turn–of–the–century Washburn pattern for instance. They don't look like much before engraving. The center cross came from the guitar's peghead.

Fig. 194—Macrophotograph of the bottom (cutting edges) view of three jeweler's gravers with a steel rule for perspective. The heavy line graver on the left is for engraving names, fine "wriggle" patterns, etc.; a fine line graver is in the center; and a multiple (12 line) lining graver is on the right.

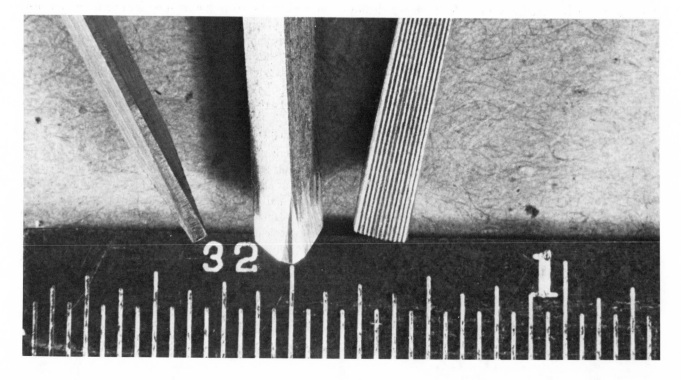

which rests in a leather "doughnut." The graver is held stationary against the workpiece, and the workpiece is rotated into the graver's cutting edge. However, on a large workpiece such as an inlaid fingerboard, this is impossible. The procedure must be reversed. I use one hand to hold and push the graver, using the thumb or a finger of the other hand to steady and guide the tool. Experiment around until you find a position that is comfortable to you.

I would suggest that you try your hand on a piece of scrap aluminum or brass first, then try it on a scrap of mother-of-pearl for the "feel" of things before trying an actual inlay on a guitar fingerboard. Get the technique down pat first. It's difficult to remove and replace a piece of fingerboard inlay if you mess it up.

Anytime you have to work down a fingerboard with engraved pearl pieces, *be sure* you make sketches of the engraving work or, better yet, trot it over to your local library or anyone with a xerox machine and xerox an exact pattern. Make a couple of patterns while you're at it and keep them on file for future reference.

I lay out all the main lines of the engraving first, using a soft-leaded draftsman's pencil sanded to a fine point. Cut out the lines with the graver, then lay out the detail and fill-in lines and do them. Of course, you can "eyeball" the engraving if you wish, but I find it much easier to follow pencil lines on the white pearl, for it's hard to see the fine lines, and if they have been penciled first, you just remove the pencil lines with the tool. I do eyeball the use of the multiple-line graver for fill-in and crosshatch work.

The angle of attack of the graver to the workpiece, usually 10 to 20 degrees, will control the depth of the cut. If you need a wide line or are doing a "wriggle" pattern, use the wide-tipped knife-shaped graver. Make the cut shallow, sharp-cornered, and clean. It needs to be only deep enough to take the filler used to bring out the pattern.

For a "wriggle" pattern (see Figure 195), hold the graver at about a 45- or 50-degree angle to the workpiece and apply downward pressure until you feel the tool "bite." The tip is then "walked" along the layout line, working the handle from side to side in a semicircular motion. One corner bites in while the opposite corner is advanced half the width of the cutting edge. Then the handle is angled over until that corner bites, and the opposite corner is walked forward. Once you have started the wriggle pattern, continue until the line is completed. It's rather difficult to stop and restart the pattern without it showing. It can be done, but you have to set the tool very carefully in the last cut to maintain the continuity of the pattern. You might try this pattern on a piece of soft aluminum with a ⅛" wood chisel instead of the graver to get the feel, and you can see what you're doing with the larger tool. Once you get the hang of it, try the smaller graver on the aluminum, then graduate to a scrap of pearl. The feel of the pearl is completely different from that of metal, and it takes practice to

Fig. 195—Macrophotograph showing a sample of the types of lines each can do in a scrap of pearl. Note the "wriggle" pattern and wide line cut by the wide graver. You will find this pattern used a lot on metal banjo parts, and it looks nice for bordering plain pearl block inlays. The engraved lines have been filled with Lacquer-Stik to bring out the lines.

do a good job. Once you get the feel, it's a snap, easier to engrave in pearl than in metal.

This "wriggle" pattern is used a lot on engraved tone rings and tension hoops on fancy banjos. It's the squiggly-looking lines that run around the circumference rather than a plain line, and it looks nice for bordering plain square and rectangular pearl-block-type fingerboard inlay pieces.

185

Fig. 196—*My favorite diamond (square) graver that I made from a 5/64" square needle file with a commercial graver handle. Note the "mushroom" shape and flat bottom on the handle.*

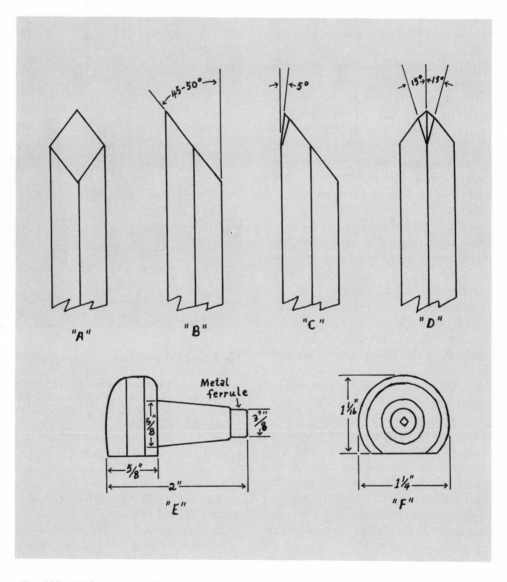

Fig. 197—*Making a graver from a square needle file. The same system of sharpening applies to any of the commercial diamond (square) gravers. Drawings "A" and "B" show the preliminary honing of the end. Drawings "C" and "D" show the finishing touches to the working edge. The angles are important for the graver to work properly. Drawings "E" and "F" show the dimensions of a comfortable handle. These may be purchased from a jeweler's supply. If you make yours, remember to flatten the bottom of the "mushroom" handle for working clearance, and insert the graver where the working edge centers on the flattened part.*

186

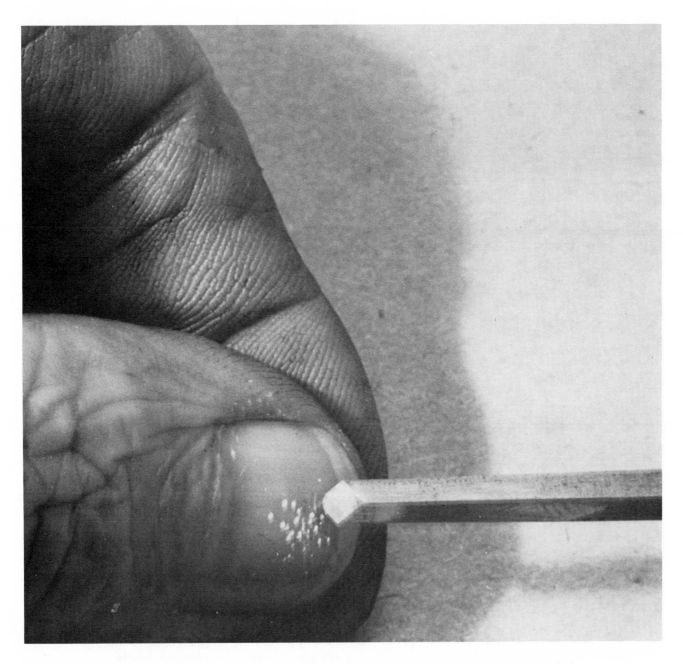

Fig. 198—When the edge of the graver digs into your thumbnail from its own weight instead of skidding across it, your graver is sharpened properly. A mutilated thumbnail is the mark of many professional engravers from testing the edges of their gravers.

For single-line detail or fill-in work I use the square- or "diamond"-style graver. You can make several kinds of cuts with this tool. Start out with a shallow cut, and you have a fine line. Increase the angle of attack and the line is deeper, appearing wider when filled, and you can end the cut abruptly by digging the cutting edge in for a "fat" square butt on the line, or you can rock the handle of the tool down to end the cut with a fine line. This graver makes a

v-bottomed cut and needs little depth to take the filler, and a shallow cut will give you a finer, more classy-appearing job. Again, experiment on a scrap before working on an instrument.

After the engraving is completed, the lines are "brought out" by filling them with a contrasting (usually black) color. One way is with waterproof India ink. Usually a product such as the Lacquer-Stik manufactured by Lake Chemical

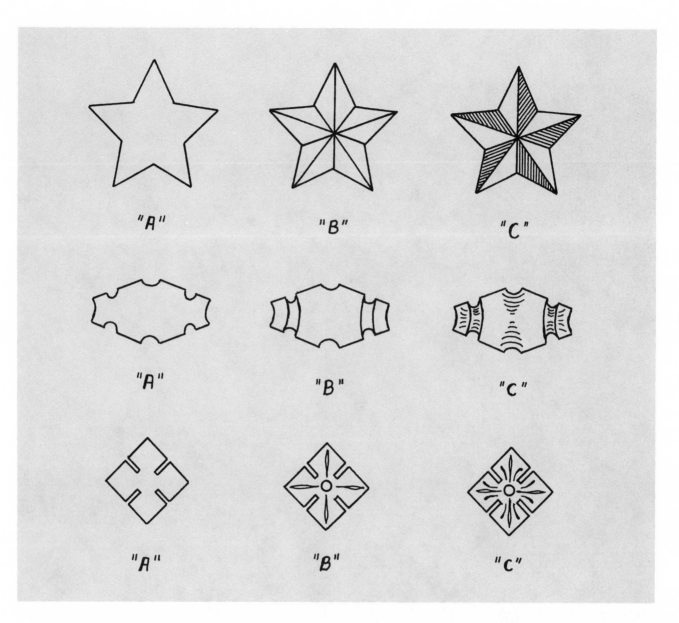

Fig. 199—Any of these pieces, including the ones in Figure 193, can be done with a single diamond graver such as the one I made from a needle file or a small commercial one. "A's" represent the inlays smoothed down on a fingerboard. Select, lay out, and engrave the major, heavier lines first as in the "B's". Follow with the light fill–in lines as shown in the "C's". The star and barrel end up with a three–dimensional aspect, and even the lowly slotted square becomes an exotic snowflake.

Company (3052 W. Carrol Avenue, Chicago, Illinois) is rubbed over the engraving lines (Figure 195), then wiped off. Your local jeweler might have some of this. In a pinch you can use black enamel or lacquer. Apply the color with a fine artist's brush, allow to dry, and sand the surface clean with fine (600-grit Wetordry) sandpaper.

Whichever method you use to fill the lines, sand lightly to clean off any of the excess color from the surface of the pearl, then heavily wax the fingerboard. If you are working on a headstock inlay, seal and finish normally instead of waxing.

With practice it's not too difficult to do a credible job of engraving, and you can add class to an otherwise plain inlay job. Once you have learned the technique, it's a lot like riding a bicycle or swimming. It's not easily forgotten. You have to practice a bit after laying off for a while, but the technique is still with you. Have fun.

14.

More on Finishing and Refinishing

There's not much to add to this chapter; I covered it pretty thoroughly in Volume I. I've had to discontinue major finishing work because of a long-developing sensitivity to the materials used. I can no longer handle the severe headaches and have had to give up experimenting along this line.

Let this be a word of warning from my experience:—*always use a chemical respirator when working with finishes of any kind*. I spent two years mixing and matching automotive lacquers for an auto supply and didn't think anything of breathing the fumes. Of course, mixing paints is a far cry from spraying them, but, as I understand it, the effects are cumulative.

I was careless after I started working on guitars too. On a small spot job with an airbrush, etc., I seldom bothered to put on my mask. Then, having only a small shop, I had these refinish jobs hanging around the shop bleeding fumes for several days after spraying. It got to the point where I would lose a day after spraying an instrument with a severe, almost migrainelike headache. The problem has now advanced to where I can no longer even use spray-type deodorants. Take a tip from my experience and *always use a respirator when working with finishes*. I wouldn't wish these headaches on my worst enemy.

That's enough about my personal problems. I do have a couple of tips and ideas for simplifying some of your touch-up problems and perhaps even eliminating some of them.

How many times have you had to refinish a small area of an instrument such as a head facing? The job is relatively simple if the head is faced with plastic, ebony, or other nonporous material. Seal, color-coat (black-faced Gibsons, etc.), and finish coats. Perhaps a week's down time allowing for sealer and finish-coat drying time. Increase that to ten days on rosewood and other porous materials requiring a fill job before you can start on the sealer.

This can be cut to *one day* from the bare wood to the spraying of the finish coats. Of course, you have to allow a few days before wet-sanding and polishing, but my technique still cuts the time involved by half, and even more on the porous woods.

Cyanoacrylate glue is the secret. Sand the wood smooth as for regular refinishing. You should graft in new wood to replace any of the larger missing chips, but small dents and chips can be filled with sanding dust to level them off. If you have several small filled spots, soak them with the water-thin cyanoacrylate first. This will penetrate the sanding dust and solidify them in place. Sand flush to the bare wood.

Use a fine Wetordry sandpaper for this, 320- or 400-grit, and work carefully so that you don't get the glue on the back of the sandpaper and stick it to your fingers. The glue will not penetrate the Wetordry backing, however, and I suggest working on a piece of scrap to get the feel of it before trying a head facing. Don't get too ambitious and try to do the whole head at one time. Apply a couple of drops of the cyanoacrylate and sand it into a small area, then spread out, working a square inch or so at a time until you have gone over the whole head facing.

Let this first application dry for fifteen or twenty minutes (you should be in a well-ventilated area because the fumes, though nontoxic, will irritate your eyes), then switch to one of the thicker cyanoacrylates. Go over the workpiece again, then a third time as soon as the second coat is dry to the (careful) touch. Let dry for an hour and block-sand with a small cork or wooden sanding block and 320-grit Wetordry. Work with the paper *dry*.

After everything is level, blow off the dust and check the surface closely for pinholes and bare wood where you might have sanded through. If you still have bad spots, repeat with another double coat of cyanoacrylate and resand. You should remove as much of the cyanoacrylate as possible without going through into the wood.

If the wood is smooth and filled this time, apply more cyanoacrylate and "polish" it down with the *smooth back* of the Wetordry sandpaper. This final coat should be very thin and smooth if you work fast and should require little sanding to level any high spots. Sand only enough to remove any shiny spots. Scuff it with 00 steel wool, and you are ready for the decal, color coat, and finish lacquer. Quick and simple.

Sealing or filling is not necessary; the cyanoacrylate takes care of that. And the finish lacquer will dry much faster since the lacquer solvents will not penetrate the cyanoacrylate into the wood as with standard fillers and sealers. A couple of days to dry and cure, and you can wet-sand the finish and buff to a beautiful luster.

Any of you who have repaired and finished broken heads, necks, etc., have experienced the next problem. You get a beautiful glue job and a nice smooth spot job over the broken area, and the customer is ecstatic with the results. But within a few weeks or months the finish shrinks into the glue line, and the repair job shows up perfectly as a sunken line in the finish.

The cure? Remember what I said about lacquer solvents not penetrating cyanoacrylate glue? Right. I usually glue a broken head or neck with Titebond, a water-soluble glue. After the clamps are removed, clean up the glue mess and wash the glue line with a damp rag to clean out the glue below the surface of the finish. Allow to dry thoroughly and sand the area smooth. Don't worry if you go through the finish in a spot or two to level the repaired area, because the next step will take care of that. Sand in a couple of drops of cyanoacrylate over the finish and all. It may take several applications to get a surface build over the repair and surrounding finish.

Allow to dry for an hour and sand smoother. If there are any irregularities left, sand some more and apply more cyanoacrylate. Do this until the glue build is over the repaired area and the surrounding finish. The final coat should be smoothed out with the back of the Wetordry sandpaper as mentioned earlier, then scuffed good with 00 steel wool.

On a natural-finished neck you might want to use a little alcohol-mix aniline dye to stain any light areas. This doesn't take too well on the cyanoacrylate, and you might have to apply and wipe lightly with a soft rag several times to blend it out before applying the finish lacquer. Again, if you haven't tried working with cyanoacrylate in this manner, experiment on a cheapie or a piece of scrap to get the feel.

A lot of my broken heads are on Gibsons or other instruments with the cutout for tension rod adjustments. Many of these are shaded or "sunburst"-finished. You can use a lacquer the color of the darker shade and shade in or darken the repaired area until the repair is no longer visible, then top the shaded area with clear lacquer.

After it is cured, wet-sanded, and polished, the repair is invisible and will remain so because the finish will not shrink into the cyanoacrylate-sealed glue line. I've seen several that I've repaired in this manner a year later with no visible evidence of the repair. Talk about happy customers.

How about sealing the whole instrument with cyanoacrylate? It's possible, I guess. The largest area I've ever tried was an old spruce top before finishing much the same as sealing with the alcohol-epoxy mixture mentioned in the

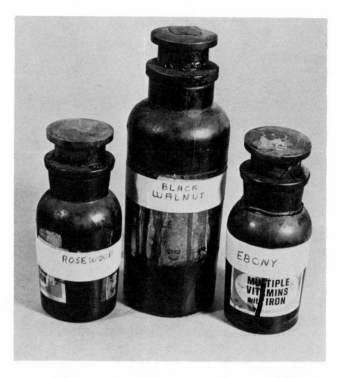

Fig. 200—Old multiple vitamin bottles with the push-on plastic caps are great for storing aniline dye stains. A small amount of dye can be poured into the cap for convenience during minor brush staining on touchup work. It sure beats trying to dip a tiny brush into a deep bottle.

finishing chapter of Volume I. This blamed allergy has put the quietus to further experimenting along that line, but if any of you wish to experiment, more power to you.

Since most of this chapter is on spot work etc., I would like to pass along another idea involving pick-scratched bare spots in guitar tops. These can be nasty to do any minor brush touch-up work on because of the character of the spruce tops. You have areas of soft wood in between the hard grain, and a flat pick will dig this out and leave most of the hard grain. On the worst areas (I've seen spots dug all the way through a top) you might have to do a graft job or replace the top.

A reasonably neat job of touch-up could be done on the minor spots if the grime could be cleaned out without sanding a deep hole. My solution is an Eraser Stick (Figure 201) typewriter eraser, the one that has a wooden shell around the rubber eraser and a brush on one end. It can be sharpened in a regular pencil sharpener. The rubber contains a very mild abrasive and can be used to "erase" the dirt and grime right out of the wood and leave the area smooth (it's also good for polishing electrical contacts). The bare spot can then be sealed with cyanoacrylate glue and brush-fin-

Fig. 201—A typewriter "Eraser Stick" is an excellent tool for cleaning small areas of bare wood that have been exposed by wild flat picks. It removes the grime and smooths the wood for brush touchup work at the same time with its mild abrasive action.

ished with lacquer for a repair that won't stick out like a sore thumb.

Another little trick I've learned concerns matching the aged yellow appearance of binding when working on an antique instrument. Many times you will have to work down the old binding past the yellowed surface or add a new piece of scrap to fill in a missing area. The white shines like a neon light and is very hard to match with most stains.

However, there is a neat trick that really works for these. Soak a common teabag in half a cup of hot water for a few hours (leaving it over the pilot light of a cookstove will keep it hot) and wring out the excess. The stained water can then be evaporated until there is little left except for a very strong, tarry-looking residue. Pour into a small bottle with a tight cap and add a small amount of alcohol and a few drops of acetone. Use a glass bottle as the acetone will destroy a plastic one, and this characteristic will also help the stain "bite" into the plastic or celluloid binding. Apply sparingly with a brush and follow with a quick wipe with a clean cloth until the proper shade is reached. When finished over, the binding looks old as the hills.

Tea may also be used to "antique" an ivory or bone nut and bridge saddles. Just soak the pieces in a strong solution of tea and water until the right color is reached. If you get them too dark, buff with fine steel wool. The tea-and-ivory trick is used occasionally by unscrupulous antique dealers to artifically age ivory artifacts, and the results are hard to tell from the real thing except by an expert.

Another question that has been thrown at me by several small shop owners in the years since I completed Volume I concerns the Model 676 Black and Decker buffer I use for polishing my finish jobs. It was available with a 1,000 rpm gear set, but several people have informed me that the model has been discontinued and that all they have been able to find were buffers spinning from 1,500 to 2,000 rpm or better.

The problem is one of heat dissipation. Most of these small buffers are designed for buffing wax jobs on automobiles, etc., and will actually melt a finish if used with a polishing bonnet and rubbing compound. They work fine on metal, but wood will not dissipate the heat generated. My 1,000 rpm job will melt the finish if I don't keep it moving, and something in the 500 to 750 rpm range would be better.

Talk to your local industrial supply house or an electrical supplier, such as W. W. Grainger, Inc. Grainger specializes in things electric and has 141 locations over the nation. Check your telephone book for an address. There are small, reasonably priced electronic speed controls available nowadays that will allow you the use of the full torque of your buffer at just about any rpm from zero to the rated rpm of your equipment. Grainger has one rated at 10 amps selling in the thirty plus-dollar range that is small enough to hook onto your belt. You can plug in your 2,000 rpm job and slow it down to a resonable 500 to 750 rpm for use on wood.

A couple more final tips, and I'll put an end to this chapter. One involves the lifting of finish from the wood. You will find this on many of the thick polyester-finished instruments that sustain impact damage. I've also had several instruments with the finish lifting around Grover Rotomatic machine heads when the retaining nut and washer were screwed down too tight around the string shaft. The latter is usually found on Martins and creates an ugly-looking bubble on the headstock face at the edge of the washer.

The water-thin cyanoacrylate glue is a lifesaver here for both types of repairs. Cyanoacrylate can be flowed into the glasslike breaks and loose chips of the polyester finishes to seal down the loose pieces and seal the cracks. Sand the area with fine Wetordry sandpaper and a drop or two of cyanoacrylate after the first application has dried. The glue can actually be used to fill in for small missing chips. Allow to dry thoroughly and sand with 400-grit Wetordry while directing a small stream of air under the sandpaper (I call this blow-sanding). After things are level and smooth, spot-finish with lacquer and an airbrush.

Repairing a lifted bubble around a machine head is a little more complicated, but not difficult if the finish has not chipped out completely. Remove the strings and the machine heads. Lift the washer very carefully so that you don't take any of the finish with it.

Use a scalpel or razor blade and slit the finish at the edge of the lifted area closest to the washer, but do not remove the chip. Wrap a piece of waxed paper around a small, flat block and have it ready, then flow a couple of drops of water-thin cyanoacrylate glue into the slit. You will see an instant penetration as the blister changes color. *There must be no delay here.* Set the waxed-paper-covered block over the blister *instantly,* applying pressure at the outside of the blister first and pressing it back toward the string post hole, and hold it in place for a couple of minutes to flatten the blister while the cyanoacrylate dries.

If you are lucky, there will be little or no cleanup to do. Should some of the cyanoacrylate bleed out onto the finish other than that covered by the washer, it's no big problem if you are working on a Martin. Martin uses a satin finish on the neck and head of its instruments. Blow-sand any seepage with 600-grit Wetordry, then use 0000 steel wool with the air hose to finish it off, applying very little pressure to the steel wool and *working with the grain.* The result is an original-looking satin finish.

Missing chips or a gloss finish on the other brands is a problem, however. You can build up the missing finish with cyanoacrylate by using several applications—letting each application dry thoroughly before applying another—but you will have to sand and refinish the face. Cut off about half the original finish with 320-grit Wetordry (blow–sanding again) to prevent too much finish buildup. Shoot it with at least two good coats of lacquer and wet sand and polish after it has cured for two or three days.

Chipped finish along the edge of the fingerboard or wear spots in the finish on the back of a neck are duck soup for cyanoacrylate glue. Clean the area with naphtha (cigarette-lighter fluid) to remove the body oils and work the glue into the bare area. It will seal the wood nicely for a bit of brush touchup or airbrush work.

On the edge of a fingerboard sand the finish lightly to knock down the sharp edges of the missing chips, wash with naphtha, and build it up with glue. The cyanoacrylate works beautifully to seal the edges on a new fingerboard too. Work with a small area at a time. Apply a drop of glue and quickly wipe it along the bare wood with a finger (keeping the finger moving until you lift it to prevent gluing the finger to the wood), apply another drop at the end of the stroke and wipe it too. Small surface irregularities can be filled by sanding the glue in.

The use of cyanoacrylate is perhaps unorthodox, but it's invaluable for saving time and doing a better job. Spot work that used to take me hours now takes only minutes, and the results are far superior in most cases. It's hardly traditional, I know, but if the results are there, who cares?

15

Care and Feeding of the Guitar

I'll make this chapter short and sweet. Everything that I covered in this chapter of Volume I pertaining to the proper care of instruments still holds true. Re-read and digest the material, and you will know how to take care of a guitar from simple polishing to packing one properly for shipping.

I still get instruments shipped in to my shop via truck lines, etc., with the strings tuned up to pitch. So far I've been lucky. None have been damaged, but anyone shipping a guitar with the strings up to pitch is tempting fate. I've repaired many that have been damaged in shipping because the strings were not relaxed or because they had been improperly packed.

Simple care with attention paid to climatic conditions, and a good guitar should serve you for years to come.

LUTHIERY AND REPAIR SCHOOLS

With the increasing demand for good craftsmen in the instrument-making and repair field, several schools have been opened to train people in luthiery and repair. I know little about the listed schools with the exception of the Roberto-Venn School of Luthiery, where I have given several talks on guitar repair during visits to Arizona; and the Red Wing school, which sent me a brochure and asked if I would be interested in teaching a course in guitar repair. I turned them down, however, as I just don't like cold weather. It gets bad enough here in Oklahoma. A letter of inquiry should bring you information on their schedules, etc.:

> Roberto-Venn School of Luthiery
> 5445 East Washington
> Phoenix, Arizona 85034

They offer a four-month course, during which you will build two instruments, one acoustic and one electric, and you get to choose from several types of instruments to make. Their course ranges from the most simple basics through the more complicated finishing, inlay work, electronics, etc.—and the owners are real nice people.

> Red Wing Area Vocational Technical Institute
> Independent School District #256
> Highway 58 at Pioneer Road
> Red Wing, Minnesota 55066

Red Wing specializes in stringed-instrument repair. Their 1,200-hour course covers most stringed instruments including guitars and the violin family, etc., with enough on playing technique to check out the repaired instruments, salesmanship, and business management.

> Acoustic Music
> 1458 Haight Street
> San Francisco, California 94117

> The Apprentice Shop
> Box 267
> Spring Hill, Tennessee 37174

> The Maine Guitar Makers School
> 16–24 Exchange Street
> Portland, Maine 04112

> The School Of Guitar Research and Design
> RFD Earthworks
> South Stafford, Vermont 05070

> Guitar Building Course
> Craftsbury Center
> Craftsbury Center, Vermont 05827

MORE SUPPLIERS FOR PARTS AND MATERIALS, ETC.

I've found a few more suppliers to add to the list in Volume I:

Gurian Guitar Ltd., Inc.
Canal Street
Hinsdale, New Hampshire 03451

Just about anything needed in the line of guitar and dulcimer making, both materials and supplies.

The Guitar Center
Division of
International Luthiers Supply, Inc.
P.O. Box 15444
Tulsa, Oklahoma 74115

Guitar-making materials and supplies.

Jim Dunlop Company
P.O. Box 821
Benicia, California 94510

Source of fret wire in just about any size and a couple of different hardnesses.

Woodcraft Supply Corp.
313 Montvale Ave.
Weburn, Massachusetts 01801

A tremendous variety of woodworking tools, regular and exotic, books, finishing materials, etc.

*Note: The numbers preceding the colon refer to the volume. The numbers following the colon are the page numbers within each volume.

Index of Figures